Society in the Novel

Society in the Novel

Elizabeth Langland

The University of North Carolina Press
Chapel Hill and London

© 1984 The University of North Carolina Press

All rights reserved

Manufactured in the United States of America

Library of Congress Cataloging in Publication Data

Langland, Elizabeth
  Society in the novel.

  Bibliography: p.
  Incudes index.
  1. Fiction—History and criticism. 2. Literature
and society. 3. Social conflict in literature.
I. Title.
PN3344.L36   1984   809.3'9355   83-23597
ISBN 0-8078-1604-3

Chapter 6 of this volume appeared in somewhat different
form in *Critical Inquiry* 9, no. 2 (Winter 1982) and is reprinted
here by permission of the University of Chicago Press

For Sheldon Sacks

Contents

Preface ix

Acknowledgments xi

1. Social Form in the Novel 3

    What Is Society? 4
    Reconsidering Novelistic Form 7
    Society as Function and Value 8
    Society's Formal Roles 11
    Society, the Individual, and "The World Out There" 15
    Historical versus Fictional Societies 19
    Society as Mimetic versus Formal Construct 21
    Thematic Approaches versus a Formal Approach
       to Society 22
    Society as Shaping Medium 23

2. Social Contexts for Judgment in Austen 25

    The Interplay of Private and Public Lives 26
    Community and Convention as Contexts for
       Evaluation 30
    Characterization through Social Discrimination 33
    Family, Society, and Self-Determination 39
    A Changing Understanding of Society 42

3. The Willing Suspension of Social Probability in Fielding,
   Thackeray, and Dickens 45

    Social Probability and Narrative Clemency in
       Tom Jones 48
    The "Author's Own Candles" and Conflicting Social
       Visions in *Vanity Fair* 57
    The Eccentric Aspect of Dickens's Social Landscape
       66

4. Society and Self in George Eliot, Hardy, and Lawrence 80

Society as Fulfillment and Frustration in *Middlemarch* 83
"The World's Opinion" in *Tess of the D'Urbervilles* 94
Society as Other in *The Rainbow* 104
Henry James's Social Aesthetic 114
Society in the Light of History 117

5. The Art of Sociological Naturalism in Zola and Dreiser 124

The Social Dialectic in *Germinal* 126
Society Anatomized in *An American Tragedy* 134

6. Society as Protagonist in *Nostromo* and *Barchester Towers* 147

Narrative Instabilities When Society Is Protagonist 150
Society Manifest in Human Lives 155
Society in Action 160
Society as Protagonist: The Artist's Intuition 166

7. Existence Beyond: Reality in Brontë and O'Connor 168

The Extraordinary in *Wuthering Heights* 171
"Rumbling Toward Heaven": Dual Contexts for Being
in O'Connor's Fiction 180

8. Society and the Problematics of Knowledge in Faulkner,
Kafka, and Pynchon 187

Mystery at the Heart of Society in *Absalom, Absalom!* 189
Through a Glass Darkly: Society in *The Castle* 196
Pynchon's *Everyman*: Searching for an Alternative
Society in *The Crying of Lot 49* 202

9. Society in the Novel 209

Basic Assumptions about Society 210
Milieu and the Artistic Act 216

Notes 223   Bibliography 249   Index 261

Preface

For several years now, critics working with structuralist and deconstructionist models of fiction have raised significant questions about how texts mean. Their questions have freed us from sometimes automatic assumptions about the relation of fiction to the world and have reminded us that fictions, or texts, are not merely mirrors of an external reality.

Structuralist and deconstructionist studies have cleared important semiotic ground, and they now invite us to build upon their understanding. This study begins with the assumption that fictions are meaningful. This meaning, however, is not simply self-referential; neither do fictions mechanically imitate a reality outside themselves. They are discrete systems of discourse, which have distinct interpretive structures.

Although critics recognize that the purpose of literature is not simply to imitate an external reality, discussions of society in fiction still rely heavily on the notion that the function of a fictional social order is to represent some outside world. Society in the novel is thus seen as replicating an historical, a contemporaneous, or an imagined milieu, its depiction governed by fidelity to an outside order. This book, *Society in the Novel*, takes as its starting point a writer's need to create a society consonant with the formal ends of the work itself. It sees society as performing a precise function in novels, that function dictated by the artistic principles governing the work. Society in novels, then, never simply replicates a world outside, and the relationship between fictional society and real world is not primarily a mimetic one but an evaluative one. We read not for fidelity to worlds we or others have experienced but for a perspective on those worlds through the autonomy of art, the ability of art to generate terms for evaluation independent of, yet connected to, an existent world.

In shaping form in fiction, an artist expresses values. As artistic function, society finds its meaning and coherence not in "truth to reality" but in those patterned values that are the corollary of form. Thus, when we talk about the function of society in the novel, we also talk about the values these formal structures embody. This book, therefore, reaches toward two ends: it defines the varied formal roles possible for society conceived as artistic function, and it articulates both general and particular meanings or values inherent in those formal paradigms.

Although we can admire the aesthetic achievement of form in novels, a key source of our pleasure in reading fiction derives from the meaning expressed by that form. This study of society in the novel offers one perspective on that interpenetration of formal and evaluative questions.

Acknowledgments

I am grateful to those who have contributed to this book. Vanderbilt University provided a semester's leave and a summer research fellowship—a portion of the time and money that allowed these ideas to flourish. A version of Chapter 6 first appeared in *Critical Inquiry*, 9, no. 2 (Winter 1982), and I thank the editors and publishers for permission to reprint it.

I am also much indebted to all those who have read and commented on the manuscript in its various stages. To Professor Sheldon Sacks, I owe a particular debt of gratitude. He was there at the inception of these ideas and so participates fully in these conclusions. I am grateful to Professor Wayne Booth, who early read the manuscript and offered substantive suggestions which I have incorporated throughout. Professor Donald Ault read a late version of the mansucript and suggested ways to polish and clarify my theoretical argument. To my husband, Jerald Jahn, belongs a special thanks. From the beginning, he provided a foundation of critical response and appreciation upon which the final book stands. He knew the book's importance to me and supported it in ways both large and small. My children, Erika and Peter, also learned of that importance, but I thank them for reminding me that society outside the novel was important as well.

Society in the Novel

1

Social Form in the Novel

It is the habit of my imagination to strive after as full a vision of the medium in which a character moves as of the character itself.
—George Eliot, letter to R. H. Hutton, 8 August 1863

It—the medium in which we are—determines our most permanent categories, our standards of truth and falsehood, of reality and appearance, of the good and the bad, of the central and the peripheral, the subjective and the objective, of the beautiful and the ugly, of movement and rest, of past, present and future, of one and many. . . .
—Isaiah Berlin, *The Hedgehog and the Fox*

Studies of society in the novel often seem to share the assumption that, just as a "pudding is a pudding and a novel is a novel," so, too, society is society. We all know, so this argument goes, what we mean by society. Reflection should quickly inform us, however, that we would probably reach no easy consensus in defining even the social environment in which we live. We experience an abstract concept, ideas about human relationships, not a concrete, codified thing. If we cannot readily pinpoint society in our everyday lives, we must be equally cautious when we turn to the novel, especially since a decade of poststructuralist and deconstructionist thought has made us acutely aware of language's limits in referring to any reality outside itself.

We did not need deconstruction to teach us, however, that the world of the novel and the world in which a writer lives are two different things. Yet critics often fail to distinguish carefully between the two, as U. C. Knoepflmacher noted in 1971: "The confusion between the invented world of the novel and the actual world in which the novelist lived persists to this day."[1] And that confusion continues to persist tenaciously.

What Is Society?

Society, as do all other aspects of novels, functions as an element in a structure that is, at least in part, self-referential. Studies of society must acknowledge, then, that society is a concept and a construct in fiction. If we begin here instead of asking questions about society's fidelity to an "outside" reality, we can raise important aesthetic questions for the novel. First, what variety exists in presentations of society in novels? Second, what diversity of formal roles can society have in the novel?

In the past, definitions of society that explicitly or implicitly see society always as an imitation of an outside world have tended to obscure the formal variety of social presentations in novels. Variety, in this framework, depended merely on the different societies writers inhabited or could imagine, rather than on the aesthetic demands of their art. Questions related to aesthetic function provide a new perspective from which to regard society. Novels that have seemed similar because they share, for example, a mid-Victorian setting—such as Trollope's *Barchester Towers*, Dickens's *Bleak House*, and George Eliot's *Middlemarch*—are markedly different when we look at the aesthetic function of a social order in them, and there are marked similarities between ostensibly different novels as well. Formal structures can be shared by a nineteenth-century and a twentieth-century novel or by a British and an American novel. A study of the formal roles of society thus provides useful insights into the working of the novel as a genre and facilitates practical insights into individual works.

The formal approach can also reintroduce mimetic questions in a new and invigorating way. While it cannot do justice to the broad question of the relationship between the aesthetic and mimetic dimensions of society—the dual aspect of the novel as aesthetic structure and verisimilar illusion of the world—it can pursue the aesthetic question to the point at which the structure of art is making a persuasive comment on life. If society is a concept and construct in art, it is also a concept and construct in life. Society in novels does not depend on points of absolute fidelity to an outside world in details of costume, setting, and locality because a novel's society does not aim at a faithful mirror of any concrete, existent thing. So, too, our everyday experience of society is not of a particular, existent thing. In life as in art, society emerges from patterned, formal relationships among aspects of our experience. When we talk about society, the aesthetic and mimetic dimensions will be already intertwined. The formal is socially defined or conditioned; the social is formally defined and conditioned. It is not possible to make simple distinctions between them.[2] This conflation between the aesthetic and the mimetic in the representation of society means that statements about the formal dimensions of society in a novel necessarily suggest statements about an author's ideas of society beyond the formal horizon of the novel. From these formal structures, on which this book will concentrate, we can then go on to infer social visions.

This intersection of art and life is important. Absolute literary realism may be impossible, but art cannot help making claims to something beyond itself. As soon as novelists select, arrange, and organize the disparate elements of culture, the arrangement takes on meaning or value. George Levine has recently addressed questions of novelistic meaning from the perspective of realism in Victorian literature, reaching conclusions similar to mine.[3] Levine recognizes the implications the deconstructionist position has for meaning in fiction, and he responds, "The Victorians, surely, did write with the awareness of the possibilities of indeterminate meaning and of solipsism, but they wrote against the very indeterminacy they tended to reveal. Their narratives do not acquiesce in the conventions of order they inherit but struggle to reconstruct a world out of a world deconstructing."[4] Levine's critical practice follows from this understanding of the Victorian's position: "Whatever else [realism] means, it always implies an attempt to use language to get beyond language, to discover some nonverbal truth out there."[5] Levine's conclusion (as I understand it) and my own is that literature can mean something besides itself. At the same time, what it depicts and means is not simply a mechanical reproduction of something "out there"; literature is free to produce its own meanings, but it is not exclusively self-referential. George Eliot said it more simply when she stated her goal was "to give a faithful account of men and things as they have mirrored themselves in my mind."[6]

This book talks about the values that inhere in formal arrangements and structures. The question of values has strong mimetic implications. Analyzing the values that inhere in a formal arrangement of society allows us to address questions of why novels mean what they mean to us and why they can affect us powerfully. Society, as depicted in the novel, thus comments on roles and possibilities of society in our lives, and I shall point throughout to ways in which it does so.

By now it should be clear that we cannot predefine society but must define it novel by novel. The flexible details of individual societies in novels help underscore the several paradigms for society, which the following chapters will articulate.

The word "society," when used by novelists, sometimes refers merely to high or fashionable class. In Dickens's *Our Mutual Friend*, the Veneering circle constitutes society, and the "Voice of Society" there gathered passes judgment. Tolstoy's *War and Peace* uses the term similarly when it early informs us that "to be enthusiastic had become Anna Pavlovna's pose in society" or that it was Pierre Besuhov's "first appearance in society."[7]

This book uses society in a wider sense, comprehending not merely peoples and their classes but also their customs, conventions, beliefs and values, their institutions—legal, religious, and cultural—and their physical environment. In short, their medium. Any one or several of these might constitute fictional society in a single novel. Its sense and purport can be expressed in a house, Poynton in "The Spoils of Poynton"; a city, Barchester of *Barchester Towers*; a country, Sulaco in *Nostromo*; an institution, Chancery in *Bleak House*; an object, the dust heaps in *Our Mutual Friend*; or a group of people—usually the flat and unchanging, what W. J. Harvey calls "background characters whose individuality need be no more than is adequate to typify social trends and pressures"—the Dodsons and Gleggs in *The Mill on the Floss*, Mrs. Costello and Mrs. Walker in *Daisy Miller*.[8] This society may also be revealed through human relationships, through characters' patterned interactions and their common expectations of one another.

Society remains potentially everything we have seen it to be

—norms, conventions, codes, background, places, people, institutions—but its particular manifestation in a novel will be dictated by its role within the work. How a writer uses society depends both on the relationship it has to his characters and on the overall role it plays in a developing action.

Reconsidering Novelistic Form

Understanding society's function or role depends upon perceiving a novel's form. Previous study of society in the novel has been limited by certain basic assumptions about form in the novel. Generally novelistic form has implied movement, usually growth. That movement may be variously characterized—thematically from innocence to experience, formally from instability to stability—but basic to its shape is the individual's encounter with society. In this basic scheme, the individual is primary, society secondary. Lionel Trilling in *The Liberal Imagination* defines the novel as a "perpetual quest for reality, the field of its research being always the social world, the material of its analysis being always manners as the indication of the direction of man's soul."[9] Maurice Shroder sees the novel's subject as an education for the protagonists "into the realities of the material world and of human life in society."[10] Alan Friedman speaks of the novel as "an onrushing double response of the self (insight and deeds) to the onrushing double trouble of the world (personal and impersonal)."[11]

In these schemes, despite potential differences in depicting society from novel to novel, society plays essentially the same formal role: antagonist to individual protagonists, a context, if not an obstacle, to the characters' growth and self-realization. Even socialist/sociological critics, such as Raymond Williams, Arnold Kettle, and John Lucas, for whom society is the focus of inquiry, conceive of society as protagonist only in thematic terms, not in formal terms; that is, the individual characters remain central to the novel's movement, but their behavior reveals social rather than individual ethics. A character does not act independently of the social forces in his or her milieu.[12] In contrast, society as formal protagonist would demand that society act in the fiction as would a human hero moving from a state of instability to stability.

The novel has traditionally been defined in such a way that it relegates society to one formal role, although allowing for enormous diversity in the depiction of society and for wide differences in the thematic interpretation of society's place. That basic role sees society as a context or background within which, and against which, characters define themselves. It would be foolish to claim that what so many critics have seen as the novel's basic pattern is not its basic pattern. This description is not wrong, but it has implicit limitations because it understands the role of society in only one way. It suggests that individuals alone are formal protagonists; it suggests an importance that society might not have; even when generally accurate, it obscures important differences in the formal relationships between individuals and society from one novel to the next. These are differences that will be explored throughout this book.

Society as Function and Value

Society conceived as a function within a novel has a limited number of possible roles that depend upon form and structure in the novel. We must here distinguish between the terms "form" and "structure," two words often used indistinguishably, to illuminate the formal possibilities for fictional society. Form is the more general term and will refer to the overall conception of the whole. When we speak of form on this broad level, we speak of value. Form and value are mutual and interdependent: form is the embodiment of value; value is the perception of form. Value does not necessarily imply ethics; it merely affirms that a novel's form makes a statement even if, as in the work of Robbe-Grillet, for example, that statement is simply of itself as phenomenal object, a pattern intended to discourage affective response.[13]

Structure, as used here, is the less comprehensive term. It includes the elements of a work subject to deliberate manipulation within the text. Questions of structure will consider the ways in which particular elements in fiction are presented, combined, and manipulated to achieve formal ends. A novel's major structural elements are the definition and development of character, the selection and order of incidents, the choice of narrator and narrative technique, and the selection of language in which to represent character and event and to reveal a point of view.

Particular values inhere in these structural elements, but they do so in ways that cut across the structural categories. Character—the protagonist or protagonists of a novel—reveals its perspectives and values through action, speech, and thought (when the narrator gives us access to a character's mind). But characters need a medium in which to act and reflect. That medium—often, but not always, society—to which they respond and in which they exist defines a set of values distinct from that of the characters. Finally, the narrator, interpreting character within the medium, whether through explicit comment, point of view, or choice of language, provides an evaluative framework for the whole. The adequacy of that evaluative framework will depend on the narrator's reliability. If the narrator is an omniscient, reliable guide to the world of the novel, then his perspective, when accessible, will be definitive in interpreting the interaction of character with medium. Such reliable narrators include, for example, the narrators of Jane Austen's novels or the commentator of Fielding's *Tom Jones*. If the narrator is the protagonist, as is Dowell in *The Good Soldier*, the reader's evaluative framework must emerge out of gaps, distortions, and contradictions in the teller's tale. If the narrator belongs to the medium in which the protagonists define themselves—a representative of society like Nelly Dean in *Wuthering Heights* or Winterbourne in *Daisy Miller*—then a broader evaluative framework will depend on our perceiving the ways in which protagonists exceed, elude, or transcend the categories for judgment.

Form, of course, derives from structure, just as formal principles determine structure. When we talk about the ways in which values cut across various structural aspects of a work, we can see that society informs both the structural elements and the formal aspects of a fiction. The way society is structured—how it is depicted, how its elements are organized—defines its formal role. So, when we speak of the formal role of society, we are speaking of the ways in which structural elements of a particular depiction are combined and evaluated to make society itself an integral part of a novel's form, a significant element in the principles generating a particular work. Because a novelist's understanding of society is a central determinant in his overall conception of his novel, it is easy to confuse a novel's larger ends with the representation of society as an end in itself.[14] The intelligible delineation of character depends on an ample presentation of a social order and its ideology as a coherent resisting force.[15] Although the ends of novels are larger than the representations of societies, artists cannot conceive of their works without understanding the formal roles of society within them. Finally we might ask whether we can ever answer this chicken-and-egg question of first causes: for example, does the destructiveness of human potential in Dreiser's *An American Tragedy* reflect the fact that Dreiser is writing a tragedy or that he takes a negative view of human society? Both, the title would suggest, and it is almost impossible to separate this simultaneity of effect in considering the artistic conception. Surely, too, for Dreiser intuition of form brought simultaneous intuition of structure.

The particular formal role or function of society depends on manipulation of three perspectives for judgment: that of the protagonists, the perspective created by the medium, and an evaluative framework that mediates between the other two.[16] Even in the face of authorial silence and absorption in one mind, our tendency as readers is to try to see character in relationship to something else in his world—whether society or ideas or nature—and to gain some perspective on that whole.

Isaiah Berlin's statement about "the medium in which we are," which opens this chapter, expresses this same concern with perspectives. Although he is speaking of life and I am speaking of art, he talks of a human impulse that art mirrors. To Berlin, the medium in which we are "determines our most permanent categories," yet "we cannot analyze the medium without some (impossible) vantage point outside it (for there is no 'outside')." In life there is no outside; in art alone can the illusion of an outside be created and maintained, and we are vouchsafed a framework within which to evaluate our lives. Art provides what life cannot, the full exploration of the immediate context or medium in which we live and think, as well as a broad, inclusive framework in which "all our thoughts and acts are felt, valued and judged in the inevitable ways that they are."[17]

The reader, then, must perceive two different, although related, judgments by the author concerning a novel's society. He must discern the way in which the fictional society is judged, and he must perceive the way in which characters are judged in relationship to that society. No major writer celebrates the status quo or espouses mindless adherence to social conventions. Great literature constructs unique visions of human possibility to question and challenge what is. Arising in the eighteenth century in response to forces that also gave impetus to economic individualism, Protestantism, and a new emphasis on personal privacy, the novel was fashioned from the beginning as an instrument of social criticism.[18] Expressing a new valuation of the individual, it brings with it a new awareness of how social values might warp or deny individual values and needs, but novelists themselves have varied widely in their judgment of society, in their depiction of society's relationship to individuals, and in their understanding of society's role in individuals' lives. These differences generate potential differences in the formal relationship of character, social order, and authorial value in novels.

Society's Formal Roles

The variable relationships among these three centers of value—character, society, and narrator/implied author—determine the range of functions or formal roles for society in the novel. There are certainly other centers of value pertinent to interpretation, notably the psychology of the actual author as well as that of the implied reader. I have limited myself to character, society, and narrator/implied author, because these all inhere in the novel and are the centers of judgment manipulated within the novel. Four basic arrangements of these centers of value seem to be most commonly used.

First, characters enmeshed in a social milieu are presented as being in conflict with it. Individual potential meets social possibility, and the result is some personal limitation or sacrifice. Here, the narrator may assume the role of detached, more or less sympathetic, observer. This is more common than the other three formal roles of society in the novel. With variations, it characterizes works by such writers as George Eliot, Thomas Hardy, and D. H. Lawrence, although not all of their novels necessarily fall within this formal paradigm. These writers are interested in exploring what it means to be an individual with special needs and particular talents in a milieu that is usually conservative, established, and generally unresponsive to particular needs. In this formal pattern, the individual may succeed or fail in establishing the validity of his values' vision.

2

Second, the narrator may choose to become engaged in the world of his novel and by his presence affect the narrative outcome. Henry Fielding in *Tom Jones* and W. M. Thackeray in *Vanity Fair* employ narrators who exempt certain characters from society's overriding effects. Charles Dickens, too, in his later novels, excuses certain characters from the logic of social organization, although he affects probability less through narrative intrusion than through the unusual techniques he has found to depict characters in society. At any rate, the potential negative effects of society in Fielding's, Thackeray's, and Dickens's novels are not fully realized in the protagonists' lives; their fates are released from strict social probability.

3

A third formal possibility exists. Society can be depicted as inevitably destructive of human possibility. The sociological/naturalistic novels weight the conflict between individuals and society in such a way that the most admirable characters are most subject to destruction since their best qualities, rather than setting them apart from society's inimical values, leave them more vulnerable. Whether he adopts the scientific objectivity espoused by Zola in *Germinal* or rhetorically heightens the "tragic" process as does Dreiser in *An American Tragedy*, the narrator is here committed to revealing society as destructive of human possibility. The artist makes a decision in advance that affects the relationships among character, society, and narrator. When critics discuss these novels in terms of their fidelity or lack of fidelity to contemporaneous social conditions, they find they are not, by and large, reliable social documents.[19] Such a conclusion should not surprise us, since we have already seen that the constitution of society, once a work is started, is largely dictated by formal conditions of the evolving work itself. Mimesis becomes secondary to a work's formal ends.

4

The fourth possibility for the formal relationship between character and society may be one of basic congruence. Society, despite its faults, can be flexible enough to accommodate the full realization of individual possibility. Jane Austen's novels offer serious depictions of social limitations from which her most deserving characters are nonetheless able to free themselves. The narrator's unspoken premise there is that social forms express individual morality and personal values. The narrator thus aligns herself with the best possibilities of that society and in that identification undertakes a scrutiny of the daily rituals of decorum and convention by which the characters conduct their lives. She ruthlessly criticizes form that has become formula, rituals that have become divorced from the values that nourished them. We do not lament the fact that Elizabeth Bennet and Anne Elliot find no scope for fulfillment outside of marriage as we do for George Eliot's heroines, because we accept the context and see that in these novels marriages express personal and moral achievements. In this fourth category, society and social convention function as yardsticks to measure individual moral growth and to make moral distinctions among individuals.

These four formal relationships among character, society, and narrator are the most common. Other arrangements are more rare, and they extend the boundaries of the novel. In one, the narrative distinction between society and individuals may be collapsed by allowing a social order to become a protagonist. Characters in these actions are agents to realize a society's fate. To speak of society as formal protagonist is not to make the general claim, common to thematic studies, that individuals act under society's dictates and influence, but to notice that a social order is the central actor, that a society functions in the text exactly as would a human protagonist. In such fictions, society undergoes a process of self-definition analogous to that of an individual hero, a process complete within the novel itself. The quality of a social order moves us rather than the quality of individual lives. Works as different in other respects as Joseph Conrad's *Nostromo* and Anthony Trollope's *Barchester Towers* illustrate how a social order or set of principles can act as protagonist.

If Conrad and Trollope discovered one way to reinterpret the relationship between individuals and society, Emily Brontë found another. In *Wuthering Heights,* society becomes so unimportant that it ceases to perform a meaningful function in realizing the characters' fates; that is, their place in the social milieu, their accommodation to it does not seem a significant measure of the characters' achievement. Emily Brontë has been praised for being a poetic novelist. What that praise seems to mean in regard to *Wuthering Heights* is that society does not have the same function that it has in most novels. The obvious social contexts and social oppositions in Brontë's novel do not exist to reveal the power of social forces or conventions over individual lives but to preclude those forces as significant sources of the fiction's meaning. As a brief example: when Heathcliff returns to the Heights a "gentleman," we see that Catherine's marriage to Edgar is not a significant obstacle to Heathcliff's union with Catherine. Social custom does not sever them: they are severed by their inability to find a human form to fulfill their powerful relationship. Flannery O'Connor's fiction shares this impetus toward establishing a transcendent or elemental realm for evaluating the quality of characters' fates. These novels are striking for positing an order other than the social one for evaluating character, an order that necessitates precluding social values from our judgment and disregarding society as function in determining narrative possibilities.

The twentieth century has also seen experiments that have altered the basic relationships among protagonists, society, and narrator. The line between objective and subjective has blurred. External reality is, paradoxically, individual and personal. The multiple perspectives that make possible the achievement of William Faulkner further cast the issue of an objective and social reality into doubt. It finally does not matter in *Absalom, Absalom!* if what an individual knows is what really is—hence the novel's fascination with epistemological questions—but it matters that each individual's conception of society has authority in his life. Likewise, in Kafka's *The Trial* and *The Castle*, and Pynchon's *The Crying of Lot 49*, "reality" is in doubt; the meaning or order discovered may be simply projections of characters' own minds, but a premise of their quests is that some essential truth, however inaccessible, remains, and that truth focuses on the ethical/social organization of mankind—on the enfranchised and the disenfranchised, on responsibility and guilt. Kafka and Pynchon acknowledge the difficulty of obtaining knowledge, but the challenge and triumph for their characters lie in pursuing truth, in searching to understand society or human organization and its relationship to individuals. So, society functions in structure as an inner imperative given objective force in the characters' lives.

These several formal roles—from society as concrete obstacle, to society as protagonist, to society as fantastic construction of a character's mind—are the foci of this study.

Society, the Individual, and "The World Out There"

Although this study appears, at times, to follow the historical development of the novel, it does so because the novel as genre has changed over time. Form or function is conditioned to some degree by historical circumstances. Thus, although this book is ahistorical in its understanding of society as a formal construct, some attention to the novel's development as a genre is in order to explain the choice of examples, primarily from among nineteenth- and twentieth-century novels.

Although the eighteenth-century novel often focuses on ordinary individuals in realistic situations and societies, eighteenth-century novelists did not, by and large, develop adequate technical means to define social values apart from personal values, a society distinct from individuals. Daniel Defoe reveals the novel's potential to analyze individuals in society, but he blurs distinctions in two ways. First, he concentrates on a single character who moves almost in isolation through his world, so that Robinson Crusoe's physical isolation is no greater than the isolation imposed on Moll Flanders by her necessity of getting ahead. Moll does not seem to exist in a nexus of relationships and of social conventions and expectations for behavior. The nameless inhabitants of her world enter only to serve or hinder her on her way to becoming a "gentlewoman." Second, and perhaps paradoxically, this physical isolation is accompanied by an individual's complete assimilation of his society's values. Although Moll ostensibly moves through her society, in fact, she and her medium constitute one set of interpenetrating values. The convincing internal life that Moll develops derives from her organic relationship to her society's monetary values, which become her personal ethic.

Tobias Smollett's interest in the picaresque tradition usually led him to explore social breadth at the expense of individual development, but his least picaresque novel, *Humphry Clinker*, begins to flesh out characters by means of their responses to the social phenomena they encounter. Responses of the various individuals—Jery Melford, Lydia Melford, Matt Bramble—stem from their own dispositions and inclinations. Yet, by focusing so consistently on the outer world, these responses provide not an increasingly complex psychological portrait but a varied kaleidoscope of society, its multiple manifestations and density. Smollett's is an enormous achievement in capturing the vitality and fluidity of society as a function of individual perception.

Samuel Richardson's characters have full internal lives. They are repositories of values and beliefs, but their self-preoccupation limits the full depiction of society. The analysis provided is that of an individual's mind. Pamela is troublesome to readers because her mind is an increasingly inadequate interpreter of objective experience; two harmless cows become ferocious bulls; Mrs. Jewkes and Mon. Colbrand take on nightmarish proportions in her imaginings. The social values that do conflict—the tension between Pamela's protestant, democratic impulses and the rigid, aristocratic, class-bound world she enters—lack a convincing external reality and seem only to reveal Pamela's confused psychological state. In Richardson's next novel, *Clarissa*'s multiple narrators offer a way of distinguishing subjective response from objective experience, but even these multiple narrators remain reflectors of individual consciousness rather than social consensus. Each expresses his or her own preoccupations; the common, shared values only begin to emerge. Joint perspectives correct the bias of one perspective without developing into shared assumptions, without creating a shaping medium.

Laurence Sterne's novels record inner lives: a mind in *Tristram Shandy* and a sensibility in *A Sentimental Journey*. Wills, articles, ordination dinners, politics, reputations, and decorum create the material of Tristram's story, but its drama lies in the narrator's effort to capture the reality of life itself through the complex workings of his mind and those of his family. Objects become incidental; the focus remains on the play of individual mind over external phenomena, so much so that mind appropriates the significance of the external world to its own private valuations. Hence, Toby cannot hear of bridges without thinking of his drawbridge and fortifications; Walter Shandy cannot hear of his son's death without converting it into a philosophical position.

In these ways, Defoe, Richardson, Smollett, and Sterne certainly anticipate later experiments in the novel, but that later experimentation is also shaped by the sharp awareness novelists have subsequently had of the divisions between individuals and social values, between individual possibility and social probability. The distinctions become clearer, the formal roles of society more carefully developed and explored. Defoe, Richardson, Smollett, and Sterne chose techniques that blur those distinctions in focusing on one or the other, either on society or the individual. They employ first-person narrators either for interior depth or social breadth, in contrast to later novelists, who seem preoccupied with articulating the potential conflict between individuals and society, even when individuals are largely shaped by their worlds. Society has existence apart from individual perceptions of it; protagonists are distinct from the medium that defines them. In the eighteenth-century novel, the individual and society as distinct and separable loci of values were only emerging, but that notion and the possible relationships between individuals and society were to dominate the nineteenth-century novel and, to some extent, the twentieth-century novel.

Although many twentieth-century writers explore the relationship between individual and society and therefore provide some of the best paradigms of the formal roles here examined, the twentieth century has also seen changes in consciousness that have diminished the centrality of society as a formal component in novels. Society has not, in these cases, disappeared from the novel, but its function has been reevaluated in light of a changed understanding of reality.

The depiction of society in the eighteenth- and especially nineteenth-century novel is predicated on a writer's beliefs that he can offer a "faithful account," a record of a life apart from himself and his particular experiences and that his characters respond and react to objective phenomena that impinge on their lives, yet are distinct and separable from them. This belief expresses no naive realism. George Eliot is only one articulate spokesperson for the subjectivity of all art when she recognizes, for example, "how inevitably subjective art is, even when it professes to be purely imitative—how the most accurate perception gives us rather a reflex of what we think and feel, than the real sum of objects before us."[20] Yet George Eliot acknowledges some objective world outside her and her characters' perceptions that is interpreted through thought and feeling. Her novels depict both that world and her characters' often painful confrontations with it.

As novelists around the turn of the century became increasingly sensitive to their partiality, subjectivity, and alienation, they reinterpreted the relationship between character and outside world. Two recent critics, W. J. Harvey and Patrick Swinden, address this issue of reality in the novel from the perspective of character and notice that one response to the shifting relationship between character and world was to cease to depend on any outside reality and to make the novel a self-sufficient artifact, "a necessary not a contingent thing."[21] As fiction becomes its own justification, however, as it turns away from "mimetic deceptions of earlier novels" out of a duty to respect what is real, the novel's reality becomes a "picture of the writer alone."[22] With such a vision of the novel's reality, there can, of course, be nothing apart from the character, called society, in which he defines himself.

Lionel Stevenson couches the problem in somewhat different terms but reaches a similar conclusion: "With the novelist's assumption of what Leon Edel calls the mind's eye view there has been an inward turning of the attention to examine not society and its varied external relationships to the individual but the human consciousness itself. How to transform this often inchoate material of the mind into a valid and ordered interpretation of life has been the novelist's problem. In our day it is clear that the most significant writers have sought to do so by conceiving the novel in terms of symbol, image, and myth."[23] Stevenson points explicitly to the twentieth-century impulse to find mediums other than society which can give characters definition and meaning. Frank Kermode echoes these reflections by defining in the modern novel "a recognizable estrangement from what used to be known as reality; and a further consequence, which can equally be defended as having beneficent possibilities, is that the use of fiction as an instrument of research into the nature of fiction, though certainly not new, is much more widely recognized."[24]

The twentieth century has opened our eyes to such alternative sources of value and alternative contexts for meaning as myth, memory, imagination, art or sensibility. In the novels of Proust, Joyce, and Woolf, the world or society is immanent in a character's consciousness and his struggle is to shape the raw materials of consciousness into some whole. The social world has been appropriated as part of the raw material of consciousness to be interpreted in terms of myth for Joyce, or sensibility for Woolf, or imagination for Proust. Having appropriated society as part of individual consciousness, Woolf, Joyce, and Proust, in effect, eliminate society's significance as a formal component of the novel. Like the eighteenth-century writers they often admired, they close the gap between individual and society, the gap that generates the formal paradigms of this study.

Historical versus Fictional Societies

In seeking to determine social values in a novel a major question arises. Is everything that might possibly fall under the rubric of "social" a part of the created society integral to a novel's effect? The novel is a "loose and baggy monster"; it will take within its folds much that arguably doesn't conduce to its formal ends. It may even accommodate irrelevant or contradictory insights. So Dickens has been praised for his overall grasp of society as organism and criticized for his local and often contradictory comments —as he speaks seemingly *in propria persona*—on social legislation and social abuses.[25] These intrusions need not disturb the mimetic critic for whom they are all aspects of a novel's reality, but they must ruffle the formalist's feathers, and they call for distinctions. A writer may, by virtue of being himself a member of society, include social details and beliefs that are not integral to a particular novel's ends. This is a sensitive point because one man's formal accident is another's key to meaning. Still, the possibility of such "extraneous" inclusions exists, and that possibility dictates a distinction between society deliberately created and included by a novelist in achieving certain artistic ends and "society" that intrudes itself into a work by virtue of the novelist's own social existence, his own investment in certain social issues.

Charlotte Brontë's *Jane Eyre* provides a famous example of this difference. In *A Room of One's Own*, Virginia Woolf points to aesthetic problems in Jane's diatribe against society's restrictions on women. As Jane Eyre paces the roof at Thornfield, she becomes defiant: "Anybody may blame me who likes."[26] Her defiance takes her into a clear articulation of the social hobbles placed on women:

> It is in vain to say human beings ought to be satisfied with tranquillity: they must have action; and they will make it if they cannot find it. Millions are condemned to a stiller doom than mine, and millions are in silent revolt against their lot. Nobody knows how many rebellions besides political rebellions ferment in the masses of life which people earth.

> Women are supposed to be very calm generally: but women feel just as men feel; they need exercise for their faculties and a field for their efforts as much as their brothers do; they suffer from too rigid a restraint, too absolute a stagnation, precisely as men would suffer; and it is narrow-minded in their more privileged fellow-creatures to say that they ought to confine themselves to making puddings and knitting stockings, to playing on the piano and embroidering bags. It is thoughtless to condemn them, or laugh at them, if they seek to do more or learn more than custom has pronounced necessary for their sex.[27]

Jane's clarion call for general equality, her cry for personal scope allows Woolf to find the voice of Charlotte Brontë in these words, writing of "herself where she should write of her characters."[28] Jane's statement does conflict with the course Jane adopts, with the emotions that fill her soul. A scant five pages later have brought Mr. Rochester to Thornfield and Jane to a new sense of purpose in helping Mr. Rochester to remount his horse: "My help had been needed and claimed; I had given it. I was pleased to have done something; trivial, transitory though the deed was, it was yet an active thing, and I was weary of an existence all passive." The woman who feels as men feel, who needs exercise for her faculties and a field for her efforts has found that scope in helping a man like Rochester, "masculine . . . dark, strong, and stern."[29] We can argue for Jane's own partial knowledge of the forces that rend her, her need yet to grow into strength beside Rochester, but what the earlier passage means by restraint and fulfillment and what the mature Jane means by restraint and fulfillment are not fully reconcilable within the terms of the novel. What Charlotte Brontë saw as the social constraints on her life and what the novel depicts, in its fictional society, as the social constraints on Jane's are not wholly compatible, and they mix uneasily in chapter 12 of *Jane Eyre*.

Occasionally, we do hear an author's voice in fiction writing "of herself where she should write of her characters." It is not surprising that these intrusions occur in the form of complaints against contemporaneous social conditions. After all, writers have themselves experienced injustice in their worlds and, when their experiences border on those of their characters, it must be tempting to voice a personal wrong, but when these intrusions occur, we know it. These interruptions are troublesome precisely because they disrupt a growing pattern of expectations in a novel, and the fact that we discern them testifies to our having recognized a coherent society, which has formal significance in the fiction.[30] Such disruptions, paradoxically, end up clarifying formal ends in a sharp and immediate way, and they incidentally reveal the care with which novelists usually build their fictional societies.

Society as Mimetic versus Formal Construct

This book is not specifically an answer to the Marxists or the sociological critics who see society essentially as a mimetic rather than as a formal construct. These critics align the novel's concerns with those of sociology and history,[31] exploring the ways in which social changes gave rise to the novel,[32] illuminating the novel's reflection of and shaping of its social milieu,[33] examining the dialectical relationship between an author and the society that made him,[34] or elucidating an historical dialectic in the development of the novel.[35] Despite differences in approaches, the foregoing studies assume the existence of something specific and concrete that we can name "society," both outside the novel and within it. They are interested in the mimetic nature of imagination and tend to turn attention away from the formal relations of a novel's parts to comment on a novel's relationship to the surrounding world, or they seek historical patterns in the formal arrangements. These issues are, of course, important. However, they do not address the question of a novel as an art form that must be true to its own coherence.

Even the neomarxists, like Fredric Jameson and Terry Eagleton, who want to wed the Marxists' traditional concern with content to a respect for form, nonetheless see form as a manifestation of history, if not an imitation of it.[36] For example, Terry Eagleton defines the text and what is signified therein—the "pseudo-real"—as a signifier of an ideology that is itself a signification of history.[37] This study demonstrates that one can understand the role of society in novels sufficiently on solely formal grounds.

While the Marxists explore a historical dialectic, social historians or sociological critics focus on details of habit, custom, and group behavior that are shared from novel to novel, a set of details detachable from the narrative. In contrast, this book articulates the ways in which diverse aspects of a fiction cohere as a center of values that we can call society. For a sociologist or social critic such as Morroe Berger who has recently traced the heritage of Jane Austen's novels to the early conduct books, which spelled out proper social decorum in varied circumstances, these novels can provide a rich source for details of proper decorum in the early nineteenth century.[38] In a formal approach, however, Jane Austen's society is a community of individuals whose patterned interactions and common expectations of one another assist the protagonists in realizing their full potential within their milieu and help us measure their worthiness.

Thematic Approaches versus a Formal Approach to Society

A thematic approach to society in the novel may share with a formal approach the understanding that society is an idea. Both approaches are ahistorical in that both are concerned primarily with a text's autonomy, with its ability to generate its own meanings, but a thematic approach to the role of society in a fiction will necessarily differ from a formal approach. Thematic criticism talks about what texts mean; theoretical or formal criticism talks about how meaning arises in texts.[39] Therefore, thematic approaches to the question of society in the novel will focus on the ways in which the aspects of a fictional society are organized to generate a theme or idea within a text. A formal approach to society does not elaborate a single thematic pattern; it rather considers how the elements of fictional society work in relationship to other aspects of a narrated action to provide the groundwork out of which all meaning must emerge. A formal study, in this sense of looking at the conditions of meaning rather than at the meaning itself, is thus theoretically prior to a thematic study.

Society in the Novel both suggests and validates certain thematic approaches without following any single thematic line to its conclusions. Whereas, for example, a thematic critic of Austen's novels will talk principally about the improvement of the estate, the re-

how meaning arises in texts — focus of formal criticism @ the conditions of meaning generation of a world represented through attention to the individual estate,[40] a formal approach speaks of the function of society as it relates to character, of the interplay of private and public lives, of the role of community and convention in determining behavior, of the narrative definition of family, and of the relationship of narrator to social medium. Its conclusions are thus not definitions of themes but definitions of formal relationships that provide a groundwork for judgment and that shape possible themes.[41] We shall define these themes to demonstrate the practical application of the theory but shall speak of meanings only as they emerge from the formal principles articulated.

A further caveat is in order. Since each novel in any author's canon is an autonomous creation, the novelist's idea of society and society's function may vary from novel to novel within any canon. This book makes no claim to have done justice to the full range of any single writer's works. It considers, instead, selected works that represent the various formal roles under consideration. We should not be surprised, however, to find that we can often draw connections among works of a particular novelist, because ideas of society are linked to novelists' values and perceptions. Such values and perceptions are often constants over a writer's canon.

Society as Shaping Medium

The only novels that will concern us here are those works that engage us in the fates of characters, works in which the moral norms or ethical beliefs have shape within their lives and actions. Utopian novels, thus, do not fall within this sphere because they take, as their primary end, the criticism or espousal of a particular social order. Although utopias do include characters with whom we become involved, they use that involvement to achieve another end, that of focusing attention on some idea or ideas about society.

For related reasons, I have not included historical novels per se and science fiction novels, although in their formal aspects these fictions might well be included. That is, a represented society within each of these subgenres—whether imagined in some future or recreated out of the distant past—has a formal role that generally conforms to one of the seven basic formal patterns here identified, in which we see society as the shaping medium for individual action.

It is in the aformal, rather than the formal aspects of the fictional society, that there is a significant difference between historical or science fiction and the novels here considered. The fact that we append an adjective to "fiction"—"historical" or "science"— signals the aformal difference. One motive in imagining a world, projecting one as in science fiction or reimagining a world as in historical fiction, is a desire to use that other world to comment on the present. The writer of such fiction usually has another goal than presenting the picturesqueness of history or depicting fantasy. The goal is thematic or didactic and gives a dimension to the representation of society in fiction that I have chosen not to consider here since it involves questions about the author's actual milieu and his opinions of it. In considering these works, then, the aformal elements—the relationship of author's world to created world and the thematic purpose implicit in setting up that relationship—demand an attention equal to that given the formal elements, the function of society within the work. Including that equal attention would detract from the formal paradigms here adumbrated.

Social Contexts for
Judgment in Austen

"Yes; but intricate characters are the most amusing. *They have at least that advantage."*

"The country," said Darcy, "can in general supply but few subjects for such a study. In a country neighborhood you move in a very confined and unvarying society."

"But people themselves alter so much, that there is something new to be observed in them forever."
—Elizabeth Bennet and Fitzwilliam Darcy in Jane Austen,
Pride and Prejudice

3 or 4 Families in a Country Village is the very thing to work on.
—Jane Austen, letter to Anna Austen, 9 Sept. 1814

Jane Austen's novels create a balance between individual needs or perceptions and social forms and values which justifies regarding her fiction as a watershed in the formal treatment of society in the novel.[1] Indeed, her work demands this approach because she is at least as different from her descendants as she is from her ancestors. Although her general techniques were to become common, the final emphasis of those techniques was not duplicated in later novels. Only Jane Austen presents that tension between social demands and individual needs as mutually enriching. Later novelists, in varying degrees, treat society as inimical to full individual self-realization. Theirs are worlds in which society implies exclusion. Theirs are worlds of class differences, class conflicts. Jane Austen stands poised between the eighteenth and the nineteenth centuries, having located the formal terms to express a congruence of social and individual perspectives while preserving clear distinctions between them.[2]

The Interplay of Private and Public Lives

Jane Austen's unique achievement rests on two formal innovations in her representation of society. First, she found techniques that enabled her to focus simultaneously on the needs and concerns of society and those of individuals. Second, although she saw the sources of tension between private and public lives, she nonetheless presented society as an adequate context for the complete fulfillment of her most deserving characters.

The two innovations are obviously related. The first speaks simply to the issue of formal balance or proportion between two aspects of the fiction; the second speaks to the formal role of society and implied value judgments. The first point can be introduced briefly, but its full development depends on a discussion of the second. Jane Austen's novels articulate and maintain a balanced interplay between personal needs and social expectations. After experimenting with the epistolary technique, Jane Austen turned to an omniscient narrator who gave her the flexibility she sought. The famous opening of *Pride and Prejudice*, for instance, establishes this balance immediately: "It is a truth universally acknowledged, that a single man in possession of a good fortune, must be in want of a wife."[3] The irony here stems from our perception of conflicting perspectives: society's need to perpetuate its structure through marriages among those of a certain class, and an individual's need to realize himself in that same institution that assures society's continuance. Against the "universal" social truth of wealthy bachelors wanting wives is set the pressure of individual needs: "However little known the feelings or views of such a man . . ." (1, chap. 1). We laugh at the juxtaposition of potentially conflicting truths here, individual and social. And, although we reject the narrow social vision of Mrs. Bennet, who espouses marriages solely on the basis of rank and fortune and who prepares to thrust one of her daughters into Mr. Bingley's arms ("You must know that I am thinking of his marrying one of them"), the sanity of Mr. Bennet's reply, which expresses individual autonomy ("Is that his design in settling here?") does not supersede the social and personal value of marriage itself (1, chap. 1). Indeed, despite his baiting, Mr. Bennet himself had always intended to visit Bingley.

Jane Austen knows that marriage is not an end in itself. It culminates individual self-realization, and it expresses a revitalized society. Marriage is thus both the paradigmatic institution for social stability and improvement and the primary relationship for personal self-realization and development. Austen understands the structural implications of this vision in forming her novels. She achieves aesthetic balance in the ability of these marriages to resolve major narrative conflicts, not the least of which is that between the individual and society.[4] Austen is formally successful in balancing the social and individual, in part because she captures the public dimensions of private lives and the private dimensions of public affairs. We are convinced that something important, both personally and socially, has been achieved when the "true friends who witnessed the ceremony [of Emma and Knightley], were fully answered in the perfect happiness of the union," or when Captain Wentworth and Anne Elliot "with the advantage of maturity of mind, consciousness of right, and one independent fortune between them" took it "into their heads to marry."[5]

By choosing marriage as the supreme social institution in her novels, Jane Austen assures the accommodation of individuals to society. This understanding pertains to my second point about Austen's unique treatment of society. Her novels are distinct in finding society an adequate context for complete fulfillment of her most deserving characters. Dominant social institutions of later novels—such as political movements (reform), educational systems, legal systems (Chancery)—dictate shaping social conditions beyond individual control. Austen limits her fictional society to one class so that no social barriers bar the marriage of any two individuals. Society, so depicted, guarantees her characters freedom and scope to fulfill themselves. This emphasis does not narrow the significance of what she writes; rather it creates a context to criticize individuals who pervert social values through mindless adherence to convention and expectation. It also allows her to reaffirm the importance of individual responsibility and judgment in fulfilling society's proper role.

Jane Austen's novels are highly critical of social formulas emptied of meaning; they make society into a battleground on which characters struggle to define themselves. In *Persuasion*, the narrator, for example, castigates the empty posturings of a Sir Walter Elliot, who "for his own amusement, never took up any book but the Baronetage" where "he found occupation for an idle hour and consolation in a distressed one" (3, chap. 1). Sir Walter embodies the bankruptcy of tradition.

Nonetheless, Austen's novels are not finally about society and social limitation.[6] They are about individual possibility. In her novels, what society needs is also what individuals need. Society makes possible individual fulfillment, and its structural role is to serve as context in which individual merit is revealed, explored, and evaluated. Social events—parties, balls, assemblies, dinners—enable us to measure individual moral natures and growth as when Darcy applauds Elizabeth's and Jane's behavior at the Netherfield Ball, recognizing that "to have conducted yourselves so as to avoid any share of the like censure [which has fallen on parents and sisters], is praise no less generally bestowed on you and your eldest sister, than it is honourable to the sense and disposition of both" (2, chap. 12).

A metaphor that Austen herself uses, that of the dance, clarifies the distinction between her techniques and those of later novelists.[7] In Austen's world there is no question of whether one will dance, only a question of how one will distinguish oneself within the dance. "Every savage can dance," quips Darcy, and in Austen's world every "savage" does. Each must choose with what care he will master the steps and so far master the discipline that the dance can become self-realizing intead of self-determining. Aspects of society are criticized in Austen's novels, but that criticism does not urge major social reform. Rather it reveals the superiority of certain individuals to the false, foolish, and petty within society. Social and moral character are intimately bound. A social deficiency points to a moral deficiency. Even agreeable villains such as George Wickham, Henry Crawford, and William Elliot, whose social polish makes a good first impression, do not escape the subtle censure of Fanny Price and Anne Elliot. These women perceive deficiencies in the manner that reveal deficiencies in the man.

Unlike later novelists, Jane Austen relies on social contexts and conventions to define character and to make subtle and complex moral discriminations among individuals. What this means in practical terms is that the values informing the novel, those of the implied author/narrator, can be expressed within the society. Put another way, Austen's fictional society, despite its particular foolishness, is not limited in its power to express the larger values that inform the novel. Those values are not necessarily expressed by individual members of a society, but the narrator is in sympathy with the larger social aims and principles of the world she depicts. She understands value to inhere in the social forms and to inform the social conventions, so much so that her novels are meritocratic in impulse. Merit is eventually recognized and rewarded. Elizabeth Bennet marries Darcy; Fanny Price finds her permanent place at Mansfield Park; Emma earns her Knightley; Wentworth deserves and wins Anne Elliot. Austen's novels deny any necessary congruence between individual merit and inherited social rank. Their marriages are democratic; they express belief in the ability of true merit eventually to win social sanction and recognition, and the novels can do so in part because the narrative and social centers of judgment are in accord.

At first glance, *Persuasion* might seem the exception to this rule. Its tone is darker than that of the earlier novels. Anne's marriage represents a lowering of class rank. Furthermore, Anne has originally sacrificed Wentworth because of her love for, and duty toward, Lady Russell, in effect, toward social class. His stubbornness threatens her with losing him permanently. The narrator in this novel no longer locates the possibility for regeneration among the Darcys—here represented by the socially bankrupt Sir Walter Elliot—but among the newly monied, but by shifting the location for social value to Wentworth and the naval people, the narrator continues to assure us that the deserving will eventually find complete fulfillment in their world and that their world will remain responsive to individual merit. This assurance links *Persuasion* with the rest of Austen's canon in holding out the possibility of accommodating individual and social needs.

Community and Convention as Contexts for Evaluation

Although marriage serves as her novels' central institution, fictional society in Austen's novels also includes a community, the characters and places constituting a particular milieu (Jane Austen's "3 or 4 Families in a Country Village"), and explicit social conventions and expectations. It is through her presentation of community and convention that Jane Austen convinces us that good marriages conduce to individual fulfillment and social revitalization. Just as marriage ultimately expresses democratic principles, so, too, do community and social rank; that is, rank and its prerogatives are finally used not to exclude characters but to evaluate them.

I noted above that the social community of Austen's novels is remarkably homogeneous. With a few exceptions—Robert Martin, the farmer in *Emma*, for example—all characters belong to the same social class. All can attend the same parties, sit down to dinner together, and intermarry. But within this class, Austen offers subtle discriminations of rank. At the top stand the titled aristocracy: Lady Catherine de Bourgh, Lady Dalrymple; next, old money, Sir Walter Elliot, Darcy, Knightley, Sir Thomas Bertram; new money, Bingley, Admiral Croft; gentry, the Bennets, Woodhouses, Musgroves, Westons; the clergy, Mr. Collins, Mr. Elton, Charles Hayter; military, Wickham, Wentworth, Mr. Price; trade, Mr. Gardiner. This survey is still rough by Austen's careful standards, which discriminate among Admiral Croft, Mr. Wentworth, Captain Wentworth, Harville and Benwick, or among the Reverend Crawford, Mary and Henry Crawford and their benefactor, the admiral. This degree of specificity in social ranking could be embalming, but we immediately perceive the fluidity of movement within those ranks. Elizabeth's reply to Lady Catherine—"[Darcy] is a gentleman; I am a gentleman's daughter; so far we are equal" (3, chap. 14)—is emblematic and expresses what we feel to be the truth. These structures and rankings do not have ultimate importance either for the narrator or for the deserving characters. Darcy's fault, stressed by the narrator, is that he feels such differences matter, and he must learn "how insufficient were all my pretensions to please a woman worthy of being pleased" (3, chap. 16). Thus we discover a special function for social distinctions, not the usual one of obstacle to be overcome, but a precise context in which to evaluate individual merit. These rankings allow characters' social responses to one another to become a subtle index to their powers of discrimination and judgment and inform our moral perception of the action.

Characters must also recognize, however, the appropriate respect due to rank. Elizabeth Bennet's awareness of Lady Catherine's social position never allows her to be rude; at the same time, her accurate perception of the Lady's personality does not allow her to be intimidated in the way Sir William Lucas, Maria, Mr. Collins, and Mrs. Bennet are. Elizabeth's own respect for that position underlines how far Lady Catherine has disappointed it in poking through Mrs. Collins's closets or in obtruding herself into the Bennets' drawing room without requesting an introduction. Elizabeth's correctness and Lady Catherine's rudeness stress Lady Catherine's bankrupt social responsibility, her failure to meet the social demands of superior rank and fortune. At the same time, Elizabeth's respect insists on the value of those distinctions and reveals her as the superior individual.

Anne Elliot makes the same acknowledgment when admitting—to her pain—that Kellynch has "passed into better hands" when her father's financial distress forces him to leave it. And Emma's failure to recognize the proper respect due someone precipitates her grievous mistake at Box Hill when she sacrifices Miss Bates's feelings to her own wit. As Miss Bates's social superior, Emma deserves Knightley's judgment and censure; "Were she your equal in situation—but, Emma, consider how far this is from being the case. She is poor; she has sunk from the comforts she was born to; and if she live to old age must probably sink more. Her situation should secure your compassion. It was badly done—indeed!" (3, chap. 7). Proper response demands judgment both of what that person actually is and of his or her situation in that world. Elizabeth Bennet appreciates both personality and social situation in her response to Lady Catherine; Emma sees the person but fails to appreciate the social situation. Darcy equals Elizabeth's triumph in his response to the Gardiners. He sees their personal worth and, as their social superior, initiates the friendship.

Since social rank in Jane Austen does not necessarily indicate personal value, the novels offer deliberate reversals: in *Pride and Prejudice* the Gardiners are vastly superior to Lady Catherine; in *Persuasion*, Mrs. Smith is superior to Lady Dalrymple. Characters who can understand the real instead of empty social prerogatives and yet distinguish individual merit are those most valued. The emphasis thus is balanced between individual and society: individual merit challenges the prerogatives of society even as vital social form expresses, shapes, and rewards individual merit.

Just as Jane Austen's communities and social rankings do not function as self-perpetuating, stultifying hierarchies, so, too, her social conventions—the second major aspect of her fictional society—do not create rigid models of proper behavior on all occasions. Conventions also function as contexts in which individuals can realize themselves and in which they are revealed, rather than as confinements and limitations of individual possibility.

The social convention at issue when *Pride and Prejudice* opens stresses the necessity of a gentleman in a neighborhood to visit newcomers of his rank. On this visit rests the immediate possibility for acquaintance with the rest of the family. Three responses to this convention are of importance to this novel: Mrs. Bennet's, Mr. Bennet's, and Elizabeth's. Mr. Bennet always intended to visit Bingley, a fact that, when revealed, indicates his pleasure in baiting his wife. His trenchant wit and skill at his object and his amusement at her foolishness apprise the reader fully of Mr. Bennet's character. His aim is to "laugh and make sport." His family members do not stimulate his parental responsibility; they serve only as a nearer object for his ridicule. Mr. Bennet clearly understands social form and prerogatives, but he is willing to exploit them and waive propriety for his individual pleasure. Lydia's later elopement becomes a chastizement for his continual irresponsibility, and he tells Elizabeth, who attempts to ease his guilt, "Let me once in my life feel how much I have been to blame" (3, chap. 6).

Mrs. Bennet's "mean understanding" is glaring in her inability to respond appropriately to Mr. Bennet's comments that she should not visit Mr. Bingley as he "might like [her] best of the party" or that he will send the girls with a note approving Mr. Bingley's choice of any. Although Mrs. Bennet holds fast to her desire to see her daughters socially established, she is incapable of any discrimination in pursuing that aim. Elizabeth, who must bear her mother's complaints over her father's "refusal" to visit, reveals to us the best understanding of the social and personal demands. Elizabeth recognizes that if Mr. Bennet does not visit Bingley, they will be introduced by someone else at the assembly. She accepts the social value of the introduction, but, in her ease, implicitly acknowledges that Bingley is not likely to be carried off by the first eligible woman to greet him. Her response recognizes the autonomy of the individual, Bingley, who has been reduced to a pawn in Mrs. Bennet's social jockeying; at the same time it accepts the propriety of seeking an introduction.

Two basic points emerge. Character is revealed through response to convention. At the same time, convention is expressed only through the characters' responses. The results of this interdependence are two-fold: we gain a precise scale for evaluating characters—a point I will later develop at length—and characters seem free to express their individuality through responses to conventions because, in Austen, that individuality is accommodated. There are few crippling social restrictions in Austen's worlds despite her constant focus on society and its rules.

Characterization through Social Discrimination

The way in which Austen's novels use social convention and rank to evaluate characters is one of her innovative narrative techniques. Equally unique is Austen's corresponding reliance on individual responses to conventions to carry forward the work of characterization. After the first few chapters in an Austen novel, we know her characters well. Yet we know little of them through what in other novelists fleshes out a character. We do not know what Austen's people look like; we do not even have objects that we identify with them. George Eliot's *Middlemarch* opens with a lengthy description of Dorothea Brooke; her response to her mother's gems and the information that she loves horseback riding give us an immediate access to her personality. Dickens's world comes alive through precisely described individual gesture and mannerism. In Thackeray, Hardy, Fielding—and the list could continue—characters have clear physical delineations and traits that set them apart from their milieus. Individualizing physical details help these authors present their characters in counterdistinction to their societies.

In Jane Austen's novels, characters are not in opposition to society. They need not be set apart from their milieu, for their individuality is defined in their discrimination of proper social decorum. In Austen's hands, this technique is capable of such precision that we know the characters completely, so completely that a physical description would add little, if anything, to our knowledge. When the narrator remarks of Mr. Collins's mistake over a trivial incident that Mrs. Bennet "declared herself not at all offended; but he continued to apologise for about a quarter of an hour," we need no more to make him vivid (1, chap. 13). We know the exact dimensions of his personality, because we know with precision how he will behave on every occasion. Social behavior, not mannerism, appearance, or personal tastes, is the key index to character in Jane Austen.

This point has been too little appreciated. In 1859, G. H. Lewes praised the then obscure Jane Austen, noting that her success lay in her having "the exquisite and rare gift of dramatic creation of character."[8] He developed this point: "If the reader fails to perceive the extraordinary merit of Miss Austen's representation of character, let him try himself to paint a portrait which shall be at once many-sided and interesting, without employing any but the commonest colours, without calling in the aid of eccentricity, exaggeration, or literary 'effects,' or let him carefully compare the writings of Miss Austen with those of any other novelist, from Fielding to Thackeray."[9] Although Lewes recognized that Austen makes each character live and breathe for us, he nonetheless concluded that she was perhaps "shortsighted" because the "absence of all sense of the outward world—either scenery or personal appearance—is more remarkable in her than in any writer we remember."[10] Lewes could not, apparently, forbear wishing for the more familiar "portrait" of a Thackeray or a Fielding, letting slip his perception that Austen's art is complete as it is, that any additions would prove merely redundant or, worse, distracting from already full characterizations.

Evidence that Austen's lack of description has not been felt as a defect by other readers may lie simply in the fact that it has rarely been mentioned. Barbara Hardy has recently praised Austen's novels for their physical density: "The reality of her social scenes, especially in *Persuasion*, depends strongly on the casual presence of objects. . . . People are what they possess, and carry objects with them like limbs."[11] Hardy's choice of simile, "like limbs," suggests that the objects are sufficiently there to convince us as we read but not significantly or symbolically there. Hardy points rather to what we in fact experience: that Austen's world feels as dense as it should; physical descriptions of characters would not improve her art.

Two aspects of Jane Austen's art of characterization reveal how intimately the representation of character is linked to the representation of society. I turn first to the function of her descriptive phrases and passages and then define those techniques by which character is developed.

The terms chosen to describe people, houses, and scenery do not body forth the places and individuals in all their concrete particularity; rather they reveal social position, proportion, and understanding. Elizabeth Bennet has "fine eyes" and a "pleasing figure." Emma Woodhouse enters "handsome, clever, and rich, with a comfortable home and happy disposition." Anne Elliot possesses "elegance of mind and sweetness of character." The Austen descriptive vocabulary features such key words as elegant, amiable, agreeable, delicate, fine, lively, clever.[12] The terms are not sensuously descriptive. They evoke no physical image in the mode of Dickens, for example, whose world is so dense with physical textures that objects often seem to have a life of their own. Nor do they evoke a quantifiable world in the mode of Daniel Defoe whose every item is catalogued for its commodity and exchange value: size, shape, weight, substance. Rather, Austen's descriptive terms develop and explore character along social lines. "Fine," "elegant," "handsome," "clever," "delicate," "rich" are words that confirm social assurance, grace, position, and poise.

The houses of *Pride and Prejudice* best illustrate how physical description in Austen's novels serves to make the social index a moral index to character as well.[13] By and large, the estates of Longbourn and Netherfield remain nondescript. The garden walk at Netherfield, where Elizabeth refuses to join the Bingley sisters and Darcy ("The picturesque would be spoilt by admitting a fourth"), has avenues sufficiently narrow to make the latters' rudeness evident (1, chap. 10). Longbourn takes on dimensions only for the purposes of Lady Catherine's visit to Elizabeth when the extent of her snub is to be evident: "You have a very small park here," and "This must be an inconvenient sitting room for the evening, in summer; the windows are full west" (3, chap. 14). Such comments reveal Lady Catherine's social and personal limitations. Austen describes Hunsford more fully so that we can evaluate the extent of Charlotte's control in her marriage. Rosings emerges principally by contrast to Pemberley, which is the most fully described estate, because it provides Elizabeth with her first full view of Darcy. Here, Austen wants to give us insight into Darcy rather than to make Pemberley tangible. The house and grounds themselves remain unvisualized for all her description.

The terms of a description are crucial in revealing places not as physical entities but as social/moral indices of a particular kind. Pemberley is "a large, handsome, stone building, standing well on rising ground, and backed by a ridge of high woody hills;—and in front, a stream of some natural importance was swelled into greater, but without any artificial appearance. Its banks were neither formal, nor falsely adorned" (3, chap. 1). The operative terms are ones of proportion and relationship, not of texture or substance: large, standing well, natural importance . . . swelled . . . without any artificial importance, neither formal nor falsely adorned. These words all express value judgments more readily than concrete settings.

Elizabeth continues into the house, where she finds a "large, well-proportioned room, handsomely fitted up." As she looks out the window she sees the "hill, crowned with wood . . . receiving increased abruptness from the distance . . . a beautiful object. Every disposition of the ground was good. . . . The rooms were lofty and handsome, and their furniture suitable to the fortunes of their proprietor . . . with less of splendor and more real elegance, than the furniture of Rosings" (3, chap. 1). The key to understanding "handsome," "beautiful," "elegant," and "good" lies in the proportions of house to land, rooms to house, and furniture to rooms. Proper understanding of proportion is a factor of social judgment and discrimination not of an innovative aesthetic sensibility. Splendor, the gaudy, or uselessly fine—ostentatious displays of one's position and wealth—are avoided. Elegance, the proper understanding of one's place and importance, is pursued. Darcy and Pemberley express an ideal that is at once social and personal.

What Elizabeth sees when she looks at Pemberley is evidence of a man in society who is properly conscious of social responsibility. Houses express a character's understanding of his place and of what is valuable. In contrast, when Dorothea Brooke in *Middlemarch* sees Lowick, she should see the soul of Casaubon, or when Pip in *Great Expectations* looks on Satis House, he should discover the destructive power of money and position enacted through Miss Havisham's life. In George Eliot's novel, a house mirrors only an individual's psychology; in Charles Dickens's novel, the house is emblematic of social process. Jane Austen's description provides insight into individual personality and simultaneously portrays social role and responsibility.

Jane Austen's descriptive terms, then, create contexts at once social and moral in which to evaluate people, but this is only part of her technique. Each individual's personality is further developed and refined through his responses to the demands of social decorum. It is important to recall that true decorum in each incident is ultimately decided by Austen's more astute and socially discriminating characters. It is not simply dictated by what is usually done. As a result, each social event offers numerous challenges to individual judgment in the assessment of true decorum.

For example, Elizabeth's decision to walk to Netherfield is a crucible in *Pride and Prejudice*. In this early episode, Elizabeth demonstrates her superiority to those around her. The episode begins with Jane's letter stating that she has become ill at Netherfield from riding through the rain to visit the Bingleys. The letter, appropriately addressed to her sister Elizabeth, provokes Mrs. Bennet's delight at her strategy's success and Mr. Bennet's stringent wit over his wife's foolishness. Only Elizabeth, knowing Jane's tendency to minimize her own interests, is "feeling really anxious" and determined to go to her. Elizabeth must walk; she recognizes that the occasion is not serious enough to warrant her inconveniencing her father on the farm by taking horses for the carriage but *is* serious enough to justify breaching decorum in this instance. If we are to admire Elizabeth, she cannot be guilty of the unthinking breaches of decorum characteristic of Lydia. Elizabeth has made a complex and precise decision, the exactness of which is confirmed in the narrator's comment: "Jane, who had only been withheld by the fear of giving *alarm* or *inconvenience*, from expressing in her note how much she longed for such a visit, was delighted at her entrance" (1, chap. 7), emphasis added. Elizabeth has avoided both alarm and inconvenience and yet fulfilled her sister's unexpressed but deep-felt wish. Austen has made Jane a horsewoman, and it would seem logical for her to have Elizabeth ride to Netherfield as well, but Austen denies Elizabeth this talent in order to intensify our appreciation of Elizabeth's judgments.

Emma Woodhouse's failure at Box Hill is significant morally, precisely because she fails to make these careful discriminations. In
Persuasion, Frederick Wentworth's obvious anger at Anne and his
irresponsibility with the Musgrove sisters is offset by the care with
which he discerns the proper course of action in the minor episodes
of daily converse: his appropriate but not excessive sympathy with
the sighings of Mrs. Musgrove over poor Dicky; his removing an
importunate, clinging nephew from a suffering Anne's neck; his
timely assistance of an exhausted Anne into his sister's carriage.

As Austen's characters engage questions of proper social behavior, they reveal themselves to us fully. Why, we might then ask,
does the narrator occasionally summarize the characters' traits for
us, as she does, for example, at the end of chapter 1 of *Pride and
Prejudice*. This paragraph and others (see, for example, the one
summarizing Mr. Collins's traits beginning chapter 15) have been
criticized for their redundancy.[14] The concluding paragraph of
chapter 1 tells us: "Mr. Bennet was so odd a mixture of quick parts,
sarcastic humour, reserve, and caprice, that the experience of three
and twenty years had been insufficient to make his wife understand his character. *Her* mind was less difficult to develope. She
was a woman of mean understanding, little information, and uncertain temper. When she was discontented she fancied herself ner-
vous. The business of her life was to get her daughters married; its
solace was visiting and news."

We should, perhaps, have deduced all of this information from
the foregoing dialogue. Although the paragraph tells us nothing
new, it serves an important purpose in limiting the range of conclusions we can draw from what has been presented.[15] If the narrator
had said, for example, that "Mr. Bennet was so odd a mixture of
quick parts, sarcastic humor, reserve and caprice that he was likely
to ruin his daughters' chances for happiness by his irresponsibility
in social matters," or that "Mrs. Bennet's mind was less difficult to
develop. She was a woman of mean understanding and little information who was characterized chiefly by a vulgar intrusiveness
into her daughters' affairs," we would have very different expectations for the characters. Yet neither of these revised character summaries provides any information that is not deducible from what
Jane Austen has shown us of the Bennets in chapter 1. By representing the social convention as no obstacle and by not emphasizing the traits of Mr. and Mrs. Bennet that might seriously harm

their daughters, she establishes at this early stage in the novel a pattern of comic expectations.

In effect, the narrator in *Pride and Prejudice* promises us a comedy, promises that individual merit will prove equal to social pressure. Likewise the narrator assures us, after Darcy has given offense at the Meryton assembly, "On the strength of Darcy's regard Bingley had the firmest reliance, and of his judgment the highest opinion. In understanding Darcy was the superior. Bingley was by no means deficient, but Darcy was clever. He was at the same time haughty, reserved, and fastidious, and his manners, though well bred, were not inviting" (1, chap. 4). The narrator has, in essence, placed Darcy's traits in an evaluative context that assigns greater weight to his cleverness than to his social pride and awkwardness. The narrator's emphasis on Darcy's judgment warrants our predicting both the immediate consequence—Darcy's growing appreciation of Elizabeth—and the eventual marriage of these two discerning and superior individuals.

In such ways, Austen uses narrative evaluation to shape our expectations for individuals and to assure us that society, in its function in the narrative, will afford a flexible balance between individual and social needs, a balance that guarantees that social class or rank will not thwart the most deserving characters. Indeed, through their efforts, the protagonists can partly free themselves from society's occasionally punctilious expectations.

Family, Society, and Self-Determination

The conclusions of Jane Austen's novels typically portray individuals marrying and leaving one family to form another. The power to constitute a "new" family is distinctive of characters in Austen's novels. Family is never defined strictly along blood lines.

The characters are, in fact, remarkably free to define their merit individually and to escape completely the disgrace surrounding their relatives. Although it is true that we can easily recall embarrassments caused by giddy, heedless, or unscrupulous family members in Austen's novels—Lydia Bennet eloping with Wickham, Maria Bertram Rushworth running off with Henry Crawford—these actions do not have lasting consequences for the protagonists. Despite Elizabeth Bennet's fears that Lydia's actions will reflect on the family, they do so largely in ways that distinguish Elizabeth's superiority. As we have seen, Darcy has assured Elizabeth earlier in his letter that she and Jane have confirmed their own merit by escaping any of the censure that falls on their family members. Finally, even Elizabeth feels that, if Darcy is swayed by considerations outside her personal merit, she "will soon cease to regret him at all."

More important, Austen's protagonists are free to establish their own "families" at the conclusions of the novels. Austen's protagonists not only free themselves from society's limitations but shape a society congenial to themselves. Darcy and Elizabeth retire to "all the comfort and elegance of their family party at Pemberley." That family party explicitly includes Mr. Bennet who "delighted in going to Pemberley, especially when he was least expected"; it includes the Gardiners with whom Elizabeth and Darcy "were always on the most intimate terms," but it excludes Wickham and Mrs. Bennet who, the narrator obliquely tells us, "visited Mrs. Bingley and talked of Mrs. Darcy" with delighted pride (3, chap. 19). This family party stresses empathy over consanguinity although it also continues to respect the prerogatives of rank in making Lady Catherine ultimately a welcome visitor. In contrast, the weaker Bingley and Jane are unable to shape a society congenial to themselves. In allowing frequent and prolonged visits from the Wickhams and also Mrs. Bennet, they fail to emerge as fully self-determining individuals. The narrator pinpoints Bingley's failure in commenting that "with the Bingleys they [Lydia and Wickham] both of them frequently staid so long, that even Bingley's good humour was overcome, and he proceeded so far as to *talk* of giving them a hint to be gone" (3, chap. 19).

In *Mansfield Park*, Maria Bertram is banished from Mansfield; Fanny is established at its center. Her duty is not to her biological parents but to her adoptive parents, Sir Thomas and Lady Bertram, with whom she shares graciousness and elegance. Anne Elliot in *Persuasion* regrets that she has "no family to receive and estimate [Wentworth] properly," but she contents herself with bringing her two worthy friends, Lady Russell and Mrs. Smith, into their new family circle, which includes the Crofts and the Harvilles.

Austen's novels conclude with characters established in new family circles that are themselves microcosms of a reinvigorated society. Later novelists will often depict family as a haven, as an environment in which the guilty or fallen individual can expect shelter, but that haven brings with it the right to censure. Although a family will defend its black sheep, it will also censure its erring member. Thus, in *The Mill on the Floss*, Tom Tulliver feels the stinging mortification of having Maggie for a sister, and, while he protects her, no one is more harsh than he in correcting her. The Poysers in *Adam Bede*, after Hetty Sorrel's child-murder, want to hide in shame and, although persuaded to remain in Hayslope, they never fully recover from the social stigma of their relationship to Hetty. E. M. Forster expresses a similar sense of family in *Howards End* when Leonard Bast realizes that he "need never starve, because it would be too painful for his relatives. Society is based on the family, and the clever wastrel can exploit this indefinitely."[16] Edith Wharton, in *The Age of Innocence*, deals with a social community similar to Austen's but assigns to it a very different role; her protagonist recognizes that "the individual . . . is nearly always sacrificed to what is supposed to be the collective interest: people cling to any convention that keeps the family together."[17] While wastrels are certainly protected by their families in Austen's novels, no individual is sacrificed to a collective familial interest. Deviant behavior of family members cannot finally reflect on the protagonists. It is precisely this larger freedom from the bonds, obligations, and imperatives of consanguinity that enables Austen's characters to be so self-determining.

In a perceptive comparison between Louisa May Alcott's *Little Women* and Jane Austen's *Pride and Prejudice*, Nina Auerbach has noted that family is a "charmed circle" in Alcott's novel, a locus for the exercise of "precious freedom." She explains, "In *Pride and Prejudice* the family fed itself to the omnipresent neighborhood, but in *Little Women* it is the heart of its world. . . . [The household of *Pride and Prejudice*] is both economic nullity and social embarrassment, while the other [that of *Little Women*] finds no greater happiness than its own being and power, transcending poverty in the creation of a community that is the most potent reality of its society."[18] However, in praising *Little Women*, Auerbach misses the fact that the Bennet family is one to be escaped in order to form a family party more congenial to Elizabeth's temperament and more conducive to her self-realization. The movement in Austen is positive; individuals in her novels are self-determining, and society, shaped in the image of its members, is a context for renewal and growth. Family, in Alcott's novel, is a shelter because society is inimical to self-realization. It is a "charmed circle" whose magic can only partially protect one from the destructive effects of social expectations.

A Changing Understanding of Society

I have stressed the ways in which society and its role are similar within Austen's canon. Her society is comprised of members of a particular class, governed by a strong sense of social decorum and by explicit social conventions. Both major and minor characters are immersed in and develop the social context. The tendency of later writers to highlight a character against a social background arises, in part, from a perception of society as limiting. Therefore the major characters must be distinguished from it. Austen's characters need not be distinguished from, only within, the context of their society, hence she focuses on multiple responses to social convention and its demands. This technique produces such precision that it obviates the need for other modes of characterization such as physical description or the identification of character with objects that grant autonomy and particularity. This is one function of objects in the novel: in association with individuals they become signifiers of values apart from society's values. Such objects are not necessary when individuals can achieve complete fulfillment in a society. Personal values and character can be fully revealed through the social forms themselves. That is Jane Austen's way. She uses description of character and place to continue her exploration of a morality embedded in social form, appearance, and behavior. Furthermore, Austen's narrator becomes valuable, not to pose or reiterate details of character and event, but to keep the whole within a comic framework that sees the role of society as nonobstructive.

Jane Austen's unique achievement in the novel seems to depend in part on the inclusion of only one social class. In order to use social conventions as a measure of moral character, and to make that revealed moral character determine an individual's fate, she must have only one class with clearly defined expectations for social behavior. Differences of rank and fortune do exist—aristocracy, gentry, military, clergy, trade—and these differences account for much of the novels' humor. But no character with proper perspective, deserving of fulfillment, is struggling to be accepted by another class. All characters can attend the same social functions, and no social bias prevents their intermarriage.

With this understanding of Jane Austen's use of society, it is interesting to consider briefly the differences between *Pride and Prejudice*, her first major novel, and *Persuasion*, her last.[19] The chief distinction lies in their definitions of normative behavior. In both novels Austen focuses on the upper-middle class, but Darcy is the standard in *Pride and Prejudice*. His formality must be matched by the Gardiners in their visit to Pemberley; beside his reticence, Wickham's openness is suspect. In *Persuasion* the Crofts and Wentworth, with their ease of manner, good humor, and marked casualness of propriety, set the standard beside which Sir Walter's formality appears hollow and Mr. William Elliot's reticence now appears suspect. *Persuasion* places greater emphasis on the individual: Sir Walter's world cannot be accommodated to Wentworth's as Elizabeth's can to Darcy's. The increasing number of personal objects in the world of *Persuasion*—mirrors, dog carts, gloves, guns, umbrellas—and the more sensuous evocation of nature suggest a world deepening its focus on individuals apart from social form, deepening its sense that social forms might no longer accommodate individual happiness. Austen still locates complete fulfillment for her characters within society, but she has sown seeds of change and anticipates later novelists' exploration of a society's inimical effect on individuals.

Jane Austen's novels provide the first boundary for this survey by depicting a society in which complete fulfillment is possible for the most deserving individuals. In them, a character's fate is decided principally by his or her own potential. Society is not simply a context or battleground for individual definition; it functions particularly as a measure of moral character; that is, as part of our aesthetic experience, Austen includes both the characters' special discrimination in enacting social decorum and their appropriate ridicule of false, foolish, and petty conventions. Austen's intention is clearly manifest in *Pride and Prejudice*'s Lady Catherine de Bourgh. Although Lady Catherine marshalls every argument available, she is unable to present any telling objection to Darcy and Elizabeth's marriage. In rejecting Lady Catherine's objections as trivial, both Darcy and Elizabeth define themselves as superior and by their perceptiveness rise above her follies. If the above example seems merely to stress Austen's rejection of the foolish confusion of social values and snobbery, the importance of fulfilling true social decorum is furthered in the contrast between the Bennets and the Gardiners. Mr. and Mrs. Bennet continually embarrass Elizabeth in failing to fulfill social decorum—whether from ignorance or carelessness of propriety—but the lower-status Gardiners, during their visit to Pemberley, win Darcy's respect and Elizabeth's grateful affection for their continually appropriate and decorous behavior and join in the triumph of a new order. Ultimately, Austen's talented and deserving individuals not only free themselves from society's limitations but shape a society congenial to themselves.

Austen keeps her characters' conflicts with their social milieu within a comic framework, not by presenting a benign picture of society, but by including narrative summaries that stress those aspects of behavior and conventions that assure us society will not stand in the way of individual fulfillment. The narrators of Austen's novels align themselves with society as a guardian of true value. Social form expresses, or is capable of expressing, enduring substance. As a result, the narrator herself becomes the most stringent critic of departures from the sane and reasonable, of form that has been reduced to formula. The formal idea of society, then, is realized and embodied in the perceptions of Austen's more discerning characters and in the judgments of her narrator. This society serves as a formal center of values by which worthy characters rise, and unworthy are identified, in our estimation.

3

The Willing Suspension of Social Probability in Fielding, Thackeray, and Dickens

I declare here, once for all, I describe not men, but manners; not an individual, but a species. Perhaps it will be answered, Are not the characters then taken from life? To which I answer in the affirmative; nay, I believe I might aver that I have writ little more than I have seen.
—Henry Fielding, *Joseph Andrews*

Yes, this is Vanity Fair; not a moral place certainly; nor a merry one, though very noisy....
   A man with a reflective turn of mind, walking through an exhibition of this sort, will not be oppressed, I take it, by his own or other people's hilarity... the general impression is one more melancholy than mirthful. When you come home you sit down, in a sober, contemplative, not uncharitable frame of mind, and apply yourself to your books or your business.
—William Makepeace Thackeray, *Vanity Fair,*
   "Before the Curtain"

Dear reader! It rests with you and me whether, in our two fields of action, similar things shall be or not. Let them be! We shall sit with lighter bosoms on the hearth, to see the ashes of our fires turn grey and cold.
—Charles Dickens, *Hard Times*, "Final"

Jane Austen found society an ample context for individual fulfill-ment; for her, the social order not only accommodated individual potential, it also rewarded individual superiority. Few other nov-elists could easily share that vision. A fully represented society, which includes the rich and the poor, the upper, lower, and middle classes, as hers did not, does not foster complete fulfillment for all deserving characters. In a carefully depicted hierarchy, wealth and social position act as barriers to individual achievement, advance-ment, and happiness.

see pattern #2, p.12

Other novelists have erected something resembling Austen's comic fulfillment, but to do so they needed to find techniques that would enable them to exempt some characters from the probable effects of living in a class- and money-based society, a society that is ultimately inimical to freedom of individual movement and self-realization. Henry Fielding in *Tom Jones*, William Makepeace Thackeray in *Vanity Fair*, and Charles Dickens in his later novels did exactly that. Each depicted a society inimical to their protago-nists' fulfillment and thus potentially precluded a comic resolu-tion, but, at the same time, each developed an approach to nar-ration that enabled him to exempt key characters from society's injurious effects. The societies they represent are largely autono-mous, but by examining carefully their narrative techniques, we can discover the seams in that fabric of society and see how char-acters are released from being totally wrapped in its logic.

The range in styles and accomplishments here is broad; these writers are diverse in their achievements and interests. Yet, in this one respect, Fielding, Thackeray, and Dickens share an essential solution to the conflict between an individual's wishes and a so-ciety's tendency to preserve the status quo: each has devised a technique that mediates between an existing social order and the fate of individual characters.

Fielding may have been one of the first novelists to recognize how thoroughly society might inhibit individual advancement. He pits an articulate, intrusive narrator against this potentially de-structive, and certainly restrictive, milieu. Class differences are clearly a major obstacle in the world of *Tom Jones*, but they do not ultimately ban the hero from his reward. From the outset, Field-ing's narrator assures us of a comic conclusion to this novel, and in the process, subverts the narrative probabilities for failure, which a very astute presentation of Tom's society has established.

By contrast, Thackeray's narrator does not interfere in the workings of a social order as it exerts its influence on the lives of the characters. Although characters' natures express their society and the consequences of being in that society, there exists, surprisingly, no necessary relationship between what a character does and what happens to him or her in that society. That surprising disjunction exists because society is depicted in two seemingly irreconcilable ways, as a set of social ideals and as a series of unspoken pragmatic laws. Because a single, coherent presentation of society is necessary to establish expectations for a character's fate, this double vision has the effect of releasing characters from clear social probabilities. What happens to each character depends on the novelist's skillful stagemanaging of these two perspectives represented by the two major characters, Amelia Sedley and Becky Sharp. Thackeray thus offers a subtle variation of the same formal role for society that Fielding and Dickens explore. His characters express society's nature, but their fates depend on the narrator's evaluative presence, because fictional society in *Vanity Fair* sets up two conflicting social probabilities.

In addition to representing society in the conflicting lives of Becky and Amelia, Thackeray uses his narrator as an important part of his fictional society. Unlike Fielding's narrator, Thackeray's narrator exploits his position to blur distinctions between good and bad, between black and white, between worthy and unworthy. This narrator forces his reader to examine the very concepts by which judgment is made in society and, by rendering them ambiguous in application if not in meaning, calls into question the nature of good and its meaning for a society.

Dickens, unlike Fielding, relies little on the privileged powers of a narrator to affect either the action of a story or a reader's perception of it, and he does not depend, like Thackeray, on a double vision of society. To suspend the expectations for individual possibility that are created by presenting a society in some depth, Dickens adopts a persuasive technique of characterizing his players. (It may be more accurate to say that the manner in which Dickens goes about creating fictional individuals produces the effect of releasing them from society's governing logic.) In Dickens, characters are not precisely flat, in Forster's sense; rather they are more or less static.[1] Personalities on the whole do not change or evolve; people do not grow. By beginning with specific quirks and then locating the general significance of those quirks, Dickens gives each individual a density not born of inner development. Characters become simultaneously representative and eccentric. They exist as part of a class structure and yet as separate and unique. They all live in the same world, but their individual eccentricities separate them, each from the next, like tiles in a mosaic. The resultant picture of society is highly detailed, but characters maintain an autonomy in their individual existence that tends to immure them from the destructive effects of a class system. In addition, Dickens chooses dominant images for social process from the landscape and elements, images that suggest a general, biological evolution rather than the consequences of specific human intentions and institutions. A society so depicted determines the general quality of everyone's life but does not necessarily dictate the particular shape of individual fates. In this way, Dickens can free characters from the probabilities of the social realm he depicts.

Dickens, Thackeray, and Fielding all adopt narrative strategies that give them a measure of control over individual characters' fates but that also allow them to represent societies which, in their fullness and range, clearly express principles of order not conducive to the success of all worthy individuals in them. Questions of privilege, class, money, and social institutions (such as Chancery) are confronted here and unlike Austen, Fielding, Thackeray, and Dickens must admit the destructive effects society can, and does, have. To a degree, then, each novelist must subvert what he acknowledges in his representation in order to extricate some characters from the fabric of society in which they live.

Social Probability and Narrative Clemency in *Tom Jones*

The fact that Tom Jones was "certainly born to be hanged" tells us at least as much about this hero's milieu as it does about his character.[2] The novel's fictional society includes both those who will be prejudiced against Tom because of his birth and those who will take active advantage of his status as foundling and of his characteristic imprudence. This society comprehends, then, both active malevolence and the passive prejudice of public opinion. Those who undertake to scheme actively against Tom—Captain Blifil and Mr. Blifil—will be aided by those generally prejudiced against the

Margin notes: even as he preaches "connection," his "individuals are separate"

foundling, for example, Mrs. Wilkins, Thwackum, Square, Dowling. Whereas Tom can "mend" his character, he lacks power to remedy the most serious offence he has committed, that of being born a bastard. His fault, in short, depends on a public attitude. Here we see the force of public opinion in this world, a fickle force that works largely against characters. We recall that Partridge, championed by public opinion when Allworthy punishes him for his putative paternity of Tom, "was in Danger of Starving with the universal Compassion of all his Neighbours" (2, chap. 6). Public opinion produces evil but not good.

Although Tom suffers from public censure, he has Allworthy's protection, since the good squire will not punish a baby for his parents' fault, but Allworthy's protection cannot make possible the hoped-for resolution of Tom's marriage to Sophia, for that requires a change in Tom's social position. In *Joseph Andrews*, too, only an elevation in social standing will free the protagonists from the machinations of the powerful and self-interested. They cease to be vulnerable at last, not through wisdom and personal growth, but through promotion within the social ranks. Joseph's identification as the Wilsons' son and Fanny's as the daughter of the Andrews guarantees their release from the malign influences of the Lady Boobys and Peter Pounces of the world.

Thus both novels depend for their comic conclusions on circumstances outside the protagonists' power. These characters cannot guarantee their own happiness or determine their fulfillments as do Elizabeth and Darcy or Anne and Wentworth in Austen's novels. What happens to them depends on forces beyond themselves, specifically on the intervention of the narrator.

Critics are quite right to point out that neither *Joseph Andrews* nor *Tom Jones* is a "whodunnit" in which we are waiting to see who parented whom.[3] We know things will turn out well although we have no idea how. It is accurate, too, to observe that, when Allworthy is revealed as Tom's uncle, the reward affirms our perception of the protagonist's worth.[4] There is justice here but not causality. Tom's worthiness itself does not guarantee his complete happiness at the novel's end as worth would in an Austen society. Only the narrator can make everything right. The distinctive power of Fielding's *Tom Jones* as a comedy stems from our recognition of society as inimical and knowledge that things need not have turned out as well as they did.[5]

Fielding's characters, then, are not the architects of their own fates. This partial divorce between character and action typifies novels in which the society generally obstructs individual possibility but does not limit the lives of the major characters, and it helps explain, for instance, our response to Tom's entanglement with Lady Bellaston. She represents a social corruption, but Tom's participation in that corruption does not taint him to the degree it would in other kinds of novels. The event's capacity to reveal new dimensions to Tom's character or to chart his growth is ultimately minimal. He remains basically good and goodnatured.

How then is character presented and developed in *Tom Jones*? Jane Austen offered a dense network of social conventions in response to which characters revealed their natures and their growth. *Tom Jones* develops character principally through the narrator's comments and observations.[6] As a result of Fielding's approach, individual fates are more easily divorced from the probabilities the narrative voice has established for us. That narrator announces, for example, that Miss Bridget is "of that Species of Woman, whom you commend rather for good Qualities than Beauty, and who are generally called by their own Sex, very good Sort of Women—as good a Sort of Woman, Madam, as you would wish to know. Indeed she was so far from regretting Want of Beauty, that she never mentioned that Perfection (if it can be called one) without Contempt" (1, chap. 3). Complex perspectives come into play here. We recognize a social group for whom jealousy provides a powerful incentive to moral stereotyping of good or bad. Beauty leads to evil; homeliness guarantees "virtue"; real virtue is confused with virginity. Mrs. Bridget's chagrin at her lack of beauty is made evident in her contempt for it. The narrator has pointed to both her social surface (contempt) and her reality (chagrin). The effect is to acquaint us with the character but to distance us, through judgment, from her, and it is done through narrative commentary. The allegorical battle waged in Black George's soul (6, chap. 13)—a battle among Fear, Avarice, and Conscience—is merely an extension of the same technique. Involvement with a character's life and inner drama is minimized and that character is securely lodged within the evaluative framework of the novel.

We *know* the characters, but we know them through the narrator's commentary, which distances us from the characters and encourages our ready judgment. In addition, because the narrator's values are always explicit and he makes sharp discriminations between his values and those of society, the characters remain basically a reflection of his ethical perspectives. They are not given autonomy. Their personalities are a function of his understanding, and he determines the scope of their influence. Henry James acknowledges the narrator's central role when he praises Fielding's accomplishment: "[Tom Jones] has so much 'life' that it amounts, for the effect of comedy and application of satire, almost to his having a mind, that is to his having reactions and a full consciousness; besides which his author—*he* handsomely possessed of a mind—has such an amplitude of reflection for him and round him that we see him through the mellow air of Fielding's fine old moralism, fine old humour and fine old style, which somehow really enlarge, make every one and every thing important."[7] It is the narrator who possesses complexity; it is the narrator who creates his social world and in his creation controls it by making his humanity, wisdom, and benevolence the standard by which characters succeed or fail. It is his voice assuring us that "Providence often interposes in the Discovery of the most secret Villainy," and the presence of such narrative commentary shapes our expectation for Blifil's unmasking and Tom's reward (18, chap. 3).

We must consider, in this light, the scope and role of society in Fielding's novels. The very need for novelistic techniques that release individuals from social probability presupposes a depiction of society that sees its destructiveness. Although society does not ultimately serve as an obstacle to Fielding's heroes, his presentation of it deepens the tone and broadens the significance of the comedy. Fictional society in *Tom Jones* includes country and city with their oppositions. It is a world of the prestigious and powerful—the landowners and aristocrats—plus those who serve them and for whom they are responsible—their servants, retainers, parishioners, tenants. It also includes, through the on-the-road sequences, innkeepers, small farmers, merchants, tradespeople, and the military. The dominant values and tendencies of that world are revealed through all of the characters but clarified through the use of digressions and through special representative characters. Fielding's society, in contrast to Austen's, depends much more on wealth of character and alternative experiences represented in the digressions than on a set of clearly defined norms and expectations for social behavior.[8] Austen's economy of representation is partly due to her developing society through conventions, the performance of which defines the characters. Society is revealed through the protagonists' actions even as it reveals them. Fielding, on the contrary, thickens his story line with digressions because his commentator cannot fully reveal society through his protagonists. Having guaranteed them his shelter from social and narrative probability, their lives cannot reflect fully the inimical power of society.

Despite his protagonists' fulfillment, Fielding created worlds in which happiness is the exception rather than the rule; in depicting society he is committed to a fidelity that recognizes good is not always rewarded nor evil consistently punished. Fielding's use of both digressions and highly representative characters guarantees that we will not see society as generally hospitable to the worthy.

Two major digressions in both *Tom Jones* and *Joseph Andrews* demonstrate this point. The first digression in *Tom Jones* is a short one, the story of Broadbrim, the Quaker, and his undutiful daughter. Tom's meeting with Broadbrim acquaints him with a story parallel in certain respects to his own—young lovers, opposition of girl's father to humble match, the father's proposal of wealthy suitor; but this story, unlike Tom's, sees the lovers eloping to the unmitigated wrath of the duped father. The Quaker and his children are left in a "limbo of permanent unhappiness," reminding us that the social fabric in *Tom Jones* is not uniformly amiable and that comedic solutions are not necessarily the rule here.[9]

The second digression and the major one in the novel, the Man of Mazzard Hill's story, also reflects on alternatives to Tom's life. It depicts one man's disastrous encounter with, and consequent retreat from, a society inimical to human possibility. Betrayed by his friends and his lover, provoked to robbery by his dire straits, the Man of Mazzard Hill has concluded that the only viable course is retreat from an iniquitous world to contemplate God's greatness. His choice ultimately leads to a complete disengagement from mankind, a disengagement destructive to his own humanity. He can hear Mrs. Waters's screams for assistance and yet sit, nursing his gun on his lap. Tom differs substantially in character from the Man of Mazzard Hill; their similarities tend to be superficial similarities of position. Nonetheless, the Man's life emblematizes one individual's experience in and response to an inimical society. We must see that neither Tom's innate goodness nor his good intentions necessarily save him from a world interested in blackening his character and destroying him.

Both digressions are related by the principal actors in them and are thus deprived of the lively presence of the narrator. This elision of the narrator is essential to Fielding's purposes, because the narrator's intervention guarantees the protagonists' happiness. Without his presence, the destructive effects of public opinion and social corruption determine individual lives. Although many readers have found the digressions tedious because of the commentator's absence, that absence changes the role of society in the characters' lives, as Fielding intended. Thus, the stories of the Man of Mazzard Hill and Broadbrim demonstrate the destructive power of that society when freed from the mediation of the benevolent commentator. Mr. Wilson's and Leonora's stories in *Joseph Andrews* carry out a similar function, defining evils and corruptions of vanity as permanent and determinative aspects of that world.

We might compare Fielding's digressions with later novelists' use of multiple plots. George Eliot and Thackeray, for example, chart the lives of a variety of protagonists both to broaden the representation of society and to suggest the power and range of social norms and expectations in shaping individual lives. In novels with several plot lines and a variety of principal characters, all characters must be equally subject to the laws of their social world. None are exempt. Fielding also desires that image of society's range and power, just as he seeks to capture that social breadth. But a single plot with major digressions allows him to reward his deserving characters, freeing them by his presence from the laws that dictate the fates of individuals in other quarters of the imagined society.

Just as digressions help broaden the moral significance of Fielding's art, certain characters serve both to flesh out the portrait of society by embodying one of its principles and to facilitate the narrator's commentary on the norms and values he prizes. The most expressive of these are emblematic, two-dimensional characters, which are "walking concepts," to borrow a term from Sheldon Sacks.[10] "Concept" aptly suggests such characters' scope and significance to the fiction. Square and Thwackum are chief examples of the technique in *Tom Jones*; each has a label attached to him, and it is reiterated frequently enough so that we do not lose sight of the emblematic principles each embodies. Square holds "human

Nature to be the Perfection of all Virtue," and he "squares" his conduct with "the *unalterable Rule of Right, and the eternal Fitness of Things.*" Square's definition of eternal fitness, of course, allows him to justify any of his own actions. Thwackum propounds "the *divine Power of Grace*" and decides "all Matters by Authority" (3, chap. 3). Thwackum's latitude lies in interpretation, which is of equal authority with the text. Although each clearly embodies a central philosophical position, both possess sufficient traits to animate them as individuals. At the same time, the evil that each represents is not confined to himself but exists in the world as a general philosophy of which they are only local particulars. Characters such as Thwackum or Square are eventually defeated of course, but the principle they have introduced into the world of the novel remains to characterize something in society and to aid in our judgment of character and event.

Even as Fielding extends the range of his social criticism through such characters, he must also see that they do not seriously threaten the protagonists' chances for success. The flatness of "walking concepts" and the narrator's derisive comments about them limit their potency. Tom encounters a variety of malign and compromising figures on the road whose transience and two-dimensional natures serve both to flesh out his adventures and to assure us that these characters will have no lasting effect on the hero's fate. When such characters are to be more permanent fixtures of the plot, Fielding takes pains to render them laughable. For example, when Square is "caught sitting" with Molly, he behaves in absolutely predictable ways. Once discovered by Jones, he is at no loss for a rationale both for lusting after a voluptuous Molly and, having possessed her, for guarding his reputation. His reason is, of course, the eternal fitness of things, the philosophical tag by which he also rationalizes Tom's destruction, but the tag now allows him to be bested by Tom, and it renders him ludicrous. His myopic self-interest deflates and defeats him. He is ridiculous and proves no match for the breadth and understanding of the narrator who contains him fully in his vision and control. So the narrator precedes Square's rationalizations with this telling observation, "Philosophers are composed of Flesh and Blood as well as other human Creatures; and however sublimated and refined the Theory of these may be, a little practical Frailty is as incident to them as to other Mortals" (5, chap. 5).

By rendering these people transient or laughable, Fielding mutes our sense of their power. We tend not to take them and their conspiracies as seriously as we might. In a similar way, the mock heroic makes laughable the churchgoers' self-righteous attack on a pregnant Molly Seagrim in the famous churchyard battle. Distance is the key. We are not allowed to fear for Molly's life; we are invited rather to laugh both at the indignation and pettiness of Molly's attackers as well as at Molly's simple vanity, which has provoked the attack. By inviting our laughter at the potentially malign, the narrator diminishes the stature and power of the antagonists.

Although muting the power of socially representative characters through laughter, Fielding guards the seriousness of those who share his norms: Allworthy and Sophia. Allworthy is a powerful but short-sighted figure, Sophia clear-sighted but powerless. Sophia's faith in Tom provides an analogue, within Tom's reality, to the narrator's faith in his hero, and Allworthy's power and justice provide an avenue, in Tom's world, for the retribution and reward that the narrator deems appropriate. Thus, the narrator expends substantial energy on assuring us of Sophia's and Allworthy's virtue. He excuses Allworthy's failure of insight: "It is possible, however, that Mr. *Allworthy* saw enough to render him a little uneasy; for we are not always to conclude, that a wise Man is not hurt, because he doth not cry out and lament himself, like those of a childish or effeminate Temper" (2, chap. 7). The narrator also points out, "If your Inside be never so beautiful, you must preserve a fair Outside also. This must be constantly looked to, or Malice and Envy will take Care to blacken it so, that the Sagacity and Goodness of an *Allworthy* will not be able to see thro' it, and to discern the Beauties within" (3, chap. 7). There is nothing risible about Allworthy although he is potentially as ridiculous in his blindness as are others in the novel. His decision to banish Tom from Paradise Hall is presented as perfectly just and reasonable in light of his information, and the narrator cautions: "The Reader must be very weak, if, when he considers the Light in which *Jones* then appeared to Mr. *Allworthy*, he should blame the Rigour of his Sentence" (6, chap. 11). The complete seriousness with which Allworthy is presented makes him a considerable force in his world. Even so, we should recognize that force as an extension of the narrator's. We are simply assured that Allworthy will respond appropriately to reward Tom when the narrator presents the set of circumstances that redeems Tom's character and changes his status as foundling.

Narrative distance is central to Fielding's art, but distance can prevent a reader's involvement in the world of the novel. We might ask, then, how Fielding's narrator engages us in his world, in his valuations, in his vision of society's relationship to individuals. Fielding himself said that he criticizes not the individual but the species. For the reader encountering Fielding's society, the danger might be that he or she will not see the ways in which this novel engages the meaning of individual human life in society. The commentator's distance and control might prevent the close identification with individual characters that vitalizes their struggles and triumphs.

To diminish that potential detachment, the commentator invokes and challenges the reader through the creation of an implied reader who is made explicitly responsible for interpreting the meaning of the represented world.[11] The commentator prefers to involve us less in the characters' struggles and more in the very process of creating and judging the world of the novel. Our intellects and imaginations are directly responsible, and to the extent that we fail in generosity or acumen, we encounter the narrator's chastisements. In Austen's novels, the characters must discriminate the appropriate responses to social conventions; in Fielding's, we must make the discriminations. It is *our* ear, not the characters', that must pick up the difference between the "prudence" of Mr. Blifil and the "prudence" enjoined on Tom by Allworthy. That is, our intelligence must distinguish between the prudence that is a social vice and the prudence that is a social virtue, *prudentia*.[12] It is, in short, we, rather than the characters, who are educable in Fielding's world.

Wayne Booth has spoken of the narrator's frequent invocations to the reader as constituting a "plot" of their own. The reader's participation in the novel is not only demanded, but the shape of that participation is defined. "Examine your Heart, my good Reader," says the narrator, "and resolve whether you do believe these Matters with me. If you do, you may now proceed to their Exemplification in the following Pages; if you do not, you have, I assure you, already read more than you have understood" (6, chap. 1). The separate plot of a growing relationship between reader and commentator has its own denouement in the narrator's farewell:

"And now, my Friend, I take this Opportunity . . . of heartily wishing thee well" (18, chap. 1). If this novel has worked for us, we are
reluctant to leave the company of this wise and urbane guide who
has become an affectionate friend.

The reader becomes an enormously important character in
Fielding's novel because Fielding explicitly expects of him certain
attributes and abilities. *Tom Jones* is a novel about judgment, and
issues of a reader's judgment are not merely implicit as they are in
most novels; they are made explicit by the narrator's comments to
the reader. The reader is invited, even forced, to consider his bases
for judgment. So the narrator argues, "the Reader makes a poor
Use of the Information I have given him." This reader is challenged
to meet the narrator's standards. He must make the discriminations that will determine the health of society; he must show his capacity to distinguish between the spurious and the valuable. Each
reader, then, is a potential architect of society. Fielding is not so
much concerned with what "really" existed as he is with each individual's responsibility to what exists in any period and to what
might exist if right-minded men and women fully understood their
social responsibility.

When we say that Fielding conceives society's role as inimical
but that he grants exemptions to a chosen few characters in his
created world, we must add that Fielding does so to enlist the
individual reader's responsibility for the shape and possibilities of
society. That responsibility is implicit in the role Fielding ascribes
to his represented society and in the attitude his commentator
takes toward that world. The characters are the commentator's
pawns, but the reader is not. He is subject to education, and the
represented world of the novel is the medium for his testing and
education. The rewarded characters are the narrator's promise for
the power of individual responsibility, commitment, and effort to
enrich the meaning and purpose of human life in society.

The "Author's Own Candles" and Conflicting
Social Visions in *Vanity Fair*

Fielding, although optimistic, presents no merely amiable comedy.
While his protagonists receive their deserts, Fielding's peripheral
characters, like Dickens's, suggest that life does not always work

out so well. Thackeray approaches a similar dark vision but by a different avenue. He does not highlight the happy story in the foreground. Instead that potentially happy story of the virtuous and deserving, Amelia and Dobbin, is not entirely happy. Thackeray's dark vision depends on two ways of looking at human interaction in society. On the one hand, one may take the Becky Sharp approach of recognizing the vanity, selfishness, and injustice in the world, and becoming pragmatic, self-interested, and calculating. On the other hand, one may adopt Amelia Sedley's sheltered perspectives and govern one's life through idealism, selflessness, and affection. But Amelia, by Thackeray's lights, is not the good girl in a corrupt world any more than Becky is the evil intruder in a haven of innocence. Both characters are emblematic of values in their society: Becky stands for society's unspoken, ruthless code of conduct, Amelia for its expressed or tacit ideals. Becky, the seeming social "outsider," often barred from the prerogatives of polite society, in reality most fully embodies the social truth beneath appearances. Amelia, the "good girl," is nearly destroyed because she tries to live entirely by untenable social ideals. Neither woman embodies the "reality" of Thackeray's world; they are equally real, and each provides a standard by which to evaluate the other.

Thackeray's achievement in *Vanity Fair* depends on this ability to suggest alternative contexts and standards for judgment. Thackeray has been praised for his novel's panoramic breadth of classes, institutions, and peoples. He does not, in fact, represent all elements of his society but concentrates on the middle to upper classes. Thackeray seems oblivious to the factory workers, or any part of England's industrial life, vividly captured in other novels of the 1840s by Disraeli, Kingsley, and Mrs. Gaskell. Thackeray's represented society suggests breadth partly by its thorough grasp of the life it does represent—that of kings, aristocracy, the Church, the military, tradesmen, old money, new money, merchant families, professionals, and the servants who serve the wealthy. More important, however, Thackeray's depiction of social values and norms gives his society dimension and scope. His portrait is complete for the same reason that he has been accused of cynicism—because he dramatizes both social pragmatism in Becky and social idealism in Amelia—and he finds both wanting. Amelia's appears to be the more moral life if only because societies are accustomed to thinking of their principles as moral ones. In fact, Thackeray exposes through her the bankrupt flaccidity of society's self-image.[13]

The narrator is essential to Thackeray's aims because, if the novel is to succeed, we cannot identify with either Becky or Amelia. To do so would sacrifice the larger analysis, which contains both visions of social possibility, Amelia's and Becky's. We might ask which vision of society is more true, Becky's or Amelia's. The narrator does not answer that question. Sometimes goodness and affection, in the person of Lady Jane Crawley and Rawdon, for example, arrive to find the "wretched woman . . . in a brilliant full toilette" and defeat the schemers like Becky and Lord Steyne.[14] At other times, the opportunists defeat the virtuous, and Becky has the triumph at the Brussels ball of leaving her "bouquet and shawl by Amelia's side" as she "tripped off with George to dance. . . . Our poor Emmy . . . was powerless in the hands of her remorseless little enemy" (chap. 29). Sometimes, the narrator seems to say, we are directed by our idealism and affection just as at other times we are motivated by our selfishness and self-interestedness. Either position is weak when ignorant of the other: the Amelias are vulnerable to the Beckys because they refuse to credit unscrupulous motives, and the Beckys become vulnerable when they refuse to believe in the power of affection and goodness. But neither side "wins," and neither one is "right." By the social standards embodied in Becky, Amelia should fail; by the values represented in Amelia, Becky should be defeated. Instead each provides an important vantage point from which to evaluate and reevaluate the strengths and weaknesses of the other. Together, they enable Thackeray to achieve his unusual effects. He has comprehensiveness in his representation of society, yet, because the representation itself leaves aspects unreconciled, his society lacks the internal consistency necessary to shape clear expectations for characters' fates in their worlds. The narrator can therefore decide those fates.

Thackeray's decision to make his protagonists women was brilliant. A pragmatic woman, Becky Sharp, living by the unspoken codes of her day would be more readily thought by readers to be ruthless. Her behavior is at odds with traditional notions of femininity. Thackeray cleverly exploits his reader's bias to dramatize social ills. In contrast to the schemer stands the pure woman, Amelia Sedley, the selfless wife and mother. Here again, women's expected role as embodiment of many social ideals makes the choice of a woman protagonist in whom to expose the weakness and sentimentality of society's conception of morality especially effective.[15]

Our responses to the two heroines keep changing. It is impossible to hate Becky all of the time, just as it is not possible to like Amelia continually. As the two women drive out of the gates of Chiswick Mall at the novel's opening, for instance, Amelia goes to a happy home, adoring parents, and waiting lover, Becky to employment as a governess. At this point both women are potentially empathetic. We may sympathize with the socially deprived Becky for whom the "happiness—the superior advantages of the young women round about her gave . . . inexpressible pangs of envy." She recognizes that the system is based on money and rank rather than merit and "determined . . . to get free from the prison in which she found herself . . . now began to act for herself" (chap. 2). This narrative commentary early in the novel inevitably buttresses Becky's famous conclusion that morality is a matter of money: "And who knows but Rebecca was right in her speculations—and that it was only a question of money and fortune which made the difference between her and an honest woman" (chap. 41). On the other hand, Amelia "best-natured of all," loved by all, eagerly anticipating a future she deserves, is admirable in her generosity and thoughtfulness (chap. 2).

Each woman has positive traits when cast in her best light; that best light, however, is only one of the varied illuminations provided by the "author's own candles." Becky possesses energy, charm, pragmatism, intelligence, vigor, resourcefulness, courage, ambition, and wit. Amelia has grace, humility, generosity, loyalty, sensitivity, warmth, and gentleness. The positive qualities of each modulate, however, into qualities less desirable when in the presence of the other. Each of these strengths or virtues, when placed in another context, can appear to be a weakness or a vice.

The young brides at Brighton and Brussels during the first third of the novel reveal this modulation at work. Emmy, newly married to George Osborne, in the light of Becky's wit, brilliance, charm, and energy finds her humility turning to humiliation, her sensitivity becoming whimpering, her guilelessness and warmth becoming brooding listlessness, her honesty, a feebleness. So at Brighton, "Rebecca's twinkling green eyes and baleful smile lighted upon [Amelia], and filled her with dismay. And so she sate . . . indulging in her usual mood of selfish brooding, in that very listless melancholy attitude . . ." (chap. 26). Becky, on the other hand, when judged by Amelia, finds her energy becoming arrogance, her charm becoming flash, dazzle, and falsity, her resourcefulness becoming remorselessness, and her courage becoming selfishness. Thus, Amelia, thoughtless of herself, mourns her husband's departure for the battlefield, "Until this dauntless worldling [Becky] came in . . . rustling in her fresh silks and brilliant ornaments," and Amelia confronts her with a spirit, volubility, and anger "which surprised and somewhat abashed her rival" (chap. 31).

Thackeray continues counterpointing the two women's lives throughout *Vanity Fair*. Its complexity and unity lie in the skill and convincingness with which Thackeray's narrator alternates contexts for judgment. The tension that exists between the women—this tension directs the action—can be resolved only in something like the parity of fortune achieved at the end of the novel, which finds Becky thriving in her charity booths "a fast and generous friend" of the "Destitute Orange-Girl, the Neglected Washerwoman, the Distressed Muffin-Man," and Amelia lamenting that Dobbin is fonder of his little Janey, possibly "fonder even . . . of his 'History of the Punjaub,' " than he is of her (chap. 67).

The novel seeks as its end the criticism of society's influence. Society encourages behavior that it then judges to be immoral, just as it warps the potentially virtuous to its narrow, self-defeating definition of goodness. In the final analysis, it is not Becky who is being criticized so much as those social laws that dictate her behavior. It is not so much Amelia who is being castigated as those social ideals by which she is compelled to live. Each woman, while illuminating the other's deficiencies, increases our sense of society's inability to maintain a sound, equitable ethical base for evaluation of its members. This formal juxtaposition creates the novel's most profound vision of the vanity of human affairs.

Even Dobbin, the novel's most admirable character, shares Amelia's weaknesses. He sees that George Osborne is a humbug and scoundrel, but he is loyal to the man out of a mistaken gentlemanly ideal of friendship, and he participates in the social idealization of womanhood, marriage, and motherhood, which so long blinds him to Amelia's failures. It is this idealization that enables Amelia to tyrannize over Dobbin—"she ordered him about, and patted him, and made him fetch and carry just as if he was a great Newfoundland dog"—and that wins him the narrator's epithet, "spooney" (chap. 66).

Dobbin, however, finally awakens to Amelia's inadequacies, which he recognizes as a product of her world. John Mathison has explored the significance of the German sections of *Vanity Fair* and has concluded that they reveal the deficiencies of English, middle-class society's idealization of women: "In the speech asserting his freedom from Emmy, Dobbin said that he had no fault to find with her. Neither has Thackeray, for both of them are unable to hold her responsible for her shortcomings. Thackeray has accounted for Amelia's deficiencies and even asks our sympathy for her; his unfavorable judgment is of English middle-class society."[16] Indeed, throughout the novel, the Victorian ideal of woman is scrutinized and criticized. Early in the novel, as Amelia anticipates marriage to George Osborne, the narrator locates her preoccupation as the center of her existence, one leading both to excess and to waste: "It is what sentimentalists, who deal in *very* big words, call a yearning after the Ideal, and simply means that women are commonly not satisfied until they have husbands and children on whom they may centre affections, which are spent elsewhere, as it were in small change" (chap. 4). Furthermore, Amelia's crippling lack of self-esteem renders her incapable of judging the objects of her affection:

> She did not dare to own that the man she loved was her inferior; or to feel that she had given her heart away too soon. Given once, the pure bashful maiden was too modest, too tender, too trustful, too weak, too much woman to recal it. We are Turks with the affections of our women; and have made them subscribe to our doctrine too. We let their bodies go abroad liberally enough, with smiles and ringlets and pink bonnets to disguise them instead of veils and yakmaks. But their souls must be seen by only one man, and they obey not unwillingly, and consent to remain at home as our slaves—ministering to us and doing drudgery for us [chap. 18].

The narrator is speaking not of individual personality but of social conditioning. As he witnesses Amelia's plight, the narrator finally finds cause to celebrate that he is a man: "O you poor women! O you poor secret martyrs and victims, whose life is a torture, who are stretched on racks in your bedrooms, and who lay your heads down on the block daily at the drawing-room table; every man who watches your pains, or peers into those dark places where the torture is administered to you, must pity you—and—and thank God that he has a beard" (chap. 37). As Victorian ideal, Amelia is finally an occasion for pity rather than celebration, and it is not only she who suffers, but also a society that makes her the guardian of its morality. This representation of Amelia's qualities forces us to contemplate the utter weakness of society and to lament that the ruthlessness and corruption encouraged by its emphasis on rank and money are countered only by a sentimental, vapid, ineffectual, self-destructive idealism.

The protagonists are thus shaped by the unspoken laws of their social milieu, whether by its idealism or by its ruthless pragmatism. Thackeray sees how the characters are variously determined, yet by representing society in its two irreconcilable aspects, he refuses the logic that determinism might suggest and creates the freedom to place his characters where he likes. In so doing, he lets the final judgment fall on society rather than on individuals.

Not only does Thackeray create parallel plots with their conflicting social visions to equalize Becky's and Amelia's fates, but he also shapes a narrator who withholds judgment along a single scale of values. As a result, he reveals the extent to which morality itself is a social issue and stresses the relativity of social ethics. "Was she guilty or not?" the narrator asks of Becky's entanglement with Lord Steyne, but he refuses to answer explicitly (chap. 53). For some readers that silence speaks eloquently. She is guilty by the standard of Rawdon's generosity to her when he left for Waterloo, but guilt implies standards, and in the realm of standards, Thackeray is subtle. The standards are not always obvious. It is not sheer perversity that keeps us wondering if Becky might have been temporarily sacrificing her husband's comfort to bargain for the higher stakes of ultimate financial security, something that she and Rawdon never possess. This alternative picture is suggested by the image of Becky in the preceding chapter, "haggard, weary, and terrible" as Rawdon slumbers opposite her, with a face he does not see because "it lighted up with fresh candid smiles when he woke" (chap. 52).

We need to look more closely at the narrator's role in shaping *Vanity Fair*'s presentation of society and its effects. Thackeray has been criticized for suddenly breaching the detachment demanded by his panoramic vision of social process and intruding into the world of his novel.[17] He has been contrasted to Fielding's narrator who has, it is generally felt, more successfully adopted the garrulous mode, has made his relationship with his world and his reader more convincing. But my observations suggest that Thackeray is not merely imitating Fielding at a time that will not countenance the imitation, but that he is responding to important narrative ends in establishing the role of society in his novel.

Thackeray partly shares the social determinism of the later sociological/naturalistic novelists, but he counters it with a general ethical commitment to individual responsibility. That commitment, however, is not expressed in the characters' lives; the controlling presence of Thackeray's narrator argues for that responsibility. His ultimate purpose, then, is not to involve us in his characters' dilemmas within their world but, by shifting between distance and proximity, to involve us with him in the moral complexities defined by that world.[18]

Key passages in *Vanity Fair* to which critics have objected are usually attempting this difficult task. For example, as Becky leaves Chiswick Mall, she flings the proffered dictionary back at a startled Miss Jemima. The narrator reports, "But, lo! and just as the coach drove off, Miss Sharp put her pale face out of the window, and actually flung the book back into the garden" (chap. 1). Arnold Kettle argues that the narrator's "actually" colors the scene, investing it with a sense of scandalized amazement, which may well reflect Miss Jemima's feelings but which "weakens . . . the objective force of the episode. . . . It is Thackeray who steps in and in stepping in reduces the whole episode."[19] These critics confuse Thackeray, the writer, with both the implied author, or shaping consciousness of the novel, and the narrator, the limited persona and speaker within the novel.[20] It is true that Thackeray reduces the objective force of the episode, but it is the narrator, not Thackeray, who interposes. The intrusion is necessary to subvert our characteristic identification with character in action and to force us to identify with questions of judgment, value, and propriety and to make us recognize our own amazement at Becky's defiance and audacity. How much simpler and easier, the implied author seems to suggest, to like the Amelias of this world, and so he begins to move us out of easy and complacent moral categories.

Amelia herself is no moral paragon, but the narrator lumbers into the Sedleys' drawing-room, ready to purchase all Mr. Lee's conservatories out of hand "for a kiss from such a dear creature as Amelia" (chap. 4). The narrator has already defined Amelia as the nineteenth-century equivalent of a contemporary Miss America—empty, vacuous, sweet, "writing to her twelve dearest friends at Chiswick Mall" (chap. 4). So by deliberately, not accidentally, allowing the narrator to participate in the sentimentality that idealizes Amelia, the implied author forces the reader to recognize and reject this easy sentimentality, to become involved not in the world of the novel but in the socially determined moral categories by which that world operates.

Similarly the narrator's comments on Becky—criticized by Dorothy Van Ghent for their "relaxed garrulity"[21]—encourage a similar involvement. As Becky daydreams over the material fruits of her imagined future with Jos Sedley, the narrator comments: "Charming Alnaschar visions! it is the happy privilege of youth to construct you, and many a fanciful young creature besides Rebecca Sharp has indulged in these delightful day-dreams ere now!" (chap. 3). Van Ghent points out that the comment distracts our attention from the "tense mental operations of Becky . . . turning it upon the momentarily flaccid mentality of her author."[22] It is a flaccid mentality, but that of the narrator rather than that of the author, and by irritating us with its flaccidity, it prevents our identification with a sentimental version of lovers' experience that is so at odds both with Becky's insecure situation and her very calculating and materialistic speculations. When the narrator acknowledges his own mercenary aims, "Ah, gracious powers! I wish you would send me an old aunt—a maiden aunt—an aunt with a lozenge on her carriage, and a front of coffee-coloured hair—how my children should work workbags for her, and my Julia and I would make her comfortable! Sweet—sweet vision! Foolish—foolish dream!" (chap. 9), the implied author provides yet another perspective on this self-indulgent sentimentality.

In short, conflicts between the narrator's perspectives and those of the implied author continually force us to participate not in the characters' lives but in the social sentimentality that governs those lives. Thackeray may not always have his sentiments under control, but the basic contrast in the novel between Becky and Amelia reveals a consistent aim to expose society's insidious flaccidity and sentimentality. By participating himself in that sentimentality and finding it an inescapable condition of that social world, the narrator partially redeems his characters' lives. Thackeray's is not Fielding's way. Whereas Fielding's narrator and the implied author of *Tom Jones* seem almost identical, Thackeray creates a distance between his narrator in *Vanity Fair* (a character in the novel) and the implied author. In so doing, Thackeray anticipates the later narrators of George Eliot and Thomas Hardy, narrators whose difficulties in judging affect their reliability. Thackeray feels no more comfortable in the oracular vein than will George Eliot's narrator in *Middlemarch* who claims, in comparing herself to Fielding, that "our chat would be thin and eager, as if delivered from a campstool in a parrot-house."[23] By participating in the ethics of his created world and by embodying a larger ethic as well, Thackeray can pardon each of his protagonists her worst offenses.

The representation and formal role of society demand this shifting narrative perspective, even if, at times, it seems clumsy. At the end, we recognize that Thackeray is not providing us with an "impression of a world, a society . . . a hundred years ago,"[24] but is using a particular period to tell us about human life in society. The characters are never aware of the extent to which social rules guide their behaviors, but the narrator is, and by pointing them out and implicating himself in them, he asks our tolerance and seeks to make us more intelligent interpreters of our own life in society. He forces us to go beyond the social pieties, the ultimate vanities, that cloud our vision and prevent our grappling with the obvious social evils. Not only is that sentimental social morality inadequate to the evil, but it is inadequate even to its own happiness. Even if we choose to retreat from the Beckys of this world and nurture our idealisms, Thackeray leaves us with only the impoverished consolation of Amelia's tears and sighs.

The Eccentric Aspect of Dickens's Social Landscape

Charles Dickens's novels are pivotal for their representation of society, a point too little appreciated by Dickens critics. Dickens discovered a technique to depict the enormous determining force of society and yet to exempt characters from it without relying on an intrusive narrator. It is a major achievement.

In the varied comments by great Dickens critics, from those of a sociological literary critic like Humphry House to critics like J. Hillis Miller and Lionel Trilling who treat the novel largely as an autonomous object, to mimetic critics with socialist orientations like John Lucas and Raymond Williams, one central theoretical issue emerges, and this broad issue reminds us of George Eliot's, Henry James's, and George Orwell's responses to Dickens, too. Focusing especially on Dickens's later novels, the issue is this: if Dickens offers a strenuous analysis of society, an analysis whose trenchancy consists in seeing society as rigid mold or as process that determines individual lives, how can he continually, novel by novel, exempt certain characters from the probabilities of the social worlds he has created? This is not a question of morality but of technique. How can a writer persuade us that society, by its nature, is inimical to human lives and simultaneously convince us that individual characters are not necessarily subject to society's destructive processes—indeed, that his protagonists will find society's values and roles a sufficient context for their fulfillment?[25] An obvious question confronts us: what are the formal terms of Dickens's novels that persuade us to accept contradictory themes?

Dickens shares his achievement with Fielding although his methods of accomplishing the trick are different. Like both Thackeray and Fielding, Dickens releases character from the strict probabilities of his fictional society, but his techniques for doing so are new.

For George Eliot, Dickens's achievement in this area required that he falsify individual psychologies: "But for the precious salt of his humour, which compels him to reproduce external traits that serve, in some degree, as a corrective to his frequently false psychology, his preternaturally virtuous poor children and artisans, his melodramatic boatmen and courtezans, would be as noxious as Eugène Sue's idealized proletaires in encouraging the miserable fallacy that high morality and refined sentiment can grow out of harsh social relations, ignorance, and want. . . ."[26] In this excerpt from "The Natural History of German Life," George Eliot worries about a possible pernicious moral effect in Dickens's seeming divorce between personality and social circumstance. John Lucas attacks George Eliot for her criticism, arguing that it exposes "her own limitations." For Lucas the innately good or ultimately redeemed characters "are not extrapolations from the process but a viable part of it," and Dickens's acknowledgement of the fluidity of social process makes him a more truly mimetic novelist than Henry James or George Eliot. Lucas regards Eliot and James as "prescriptive rather than truly mimetic." They "protest against Dickens's method of showing human probabilities, since it upsets their own calculations or judgments of the probable."[27]

One reason for Lucas's energetic defense of Dickens's technique stems from the work of other critics who, taking the novels as autonomous objects, are quite willing to sacrifice their "reality" in order to explain seeming incompatibilities of vision. For example, Lionel Trilling, writing on *Little Dorrit*, concedes in conclusion, "[Little Dorrit's] untinctured goodness does not appall us or make us misdoubt her, as we expected it to do. This novel at its best is only incidentally realistic; its finest power of imagination appears in the great general images whose abstractness is their actuality, like Mr Murdle's dinner parties, or the Circumlocution office itself, and in such a context we understand Little Dorrit to be the Beatrice of the *Comedy*, the Paraclete in female form."[28] Trilling thus answers the problem of probability by denying that the novel's reality is convincing. Even J. Hillis Miller, in an exhaustive study of Dickens's worlds, seems rather to avoid this problem than to confront it. Miller charts in Dickens's novels the changing relations of self to society and has no difficulty concluding that in *Bleak House* Esther Summerson learns not to rely on society and finds an identity outside of prescribed social roles by a process of transcendence. In *Our Mutual Friend*, the characters learn they must have their identity in society and by a process of negative transcendence, "a purifying descent into the dark waters of death" are liberated "to new attitudes toward their situation, an attitude which recognizes that value radiates not from any thing or power outside the human, but outward from the human spirit itself."[29]

One thing is clear; characters in Dickens are finally absolutely free of social determinism, whether they choose the route of transcending society or of descending to its murky depths to arise reborn, fashioned in the image of their own salvation. Yet few writers give us such a compelling vision of society's determining processes as does Dickens, and the problem of how he manages to do so and grant individuals such freedom from those processes persists.

Understanding how Dickens manages it begins with the recognition that his techniques for representing society are unlike those of his predecessors. G. H. Lewes pinpointed early one aspect of Dickens's genius: that he does not see his world in the "vague schematic way of ordinary imagination, but in the sharp definition of actual perception, all the salient details obtruding themselves on his attention."[30]

Dickens's world, in other words, seems to present itself complete to his imagination, and we are struck on entering that he sees the whole as a collection of vital, visual, and autonomous details. Dickens starts with a specific detail—the quirk, the mannerism—and then enlarges to its general significance.

This technique is quite different from that of most writers. They seem to begin from the outlines of their world, especially of their society (its distinctive types, its norms and values, its characteristic scenes), and specify a world for us. Their characters may be credible personalities or two-dimensional abstractions, but individual behavior will be explicable in terms of social beliefs and attitudes. For example, Fielding uses his walking concepts and the rather cardboard figures encountered on the road to generalize the attitudes that govern his represented society. Thackeray's protagonists as well as his minor characters broadly and brilliantly emblematize social value and expectation. Jane Austen emphasizes clear social conventions that all her characters share and understand. These writers locate the general in specific characters and actions.

One result of moving from general to specific is that society in a novel is inhabited by all its characters. Society is largely conceived as types, norms, values, and conventions; the characters recognize these principles and share a common social order even if they do not inhabit the same locale. Society there exists as a continuum of values and classes. Despite the obvious and marked connections in such worlds (George Eliot's "web" offers a convenient image for them), social gulfs seem unbridgeable. George Eliot's Hetty Sorrel cannot marry Arthur Donnithorne; Mrs. Gaskell's John Barton is always a worker, never a master; Flaubert's Emma Bovary cannot escape her pedestrian life with Charles; Hardy's Jude Fawley cannot go to Christminster. The more convincing the order is, the more oppressive of individual fulfillment it seems.

Dickens's society, too, is comprehensive; it depicts a wide range of classes and values, yet it suggests not a continuum but rather a series of contiguous circles for its dominant image.[31] This fragmentation derives in large measure from Dickens's visualization of character. Each character exists as eccentric individual as well as a representative of a social position. As a result his representative capacity is always somewhat limited. I will turn to this point in a moment.

These circles, however, need not remain in absolute configurations; patterns and relationships can change; key boundaries are fluid. Seemingly isolated in their discrete circles, characters have real mobility: Little Dorrit finds her Clennam, Lizzie Hexam marries Eugene Wrayburn. Noddy and Henrietta Boffins's juxtaposition of fashion and comfort—separate yet contiguous realms in one room—provides a comic analogue for the very real social boundaries that exist. She likes fashion; he favors comfort, and both keep their quarters, but one or the other may advance if the inclinations of the other shift. These shifts are dictated by temperament and disposition rather than by class or other social conditions. In analogous fashion, characters throughout Dickens's novels move from one condition to another.

Examining the interaction between individualized and representative traits clarifies Dickens's method for divorcing individual fates from the exigencies of social process. J. Hillis Miller, contrasting Dickens with George Eliot, explains that Dickens "achieves inclusiveness by making the part explicitly stand for the whole. He emphasizes the synecdochic, representative, emblematic quality of his characters. . . . Moreover, the range of examples includes by this method of synecdoche all of England."[32] Several critics have testified to Dickens's seemingly inexhaustible ability to populate his world and to make that population representative. His characters strike us as emblematic because they are so often two-dimensional, but what we often fail to see is that their superficial representative clarity masks a counterposing resistance to social typing. Miller's examples of the synecdochic emblematic character include Sir Leicester Dedlock who is "presented as an example of the whole class of aristocrats," Krook who "stands for the lord chancellor, his shop for the Court of Chancery," and Gridley, the Man from Shropshire, who is an "emblem for all the suitors who are destroyed by the delays of Chancery."[33]

There is nothing to dispute in Miller's conclusions; in fact, they stimulate important further questions—such as what makes characters who supposedly represent little more than an idea of something else so memorable and distinct as individuals? The answer lies in a direction other than that of their representative functions.

The Man from Shropshire is an abstract form when protesting delays in Chancery, but in nurturing the infants Tom and Emma Neckett and in his touching deathbed longing for Miss Flite, Gridley assumes characteristics not germane to rendering his representative nature. A victim of the system on one level, he rigidly resists its coercion on others. It is clear that he represents a "class of suitors," a class that Miss Flite and Richard Carstone also share in the current generation, but this "social group" is not organized around a set of norms or conventions.

In most novels, characters are typed by values; they become representative by embodying shared norms or social codes. For example, Miss Bingley in *Pride and Prejudice* characterizes the snobbery of the nouveau riche. Newly elevated in social status herself, she adheres rigidly to the most mechanical social distinctions. For her, it will always be a mark against Jane and Elizabeth Bennet that their uncle lives in Cheapside "within sight of his warehouses." In Fielding's novel, Square and Thwackum represent complementary perspectives, which align them with general attitudes and values. Thackeray's Sir Pitt, remarkable in his crudity, is memorable precisely for those qualities Thackeray wants to criticize in the aristocracy. His arrogance and disdain are of a piece with those of Lord Steyne and Lady Crawley.

In Dickens's novels, a representative figure like Gridley shares circumstances and a fate but not a set of values or behaviors with the Miss Flites and Richard Carstones who also share his position. Sir Leicester, too, clearly stands for a set of class values, those of the moribund aristocracy, which is complacent and insensitive, upholding the status quo and defining merit solely by class. Though memorable in his cotton wool padding and resistance to social change, he is equally remarkable for the startling transformation wrought by his love for Lady Dedlock: "His noble earnestness, his fidelity, his gallant shielding of her, his generous conquest of his own wrong and his own pride for her sake, are simply honourable, manly, and true."[34] He is capable of transcending his representative self in ways inaccessible to Lady Catherine de Bourgh or Sir Pitt or Sir Willoughby Patterne, to name characters whose fates express narrative evaluation of the social values they represent.

Krook represents the Lord Chancellor—we are explicitly told so—yet he is memorable for the jealous guarding of his documents and his narrow suspicion that, should someone teach him to read, "they might teach me wrong!" (chap. 14). Chancery thrives on precedents and jargon; Krook's suspicious illiteracy reflects only obliquely on the Lord Chancellor and the legal profession reprented by such language merchants as Conversation Kenge. Indeed, if Krook is representative of institutional behavior, he, like Sir Leicester Dedlock, is also individualized in ways that exceed his representative qualities.

We can draw two major conclusions about Dickens's representation of society: (1) the emblematic characters, at crucial points, do not represent shared class values or norms; they are rather representative of a group that shares similar external conditions, and (2) characters often spring to life in contexts that individualize rather than reinforce their representative natures so that even a Sir Leicester can transcend the class values of his condition.

Dickens's characters, then, are not socially representative in traditional ways. They do not consistently embody social values so that those values may be systematically criticized through their lives and their fates. We may be momentarily deluded into thinking they do, because, for example, Krook spontaneously combusts and Gridley dies pursued by the system in the person of Mr. Bucket. These deaths derive from general probabilities in the social world—that Chancery is destructive of its suitors, that it is a self-consumptive organism—and they are fitting conclusions to a general condemnation of society. Yet the fates of Dickens's characters do not ultimately express a careful criticism of social convention, or the abuse of social decorum that is characteristic of Austen, or a systematic exploration of the abuse perpetuated by social class and social idealism found in Thackeray, or a close examination of the determinative pressures of social opinion that we shall see in George Eliot.

The protagonists of *Bleak House* reveal even further Dickens's unique methods of broad social analysis. Against whom or what is Esther Summerson pitting herself? Of what is Lady Dedlock guilty? Esther fights a system marked by impersonality and by the abnegation of moral responsibility. Her antagonist is much more amorphous than that in other novels. For example, Elizabeth Bennet struggles against attitudes that define merit in class rather than individual terms. Becky Sharp struggles with a society that discriminates against her on account of her birth, and Dorothea Brooke challenges a world that limits women's fulfillment to marriage and children. Esther, in contrast, does not confront particular limiting attitudes. Esther Summerson could be a Becky Sharp, discriminated against on account of her birth, but John Jarndyce's early protection of her removes major potential instabilities in her life that stem from social questions, and Dickens makes the agent of her destruction as impersonal as the typhus fever spreading from Tom-All-Alone's.

Dickens rarely imbeds destructive social forces in any particular person. They seem rather to inhere in the landscape or to be exhaled into the very air the characters breathe. The novel's dominant images of mud and fog, emblematic of Chancery's obfuscation and miring in precedent—"Chancery, in turn, is a synecdoche for the state of 'wiglomeration' of English Society as a whole"[35]— create the impression that this condition has so long existed that it is part of the very nature of things: "it would not be wonderful to meet a Megalosaurus, forty feet long or so, waddling like an elephantine lizard up Holborn Hill" (chap. 1). This world as natural process seems to be devolving back to its original, primeval state. Dickens finds powerful images for social decay and corruption, but by rendering them into landscape he makes them seem that much more impersonal, that much more a function of natural process, that much less a function of personal will or intention. This is evolutionary process instead of social process dictated by laws and expressed in conventions, beliefs, and attitudes.

In *Our Mutual Friend*, too, we slide with Mortimer Lightwood and Eugene Wrayburn from the glitter of fashionable society at the Veneerings down the banks of the Thames "where accumulated scum of humanity seemed to be washed from higher grounds, like so much moral sewage, and to be pausing until its own weight forced it over the bank and sunk it in the river."[36] This process is dictated by gravity and water flow rather than by society's laws, attitudes, and customs.

Such processes would seem to be inescapable, but once we move beyond them, characters strike us as autonomous and remarkably free of social determinants. For example, in *Our Mutual Friend*, Gaffer Hexam can enforce his isolation by barring his children from education with its possibilities for upward mobility. Gaffer Hexam's restrictions are not born of the suspicions of *Bleak House*'s Krook, who is afraid that people might teach him wrong. Hexam's convictions originate in an identification with the river.

"As if it wasn't your living! As if it wasn't meat and drink to you!" (chap. 1). In chastising Lizzy, he reveals a profound bond with the river which prevents us from seeing him simply as a social victim, one of the poor, relegated to his place, according to Podsnappery, by the dictates of providence: "The fault lies with the sufferers themselves" (chap. 11). Jesse Hexam's life, nourished by death and corruption, is nothing like the abstract complement to himself, which Podsnap imagines. Dickens creates a life for his poor, which is not defined simply in terms of social disadvantage and lower class, and not simply in terms of consciousness of that class difference. The poor, in most novels, are depicted primarily in class terms, as socially disadvantaged because of their position in life. *Bleak House*'s Jo is typical of that depiction, but certain of Dickens's impoverished characters, like Gaffer Hexam, relish their situation and do not see it strictly in class terms or themselves as social victims.

A brief look at George Eliot's *Middlemarch* will further highlight the unique quality of social worlds in Dickens's novels. When Dorothea Brooke visits the poor and wants to improve their lot, they exist for her and for us as individuals to whom she has a social responsibility; they lack the autonomy and individuality of Dickens's poor. Mr. Brooke is verbally assaulted by his abused tenants, and his complacency is reminiscent of Podsnappery, but we understand from George Eliot that Mr. Brooke, unlike Podsnap, must acknowledge that reform begins at home, that abstract public sentiments must have concrete private results. Mr. Brooke's fatuous foolishness masks from him the inevitable logic of his social responsibility to rectify the ills of those less fortunate. Likewise, Hetty Sorrel, from *Adam Bede*, dreams of marriage to "Squire" Donnithorne and ignores the logic of social behavior and expectation that her world accepts and that we are brought to understand. Her ignorance and egotism cause her destruction.

Dickens's characters do not share a similar, underlying logic of social values and relationships. When Mr. Brooke and Hetty Sorrel fail to grasp the logic of class relationships, they are punished. When Mr. Podsnap in *Our Mutual Friend* and Mrs. Pardiggle in *Bleak House* fail to do so, they remain unpunished. Mrs. Pardiggle can sweep into and disrupt the brickmakers' world by knocking objects about, but the physical impression she makes only underlies the absence of any personal or moral impression and connection. Esther remarks that she and Ada "both felt painfully sensible that between us and these people there was an iron barrier, which could not be removed by our new friend [Mrs. Pardiggle]. By whom, or how, it could be removed, we did not know; but we knew that" (chap. 8). The brickmakers are—and the omniscient narrator underlines the fact—as remote to Mrs. Pardiggle as the Tockahoopo Indians. So it is with Jo: "He is not one of Mrs. Pardiggle's Tockahoopo Indians . . . he is not a genuine foreign-grown savage; he is the ordinary home-made article" (chap. 47). She cannot affect them and they cannot affect her; those usual connections engendered by society are absent.

Dickens is vitally aware of social inequities; he offers no foolish sentimentality that the poor are happy in their poverty. Rather, Dickens grants them unusual individual authority and vitality which endow the realms they inhabit with autonomy. They do not strike us as existing at the tail end of a continuous social spectrum, a fact with both positive and negative implications. The workmen in *Mary Barton*, for example, can strive to become more equal to the masters; Hetty Sorrel can imagine life as a squire's wife; Becky Sharp can see herself presented to the king, as Jude Fawley can see himself at Christminster. But in *Bleak House* Jo will never participate in the meaning of St. Paul's Cathedral: "He is not of the same order of things, not of the same place in creation. He is of no order and no place; neither of the beasts, nor of humanity" (chap. 47). Jo obviously belongs to humanity, and we can acknowledge the narrator's bitter irony. Yet, because of the autonomy of Dickens's characters, we recognize that Jo is not represented as a part of the "same order of things," even though his existence is a logical consequence of that social system.

This is how Dickens achieves his special fidelity to social representation and yet exempts key characters from the consequences inherent in their social position. The authority he invests in each aspect of his society creates seemingly unbridgeable social gulfs, but those gulfs are in fact bridged by the same narrative techniques that created the distances: the vitality and autonomy of individuals is a vitality and autonomy of individual values and behavior. Values are not ultimately determined by society. This was George Eliot's point about the frequently false psychology of Dickens's characters "encouraging the miserable fallacy that high morality and refined sentiment can grow out of harsh social conditions, ignorance, and want." But Dickens's techniques convince us. They generate a fluidity among the various social spheres much greater than when society is conceived of as a spectrum of values, attitudes, and behaviors. Lizzy Hexam can finally marry Eugene Wrayburn; Esther Summerson, without Morgan-ap-Kerrig lineage, can marry Allan Woodcourt; Sir Leicester can mourn his Lady, Little Dorrit can find her Clennam. It should not surprise us that, through these techniques, Dickens increasingly wins our sympathy for outsiders or outcasts, even the criminals of his fictional world. They are equally a consequence of his formal role for society that presents characters as divorced from their conditions and thereby allows them to be evaluated independently of their effects in the world.

Dickens is thus at once a trenchant social critic and a celebrator of human life and individual possibility. Most writers in criticizing society demonstrate society's capacity to mold and destroy human lives. Dickens's characters walk curiously intact upon the earth, free to feel, to act, and to think in individual ways, whatever their external conditions. So the Twemlow in *Our Mutual Friend* is hauled out for the Veneerings' dinners—Twemlow with one leaf or Twemlow with twenty—a flat two-dimensional character eternally puzzling over whether he is the Veneerings' oldest or newest friend. Seemingly a moveable piece of furniture, he suddenly possesses the capacity to flout fashionable society, to defy his "noble relation," and to support Eugene Wrayburn's marriage to the lower-class Lizzy Hexam: "I could not allow even [Lord Snigsworthy] to dictate to me on a point of great delicacy, on which I feel very strongly" (Chapter the Last). Although his situation is socially determined, his inherent values are not socially conditioned.

Likewise, in a more substantial transformation, Sir Leicester throws off encrusted tradition, the seemingly impenetrable armor of social custom and pride, in mourning and compassion for Lady Dedlock: "His noble earnestness, his fidelity, his gallant shielding of her, his generous conquest of his own wrong and his own pride for her sake, are simply honourable, manly, and true. Nothing less worthy can be seen through the lustre of such qualities in the commonest mechanic, nothing less worthy can be seen in the best-born gentleman. In such a light both aspire alike, both rise alike, both children of the dust shine equally" (chap. 58). In Dickens's world, good and evil still exist, and they transcend social categories. The images of light that irradiate Sir Leicester are those that have illuminated Esther—"sunshine and summer air"—and that associate Jo in this select group: "Thou art not quite in outer darkness. There is something like a distant ray of light in thy muttered reason for this: 'He wos wery good to me, he wos!' " (chap. 11). And at Jo's death, "The light is come upon the dark benighted way" (chap. 47). In succeeding novelists, the tendency will be increasingly to find evil mitigated by social circumstance, good hampered by social limitations. There exists little sense of transcendent good or evil in the worlds of George Eliot or Henry James.

Charles Dickens's protagonists do not, of course, emerge unscarred from their participation in a corrupt and corrupting world. Eugene Wrayburn is physically marked after being beaten by Bradley Headstone; in Esther Summerson's face is etched the social corruption and contagion that has spread as typhus fever to infect her haven at Bleak House. Esther has also lost her mother and must share in her dearest friend's widowhood. Yet characters make no great internal sacrifices and compromises of their essential natures or aspirations. Esther is as good at the end as she was at the beginning; her potential for doing good, is, if anything, greater. Eugene has, for the first time, hope of self-realization and fulfillment. That world cannot finally infect the will or purpose of its noble creatures however it transforms their external circumstances. In Dickens, in fact, a character's external circumstances often mirror his or her deserts. Esther is awarded Woodcourt and the idyllic new Bleak House. Wrayburn marries his Lizzy and Harmon his Bella, but only after he has won her love for himself alone. We need only consider what society will do to a Tertius Lydgate in *Middlemarch* or to a Jude Fawley in *Jude the Obscure* to have a measure of how much novelists' visions will change.

The possibility for individual redemption or exemption always exists in Charles Dickens's novels despite the overarching presence of adverse social forces. The individual is free because society can infect his situation but not his will, and morality is always individual. Dickens puts the burden of moral responsibility on each person. The individual, he says, has power; this power belongs not only to his characters but to his readers. Thus, in his fable, *Hard Times*, Dickens can express, without irony, the truth of all his novels: "Dear reader! It rests with you and me whether, in our two fields of action, similar things shall be or not. Let them be!" Ours is the power to choose. His full assurance that we can personally become avenues for the concrete realization of good is not equalled by later novelists.

Novelists like George Eliot, Henry James, and Thomas Hardy insist on the hampering, thread-like entanglements of social existence. They will extricate none from the fabric of social value, behavior, and attitude although some figures will withstand the pressures better. Individual potential will be pitted against social possibility, and protagonists will make sacrifices and achieve partial triumphs. Our identification of the worthy will no longer bring with it expectations of complete success. Although society clearly includes the protagonists, it is also apart from and, as Dickens is already suggesting, increasingly alienated from them.

Dickens, Thackeray, and Fielding all recognize society's inimical effects, but they discover techniques that free certain characters from the logic of social process. Fielding pits his values against society's and, by making character complexity a function of a narrator's evaluation, he is able to base the expectations for his characters' fates on the narrator's values and attitudes rather than on society's. Thackeray expands his vision to attack both the unspoken codes by which people thrive and the ideals that society openly espouses. His representation of both social realities bars any single coherent logic of society to shape and determine individuals' fates. Finally, in Thackeray's encompassing vision, the seemingly evil and the seemingly good are both revealed as socially conditioned and are both partially excused and partially condemned.

Both Fielding and Thackeray give us "bar-parlour chattiness."[37] They talk about their characters almost as if they were puppets; they do not invite us to share the characters' perspectives; they maintain narrative distance. Our locus of identification is the narrator himself, and his wisdom in Fielding's case, or fallibility in the case of Thackeray, determines how we see the characters and what we anticipate for them. Thackeray's fallible narrator partially excuses Becky Sharp; perhaps more important, he partially condemns Amelia Sedley. She is not as good as her society would like to believe. The contrasting visions of society embodied in the two women prevent any single depiction of society from shaping our expectations for the characters. Thackeray accomplishes in this way what Fielding accomplishes through his commentator: he releases characters from the strict logic of social probability and engages his readers in the constructive enterprise of social criticism, making his novel about our social education and responsibility.

By very different techniques, Dickens also divorces his characters' fates from the strict logic of social probability. He often begins his characterizations from quirks and striking details and then lets the representative significance emerge. As a result, we tend to continue seeing characters as separate and distinct individuals. They represent not class values and attitudes but situations and conditions determined by their milieu. Furthermore, Dickens's images for social process derive from the landscape and the elements, images that suggest a biological evolution of mankind rather than a consequence of specific human will and intention. When his images do include a social institution—like Chancery in *Bleak House* or the prison in *Little Dorrit*—that institution is itself associated with human evolution and is depicted as divorced or remote from human control and intention. Dickens's medium takes its formal coherence from these dominant images of natural process. As a result, society is at once generally determinative of individuals' lives and yet not specifically, in class terms, determinative of their individual fates. Thus, characters can live in society and maintain free souls. The values of class and rank, the attitudes of their world and its expectations, have not become an inseparable part of their personalities and fates as they will in the novels of George Eliot, Thomas Hardy, and D. H. Lawrence.

The formal idea of society, then, in Fielding, Thackeray, and Dickens, differs in function from that of writers who insist upon their novels' fidelity to strict social probability. The exemption these writers grant characters from the probabilities of the societies they create points to the formal role society plays in their novels. Fictional society in these novels functions to teach us about the nature of societies in general and to encourage us to exert ourselves for the good within our worlds. The insistence of the narrator that human life should and can be otherwise makes social probability secondary to moral imperatives.

Society and Self in George Eliot, Hardy, and Lawrence

It always remains true that if we had been greater, circumstances would have been less strong against us.
—George Eliot, *Middlemarch*

The letter killeth.
—Thomas Hardy, epigraph to *Jude the Obscure*

You musn't look in my novel for the old stable ego of the character. There is another ego, according to whose action the individual is unrecognizable, and passes through, as it were, allotropic states which it needs a deeper sense than any we've been used to exercise, to discover are states of the same single radically unchanged element.
—D. H. Lawrence, letter to Edward Garnett, 5 June 1914

W. M. Thackeray's commentator walks directly into the world of his novel and identifies himself with the schemes and weaknesses of Becky and Amelia. Gustave Flaubert may claim, outside his novel, "Emma Bovary, c'est moi," but the work itself does not betray that identification. The consequent differences between a Thackeray and a Flaubert are enormous. Flaubert provides an example of the novel's increasing commitment to characters' autonomy and of the novel's organic understanding of character, incident, and milieu. The "bar-parlour chattiness" of a Thackeray or a Fielding has become unacceptable; perhaps more important, it has become inadequate for a new vision of human life in society.

George Eliot in *Middlemarch*, Thomas Hardy in *Tess of the D'Urbervilles*, and D. H. Lawrence in *The Rainbow* all perceive a vital dynamic between individual nature and social nurture, a dynamic that announces, paradoxically, that society is at once necessary and inimical to the fulfillment of human possibility. A majority of writers share this understanding of the individual and society. Eliot, Hardy, and Lawrence, however, offer a range of complex examples through which we can explore the presentation and formal role of society so conceived.

Thackeray, Fielding, and Dickens emphasized society's influence on individuals by making certain characters emblematic of social values, attitudes, or situations. These writers do not, therefore, use incidents as a primary means of revealing or developing character. Character is basically static. We cannot, for example, say that Tom Jones's involvement with Lady Bellaston significantly reveals his personality. The incident functions to reveal society and its corruption.

In contrast, George Eliot, Thomas Hardy, and D. H. Lawrence rely on actions fully to reveal their characters' personalities. Further, personal behavior is conditioned by social expectation and opinion, because individuals care about what others think of them. Individual personality includes a particular valuing of social reputation. Thus, individual personality is conceived of as being partially a fabric of social opinion. Society is internalized in all individuals rather than embodied in certain ones who serve as emblems of distinct social values, as in Thackeray or Fielding. Character may thus be in conflict with itself, torn by contradictory impulses as it struggles to liberate itself from received notions and to see individual self and socialized self in a larger perspective, which partially liberates one from the coercions of social conditioning. It follows that varying degrees of personal liberation from social coercion are possible.

As the admirable characters in Eliot, Hardy, and Lawrence struggle to liberate themselves from social constraints, they approach their novels' visions of individual possibility and morality and also the relationship of these two to social organization. At the beginnings of these novels, a wide gap exists between narrator and character. From his superior perspective, the narrator watches characters struggle to realize themselves within certain social limitations. Increasingly, those characters capable of education approach the norms informing the novel. They grow to understand themselves and their worlds in ways inaccessible to the protagonists in novels by Fielding, Thackeray, or Dickens. The triumphs of Eliot's, Hardy's, and Lawrence's protagonists are defined by their struggles and accomplishments in growth.

The larger vision these protagonists attain sees society, with all its problems, as a positive community. Although the achievement of such community is tenuous, the possibility of such a community exists. The tension between society as constructive community and society as destructive milieu informs the visions of Eliot, Hardy, and Lawrence, each of whom expresses, above all, the sense that human beings cannot divorce themselves from society and still be whole.

This chapter examines what is perhaps the most common formal role for society in the novel, one in which there is a continual interplay between individual nature and social nurture. Communal values are in conflict with the protagonists' values, but community is ultimately necessary for the individual to realize himself, and each individual's fate depends both on his own potential and on the limitations put on that potential by society.

George Eliot understands the hampering pressures of social existence but insists through her narrator that society is a context for the world's "growing good." The tensions inherent in this understanding of society's positive and negative aspects produce a complex, and at times seemingly contradictory, reading of individuals' fates.

Thomas Hardy follows George Eliot in important ways. Increasingly his novels reflect an awareness of how society shapes individual lives. The early novels recognize the value of community, but society clearly functions as agent of destruction, especially in his last two novels. Hardy's answer to the dilemma confronting him was to concentrate on his protagonists as loci for conflict. Their lives could express the consequences of living as a social being in a society poorly attuned to the needs and problems of exceptional individuals.

Both Hardy and Eliot recognize that society is determinative of individual lives. But they avoid the determinism characteristic of naturalistic/sociological novels by insisting on individual responsibility. For George Eliot, the fact that we feel free provides the basis for morality. No matter how socially determined the reader may see them to be, Dorothea Brooke and Tess Durbeyfield always accept responsibility for their actions. The triumph of Hardy's and Eliot's art lies in its fidelity to social pressures coupled with its refusal to allow characters to substitute social pressures for individual responsibility. Thus, Hardy and Eliot preserve a sense of society's potential for supporting individual growth and encouraging a general improvement of human community through individual betterment.

D. H. Lawrence could not create a realistic social milieu adequate to the needs of his exceptional individuals in *The Rainbow*, but he values, nevertheless, the idea of community as stimulus to individual growth. Society presents the most vital challenge to individual expansion, and characters who meet that challenge are granted a vision of revitalized human community. This vision of society as positive community—evident in George Eliot's novels, still glimpsed in Hardy's—has largely disappeared from the modern world, but D. H. Lawrence found a means to affirm it, in spite of an enormous impulse toward negation and alienation.[1]

Although this chapter concentrates on Eliot, Hardy, and Lawrence, three writers who exemplify the most common formal role of society in diverse manifestations, it also looks briefly at three other novelists, Gustave Flaubert, Henry James, and Leo Tolstoy. These writers share with the former novelists some assumptions about the influence of society on individual lives, but they develop those assumptions in ways that diminish society's function in our interpretation of characters and their fates.

Society as Fulfillment and Frustration in *Middlemarch*

When Raffles threatens to destroy Bustrode's reputation by revealing his past, the narrator of *Middlemarch* reflects: "Who can know how much of his most inward life is made up of the thoughts he believes other men to have about him, until that fabric of opinion is threatened with ruin" (chap. 68). That reflection posits a relationship between social reputation and self-conception which offers a key to the novel's depiction of society. For the characters in

Middlemarch, society is a fabric of opinion, a set of attitudes, real or imagined, that individuals believe others to possess about them.

This perception of what society means to the individual, this understanding of how "inward life" is inextricably bound with social role and bearing, marks George Eliot's earliest fiction as well. "The Sad Fortunes of the Reverend Amos Barton" opens not with the central character but with a social clique anatomizing the reverend's merits. The narrator, after reporting these unflattering reflections, concludes, "Indeed, what mortal is there of us, who would find his satisfaction enhanced by an opportunity of comparing the picture he presents to himself of his own doings, with the picture they make on the mental retina of his neighbours?"[2] That narrator argues further: "Thank heaven . . . that a little illusion is left to us, to enable us to be useful and agreeable—that we don't know exactly what our friends think of us."[3] "Amos Barton" toys with this interplay between private and public selves, but the full exploration of this theme waits for George Eliot's great novel, *Middlemarch*. There, she merges her presentation of society as a fabric of opinion with other dimensions to her understanding of society that enrich her portrait of human meaning and its relation to social life.

Middlemarch depicts a complex society that has three interconnecting structural roles. First, fictional society includes the town of Middlemarch, conceived of as a microcosm of English society as a whole. That is, society functions as a milieu in which characters live and to which they relate. Second, society functions as a fabric of opinion; social attitudes, beliefs, and values are crucial determinants of individual personality. Nurture and nature are thus inextricable. Third, society functions as an ideal community, a perspective created and developed by the narrator and glimpsed, finally, only by her most perceptive characters.

Society, then, in its three aspects, provides the context for individual action, functions as a major determinant of individual personality, and informs us of the implied author's values. In our experience of *Middlemarch*, these three are not separate and distinct but weave together to shape our understanding of the whole. We see these three aspects of society enacted in the lives of two major characters, Dorothea Brooke and Tertius Lydgate. Their fates are made rich and complex by virtue of these three dimensions.

Various critics of *Middlemarch* have pointed to each of these aspects of society, but the three have not been fully considered in their necessary interrelationships. J. Hillis Miller signals the first: "*Middlemarch* presents a large group of the sort of people one would in fact have been likely to find in a provincial town in the Midlands. Their representative or symbolic quality is not insisted upon. . . . The relation of Middlemarch to English society is rather that of a part to whole . . . a fragment is examined as a 'sample' of the larger whole of which it is a part."[4] Miller is right to note that characters are not strictly representative of social types or values as they are in, say, Thackeray's or Fielding's or even Dickens's novels. Indeed, he adds the astute observation that George Eliot's method of depicting society encourages a full development of character "whose specificity and even uniqueness is indicated by the completeness of the psychological portraits of each."[5]

To refine Miller's observation somewhat let me suggest that George Eliot does think of some characters as types (Sir James Chettam), as embodiments of values and expectations (Mrs. Cadwallader), and as representative of class (Mr. Brooke), but she enriches their potentially two-dimensional nature by adding another dimension to her presentation of society, the second just mentioned, society as a fabric of opinion. Society in this light contributes to psychological depth. Each of these characters, unlike a character who is typed, is shown to be sensitive to how he is seen and regarded by others, and those opinions become bound up with his self-image.[6] In this regard, George Eliot's use of public opinion differs from Fielding's. For Fielding, public opinion influences characters' fortunes, but society's judgments are not internalized, as they are in *Middlemarch*.

The third dimension to Eliot's presentation of society, that of ideal community, derives partially from her choice of metaphors. For J. Hillis Miller, Eliot succeeds in her goal of making a "part stand for the whole" through her choice of images that are posed as models for the whole of Middlemarch society. Each metaphor (a labyrinth, flowing water, web) is "an interpretive net which the reader is invited to cast over the whole society, to use as a paradigm by means of which to think of the whole."[7] Miller glances briefly at the idea of society implied by these metaphors, but he is more interested in pursuing epistemological questions posed by contradicting metaphors.

As our purpose is to examine that society, we need to consider

George Eliot's principal choice of metaphor for society in *Middlemarch*: the web. Distinguishing herself from a writer like Fielding, Eliot's narrator sees her task in light of a web of interconnections: "I at least have so much to do in unravelling certain human lots, and seeing how they were woven and interwoven, that all the light I can command must be concentrated on this particular web, and not dispersed over that tempting range of relevancies called the universe" (chap. 15). This web, as she sees it, is not static, but fluid and supple, responding to the slightest tremor and reflecting the minutest action. The web as responsive medium has both positive and negative implications. When one strand of it is pulled the vibrations or ramifications are felt throughout, and the effects of good and evil actions, or even intentions, radiate generally. Eliot's first novel, *Adam Bede*, explores this process systematically. On the one hand, clumsy Molly's intentions have "beneficent radiation": "The raw bacon which clumsy Molly spares from her own scanty store, that she may carry it to her neighbour's child to 'stop the fits,' may be a piteously inefficacious remedy; but the generous stirring of neighbourly kindness that prompted the deed has a beneficent radiation that is not lost."[8] And, on the other hand, the Reverend Irwine warns Arthur Donnithorne that consequences of actions are "unpitying": "Our deeds carry their terrible consequences, quite apart from any fluctuations that went before—consequences that are hardly ever confined to ourselves."[9]

In *Middlemarch*, the narrator's central philosophy of the "growing good"—the accumulation of small beneficent actions—depends on presenting society as an interconnected web. It is this sense of effects "incalculably diffusive" that informs our understanding of Dorothea's triumph. She does not reform a conventual order but the "growing good of the world is partly dependent on unhistoric acts; and that things are not so ill with you and me as they might have been, is half owing to the number who lived faithfully a hidden life, and rest in unvisited tombs" (Finale). Dorothea has contributed to that growing good; each of her actions has radiated outward.

The metaphor of the web—a community of interconnected beings—leads logically to society in its third sense, in its highest and final sense, that of an ideal community of fellow beings. This aspect has been explained by Steven Marcus:

> Society, in these novels, is represented as a living whole, composed or articulated of differentiated members, each of which fulfills or possesses a special function. As a consequence, the individual person is not separable from the human whole. . . . Society and individual persons, then, are not separable or distinct phenomena, but are in reality the collective and distributive aspects of the same circumstance or thing. . . . Because of this inseparability, it is both a logical error and an existential impossibility to conceive or speak of an opposition between the (or an) individual person and society—one can legitimately only speak of one individual opposing one or several or many other individual persons.[10]

This third, important function of George Eliot's represented society, its presence as a "human whole," something positive in which each individual inevitably participates and to which he contributes, cannot be seen as separable from the individual. Since the individual is part of that human whole, individual actions and attitudes are a part of "society," even if they contradict opinions and actions of a majority of other persons.

These metaphors and philosophical perspectives belong, however, to the narrator and express her vision of human community. The characters share in that vision only partially. Their perception of society manifests itself in their sensitivity to the climate of public opinion, the second and complementary aspect of George Eliot's representation of society. The characters recognize those webs of interrelationship not as potential contexts for their widespread good or harm but as a series of subtle or not-so-subtle pressures and social demands. In this context, the web, now as fabric of opinion, has negative implications. Dorothea's introduction includes the narrator's broad and humane understanding: "Her mind was theoretic . . . she was enamoured of intensity and greatness, and rash in embracing whatever seemed to her to have those aspects; likely to seek martyrdom, to make retractations, and then to incur martyrdom after all in a quarter where she had not sought it" (chap. 1). It also includes the social evaluation of such a character: "Women were expected to have weak opinions; but the great safeguard of society and of domestic life was, that opinions were not acted on. Sane people did what their neighbours did, so that if any lunatics were at large, one might know and avoid them" (chap. 1). The narrator's reduction of sanity to conformity with social convention is only partially ironic. Each individual internalizes social opinion to some extent.

This sense of a shared social opinion has two corollaries: (1) society expects individuals to fulfill general roles and responsibilities based on gender and class; and (2) society then judges particular individuals for their fulfillment of these roles and responsibilities. This judgment will constrain the unique and protect the conformist. Rosamond Vincy is perfectly invulnerable as an individual because she perfectly fulfills society's estimate of her general role and responsibility: to adorn her husband's new home. If she continues to fill that role, she is basically assured of society's continued approval. Her response to Lydgate's crisis, her little speech of four words—"What can *I* do, Tertius?"—capable by varied inflexion of expressing all states of mind, expresses "as much neutrality" as it can hold (chap. 58). She has done all that is expected of her within her society. By the narrator's lights, of course, she is deficient, but she fulfills her social role and wins social approbation. It should not surprise us, then, that society never recognizes the source of Lydgate's misery: "It did not occur to [Farebrother] that Lydgate's marriage was not delightful: he believed, as the rest did, that Rosamond was an amiable, docile creature, though he had always thought her rather uninteresting—a little too much the pattern-card of the finishing-school" (chap. 63).

George Eliot's representation of society finds its richness in merging a philosophical understanding of society with an experiential reality. On the one hand, society is the only context for meaningful individual action, the only context for personal self-realization, but, on the other hand, that society can celebrate the "pattern-card of the finishing-school" and limit, fragment, or destroy the possibilties of its more substantive and rare creatures. So the narrator concludes about Dorothea, "Many . . . thought it a pity that so substantive and rare a creature should have been absorbed into the life of another, and be only known in a certain circle as a wife and mother. But no one stated exactly what else that was in her power she ought rather to have done" (Finale). At this point, Steven Marcus's conclusion that "it is both a logical error and an existential impossibility to conceive or speak of an opposition between the (or an) individual person and society" is inadequate. Logic and existential possibility aside, Dorothea opposes not one or several or many, but a whole set of values given extension, through the narrator's power of generalization and evaluation, into all of English society. For example, the narrator's opening remarks in the Prelude—focusing on later-born Theresas who possess "spiritual grandeur ill-matched with the meanness of opportunity," who are "helped by no coherent social faith and order which could perform the function of knowledge for the ardently willing soul"—generalize the attitudes, values, and beliefs beyond the possession of any group or groups of people.

The very richness of George Eliot's depiction of society gives rise to the central tension in her novels, a tension anticipating the modern age: that between society presented as "human whole," an ideal human community, and society presented as social opinion, convention, and expectation, divorced from human needs, limiter or destroyer of human possibility. The context in which this tension plays out is Middlemarch itself, a sample of the whole texture of society. The key to interpretation lies in metaphors like that of the web by which, in its positive implications of interconnectedness, the narrator depicts and interprets her world as human community, and by which, in its negative implications as current of social opinions, the narrator explores the ways in which characters understand and evaluate themselves and each other.

When society provides both a medium for growing good and a context for gossip and opinion, obvious conflicts result. This representation allows for the general tendency of the world toward good and provides a context for the consolidation and expression of the good of the world, but the same medium, with its "threadlike pressure" on individuals, conduces to personal sacrifice and limitation. Lydgate, for example, continually feels "the hampering threadlike pressure of small social conditions, and their frustrating complexity" (chap. 18). For talented individuals, society is a prison of pettiness and convention. Only in unusual moments is an individual vouchsafed a glimpse of the larger human community to which he or she belongs. In *Middlemarch*, Dorothea alone shares that transcendent vision with the narrator as physical sight becomes moral illumination and insight:

> It had taken long for her to come to that question, and there was light piercing into the room. She opened her curtains,

and looked out towards the bit of road that lay in view, with fields beyond, outside the entrance-gates. On the road there was a man with a bundle on his back and a woman carrying her baby; in the field she could see figures moving—perhaps the shepherd with his dog. Far off in the bending sky was the pearly light; and she felt the largeness of the world and the manifold wakings of men to labour and endurance. She was a part of that involuntary, palpitating life, and could neither look out on it from her luxurious shelter as a mere spectator, nor hide her eyes in selfish complaining [chap. 80].

Dorothea here glimpses her part in involuntary, palpitating life. The experiential reality is, however, marked by constraint and suppression of self, not by self-realization. George Eliot tries to mediate by making constraint and self-suppression an avenue for transcending the narrow self, for discovering a larger self whose identity belongs to the human whole.

The narrator of *Middlemarch* thus plays a complex role in relation to individuals and society, at once mediator and mere reporter. We have seen that the final dimension to society (as ideal community) is one created by the narrator and shared only by her superior characters. This dimension represents the narrator's vision of society's significance. The other two dimensions to society—as milieu and fabric of opinion—represent the world as it is experienced by characters. George Eliot's narrator will not meddle with the consequences of this experience; she adopts the stance of scientific observer who must unravel and seek to understand fates but not alter them. Her role as observer of complex events enforces humility and a hesitation to judge. This narrator continues to probe because of her dual commitment to the extreme difficulty of knowing truth and to the vital importance of pursuing it. *Adam Bede*'s narrator remarks, "Falsehood is so easy, truth so difficult" as a preface and caution to attempting to define a truth. At best, such difficult truth can be approached only by providing multiple points of view.[11] Then we face the inescapable paradox that our guide to that truth can herself possess only *one* opinion, no matter how many others she presents. The tension between omniscient narration and a truth that is multisided produces the distinctive "unreliability" and limitation of George Eliot's narrator. In conjunction with a multifaceted representation of society, this "unreliability" ultimately generates an irresolvable tension between the individual and society.

This tension finds apparent narrative resolution, but a resolution unsatisfactory to many critics.[12] George Eliot asks us to accept Dorothea's contribution to the "growing good" as a worthy fulfillment, yet she teases us with the "pity that so substantive and rare a creature should have been absorbed into the life of another." Our study of society in Eliot's novel makes clear that we cannot finally resolve Dorothea's fate into some harmonious whole. The complex nature of Eliot's representation of society and of her judgments of individuals in society prevents our seeing human life in any single light.

George Eliot's narrator articulates the often crippling effects of particular social conventions on any individual: "For there is no creature whose inward being is so strong, that it is not greatly determined by what lies outside it." It is to that melody that most of the novel is piped; it is that refrain that echoes in the characters' lives. In the novel's first edition, Eliot allowed that chorus a share of her conclusion: "Among the many remarks passed on [Dorothea's] mistakes, it was never said in the neighbourhood of Middlemarch that such mistakes could not have happened if the society into which she was born had not smiled on propositions of marriage from a sickly man to a girl less than half his own age."[13] In the first edition, the narrator forcefully describes the ways in which social opinions have restricted or determined Dorothea's life. The fact that Eliot decided to omit these remarks in later editions suggests that she may have seen how they conflicted with her other final vision—also one of society, but positive—in which Dorothea contributes to the "growing good" of the world.[14]

Nonetheless, social opinion, not simply as something outside personality, but as woven into the very fabric of an inner life, dominates the novel's characters, and when a character fails to glimpse any human community and fails to share in the narrator's vision, his fate seems that much more determined by the hampering, threadlike pressures of social opinion. Lydgate offers an obvious example. The narrator immediately acquaints us with his "noble intention and sympathy" lying side by side with his "spots of commonness." His "spots of commonness," as she discusses them, stem from social opinions and attitudes Lydgate has imbibed, they "lay in the complexion of his prejudices, which, in spite of noble intention and sympathy, were half of them such as are found in ordinary men of the world: that distinction of mind which belonged to his intellectual ardour, did not penetrate his feeling and judgment about furniture, or women, or the desireability of its being known (without his telling) that he was better born than other country surgeons" (chap. 15). The narrator later comments: "We may handle even extreme opinions with impunity while our furniture, our dinner-giving, and preference for armorial bearings in our own case, link us indissolubly with the established order" (chap. 36). The divorce in Lydgate's personality becomes, for the narrator, "two selves" that can be seen as a product of nature and nurture although for George Eliot this divorce is not absolute— nature and nurture interpenetrate: "He had two selves within him apparently, and they must learn to accommodate each other and bear reciprocal impediments" (chap. 15).

The determinative fabric of opinion can be unspoken or spoken. Its unvoiced manifestation, in the form of received notions of class- and gender-related prerogatives, generally undermines a character, but voiced public opinion may also serve as a corrective to certain complacencies engendered by social conditioning. Mr. Brooke is muffled in inherited assumptions of his superiority and virtue. Reverend Cadwallader suggests that his friends let him run for parliament, "let him try to be popular and see that his character as a landlord stands in his way" (chap. 38). Indeed, Brooke experiences this corrective of public opinion to his self-conception when he visits his tenants. "It is wonderful how much uglier things will look when we only suspect we are blamed for them. Even our own persons in the glass are apt to change their aspect for us after we have heard some frank remark on their less admirable points" (chap. 39). Though this passage seems to echo the earlier-cited passages from "Amos Barton," now public opinion leads to good. Fred Vincy, also well-wadded with stupidity of this kind, experiences his antidote when he uses the Garths for security on his loan. Here, again, the sting of public opinion impels that essential movement outside self which characterizes all of the best characters.

Public censure, when deserved, may act as a corrective because inner lives are so deeply interwoven with public opinion. Conversely public censure can be destructive, when undeserved, for the same reason. Lydgate's dilemma, after prescribing for Raffles at Bulstrode's request, revolves around the question: "How was he to live on without vindicating himself among people who suspected him of baseness?" (chap. 73). Despite the fact that his "association with [Bulstrode] had been fatal to him," it "belonged to the generosity as well as defiant force of his nature that he resolved not to shrink from showing to the full his sense of obligation" (chap. 73). But Lydgate can fulfill his obligation to Bulstrode only at the price of acceding to all of Rosamond's wishes because the tide of public opinion has been too strong against her husband to make their continued life in Middlemarch tolerable. Mr. Vincy sums up: "I think Lydgate must leave the town. Things have gone against him. . . . I don't accuse him of any harm" (chap. 75). Vincy's tardy admission that Lydgate is not necessarily guilty makes the point. Lydgate is guilty of no harm, but public opinion has turned against him and that, alone, is sufficient to ruin him.

No matter how determined they are by social forces, however, George Eliot never absolves her characters from individual responsibility for their actions. The characters themselves feel free and that felt freedom is the basis for moral behavior even as it supports the notion of ideal community. The narrator may sympathize that "there is no creature whose inward being is so strong that it is not greatly determined by what lies outside it," but the characters themselves are held accountable for their actions and fates. Lydgate wins approbation because he accepts his crippling marriage as his duty: "Lydgate had accepted his narrowed lot with sad resignation. He had chosen this fragile creature, and had taken the burthen of her life upon his arms. He must walk as he could, carrying that burthen pitifully" (chap. 81). Although he never participates in the human community that Dorothea glimpses or contributes as directly to the "growing good," Lydgate shoulders his responsibility and becomes, the narrator tells us, "what is called a successful man." The doctor treating gout in Bath fulfills society's notion of success, and we can admire him for his duty. While Lydgate sees little of society in Eliot's wider sense of ideal community, he strengthens that ideal by his fidelity to his choices and commitments. The narrator can present this complexity but not, as we have seen, fully resolve it, committed as she is to a complex portrait of society and a multifaceted truth.

Lydgate's fate in *Middlemarch* anticipates the fate of Gwendolen Harleth in George Eliot's last novel, *Daniel Deronda*. There, the possibility of actual community has become even more tenuous.

Daniel leaves to create his own community, a Zionist state, something never realized within the bounds of the fiction. Gwendolen is thus deprived of her link, through Daniel, to a larger ideal community. At the novel's conclusion, when she discovers he is leaving, she cries, "I will try—try to live. I shall think of you. What good have I been? Only harm. Don't let me be harm to *you*."[15] She writes to Daniel on his wedding-day: "I have remembered your words—that I may live to be one of the best of women, who make others glad that they were born. I do not yet see how that can be, but you know better than I."[16] Her experience, when the novel ends, is one of separation, loss, and failure.[17]

Later novelists perceive a similar tension between society as positive community and society as network of hampering opinions and values. This perception forces Hardy toward the tragic mode; Lawrence's understanding causes him increasingly to define fulfillment as an achieved internal state not marked by any success within or accommodation to the actual community of human beings without.

"The World's Opinion" in *Tess of the D'Urbervilles*

George Eliot's vision of individual fulfillment within society includes both a Lydgate and a Dorothea. The doctor's fate particularly suggests the increasing remoteness of community. Thomas Hardy explores one inevitable consequence of seeing society as at least partially inimical to human possibility: tragic failure of the individual. For Hardy, the probability that social values and roles will sustain the individual becomes increasingly remote, the possibility of sustaining human community more precarious. His *Tess of the D'Urbervilles* demonstrates this emerging vision of society's role in human lives.

Hardy's early novel, the comedy *Under the Greenwood Tree*, takes its title from a song in Shakespeare's *As You Like It* and suggests a search for that revitalized community. The novel assimilates the city-bred and educated Fancy Day to the country mores and manners of Dick Dewey. Such assimilation, resting on Fanny's lies to her new husband, is a tenuous resolution at best, and Hardy's subsequent turn to more tragic modes suggests he found individual defeat more faithful to the probabilities of the world he envisions. Increasingly, the desire for education—which often amounts to the inculcation of modern social attitudes and values— jars with the natural world and supportive traditions to which Hardy's protagonists are also attracted. The educated and socially refined Grace Melbury unwittingly destroys simple Giles Winterborne in *The Woodlanders*; Angel Clare serves as a primary agent in Tess Durbeyfield's destruction.

The voice of Hardy's narrator is often ambiguous or ambivalent, and this locus of a novel's values has presented problems for Hardy's critics. The real strength of his novels derives instead from the stature he affords his protagonists. As does George Eliot, Hardy makes a character's conflicts with society reveal individual superiority. Real issues of choice and responsibility exist, especially in the later novels, so that Hardy's protagonists are not defeated merely by society but by individual failings, misperceptions, and weaknesses as well. Hardy holds to the possibility of a better meshing of man and circumstance, and that possibility gives tragic dignity to his protagonists' struggles to realize a larger vision of their lives and fates. Hardy's understanding of human fate, as expressed in his protagonists' lives, draws its power from his moving and convincing depiction of the interaction between those lives and their environments. In the later novels, particularly, those environments are largely social or fraught with social overtones.

Hardy's earlier novels, *Far From the Madding Crowd*, *The Return of the Native*, and *The Mayor of Casterbridge* rely on impersonal fate, doom, and nature for their tragic effects more conspicuously than the later novels, but in *Jude the Obscure*, his last novel, Hardy clearly focuses on the social limitations barring his hero. Jude can finally respond to Sue Bridehead's lament that the Gods are punishing them by saying they suffer only at the hands of "man and senseless circumstance." Jude's cathartic understanding focuses on the social mechanisms that have shaped his lot, and he perceives that "there is something wrong somewhere in our social formulas."[18]

Tess of the D'Urbervilles, Hardy's last major novel before *Jude*, toys with the notion of fate and "Aeschylean justice" to explain what happens to Tess, but its vision of inimical social attitudes in fact parallels *Jude*'s. The narrator's comments on impersonal fate and the tragic nature of the world have become largely rhetorical and do not form a substantive structure of meaning and probability in the text. Here, too, society is the real agent of destruction.

Society in *Tess of the D'Urbervilles* is represented both as something outside Tess and as a part of her personality. On the one hand, social values and expectations that threaten to limit or destroy Tess are concentrated in external forces: in the natural environment and in other persons, particularly those close to Tess—her parents, Angel Clare, and Alec D'Urberville.[19] Hardy lends breadth to Tess's experience, without sacrificing the concision essential to tragedy, in her wanderings over the face of England, from the lush, rural farmland of the south to the flinty, harsh soil of the north, from warmth to cold, but the forces that pursue her are endemic to her whole world and are grounded in the personalities of Alec, Angel, and Tess's parents.

Society also comprehends that "fabric of opinion" characteristic of George Eliot's novels. Hardy's protagonists are not creatures helpless before an impersonal and remote society; they are instead burdened, like Eliot's characters, with a set of social values that hampers their self-realization. Tess herself is partially responsible for her fate because she shares others' evaluations of herself throughout most of the novel. In Hardy, as in Eliot, then, society is both an internalized texture of attitudes and opinions and an environment outside the individual. Critics have seen *Tess of the D'Urbervilles* as the story of a "pure woman" caught in the meshes of society: the character as pure nature, the medium as society.[20] This reading overlooks, however, the two forms society takes in the novel and diminishes its richness. Hardy wishes to explore the ways in which the "Pure Woman" of the subtitle becomes complicit in her own fall, how, in short, Tess is both victim and agent of her own doom.[21]

Tess is Hardy's attempt to understand the destructive conflicts generated by a society in transition.[22] The imagistic oppositions (havens of nature versus the engines of society), environmental oppositions (north versus south, cold versus warm), and the elemental oppositions in character (sensual Alec versus spiritual Angel) serve as contexts to explore the action of society on character. Ultimately and ironically these oppositions are not opposite in their effects. Both Alec and Angel insist on Tess's naturalness, yet both want to adorn her. Alec smothers her in roses; Angel decks her in diamonds. Both, in the process, make her something artificial. For Hardy, these oppositions are not absolutes—nature on the one hand, society on the other, or sensuality on the one hand, spirituality on the other. They represent, rather, a cumulative weight of contending social ideas that bear upon Tess, and she embodies the complex aspects of the world she experiences. Tess is both a child of nature and a child of society, sensual and spiritual, a child of an old world and of a new. *Jude the Obscure* culminates aspects present in *Tess*. It, too, presents a world in transition, but the old traditions and sustaining values are here more remote. The widow Edlin, with her talk of former days, seems the last positive remnant of that world. Jude's own comments and actions are marked by conventional and unexamined attitudes that cripple his attempts to break out of his social sphere.[23]

Both the rural world, with its customs, traditions, and superstitions, and the urban world, with its industrialization, progress, and education, constitute society in *Tess*. Tess is prey both to her parents' simple ideas of former family grandeur and to Angel's bookish, yet naive, notions of purity and innocence. Tess can make only a verbal resistance to these notions; her life expresses their consequences.

The novel's opening stresses a world in change. The rural community of Marlott still celebrates the local Cerealia: "It had walked for hundreds of years, if not as benefit-club, as votive sisterhood of some sort; and it walked still."[24] The other clubs have ceased May-walking, and in the abandonment of these customs the narrator sees signs of larger social change; the white gowns are "a gay survival from Old Style days when cheerfulness and May-time were synonyms—days before the habit of taking long views had reduced emotions to a monotonous average" (chap. 2). This rural world set in the Vale of Blackmoor is rich in its contact with nature, but it is not, therefore, "natural" as opposed to social. Rather, the social customs and habits still reflect a sustaining identification with nature. The rural world, then, is one of customs, traditions, values, and attitudes that mark social beings.

Tess can therefore return to this world to bear her illegitimate child and be more readily accepted by her neighbors than she feels herself to be. Their country-bred fatalism—"It was to be" (chap. 11)—guarantees her acceptance among them. That fatalism stems partly from the logic of natural process in which their lives are imbedded and partly from a deep unconcern at her dilemma: "She might have seen that what had bowed her head so profoundly—the thought of the world's concern at her situation—was founded on an illusion. She was not an existence, an experience, a passion, a structure of sensations, to anybody but herself. To all humankind besides, Tess was only a passing thought" (chap. 14).

Of course, Tess, "living as a stranger and an alien here" (chap. 14), does not feel accepted. Hardy, like George Eliot, recognizes the limiting, even destructive effect of social norms on individuals, a destructive effect that often operates as much from within a character as from without. Hardy's novels share, too, a poignancy of lost community, a sadness that for individuals society has become a series of hobbles and harnesses rather than a structure of support and nurture. The narrator can conclude, "But for the world's opinion those experiences would have been simply a liberal education" (chap. 15), but Tess can never fully share this lofty perspective. Although she escapes the confines of Blackmoor, the "world's opinion" lives in her soul and continually argues her unfitness for happiness and fulfillment. Jude Fawley, likewise, embodies the conflicts that cripple him. On the one hand, he hotly defends his conventional "honour" and sense of duty by first marrying and then remarrying Arabella; on the other hand, he chastises Sue Bridehead for her enslavement to convention. Of Christminster, which Jude loves, Sue says, " 'He still thinks it a great centre of high and fearless thought, instead of what it is, a nest of commonplace schoolmasters whose characteristic is timid obsequiousness to tradition.' "[25] Jude cannot emotionally divest himself of values that he can intellectually reject.

Hardy's narrator thus expresses what is also George Eliot's understanding of the role of public opinion in shaping a character's personality and action, but in order to heighten tragic expectations, Hardy's narrator seems to suggest that this fabric of opinion has no real validity; it is a "cloud of moral hobgoblins by which [Tess] was terrified without reason":

> But this encompassment of her own characterization, based
> on shreds of convention, peopled by phantoms and voices
> antipathetic to her, was a sorry and mistaken creation of
> Tess's fancy—a cloud of moral hobgoblins by which she was
> terrified without reason. It was they that were out of har-

mony with the actual world, not she. Walking among the
sleeping birds in the hedges, watching the skipping rabbits
on a moonlit warren, or standing under a pheasant-laden
bough, she looked upon herself as a figure of Guilt intruding
into the haunts of Innocence. But all the while she was making a distinction where there was no difference. Feeling herself in antagonism, she was quite in accord. She had been
made to break an accepted social law, but no law known
to the environment in which she fancied herself such an
anomaly [chap. 13].

Although the narrator's tone differs markedly from that of George
Eliot's, the insight here does not differ greatly from hers: individuals' self-conceptions reflect social opinion. Society is woven firmly
into the fabric of individual psychology. Hardy's narrator sets up
opposing categories of nature and society and suggests a possibility
of pure identification with one and escape from the other. The
purely natural world does not exist, however, in the novel as a
separate medium for individual definition. All contexts the characters meet are social. Some are more firmly rooted in tradition, their
characters' occupations more firmly tied to the soil and season, but
purely asocial "nature" no longer exists as a retreat for Tess. Society and nature are set apart rhetorically only to increase our expectations for Tess's doom.

In his representation of Tess's character, Hardy is far less schematic than his rhetorical narrator. Tess is not natural or social, but
a combination of natural attributes and social conditioning. She
is, on the one hand, "a fine and picturesque country girl," her
personal charms are probably her mother's gift and "therefore un-
knightly, unhistorical," yet a dignity and pride, seemingly of D'Urberville lineage, separate her from her fellows, just as her education "under an infinitely Revised Code" creates a two-hundred-
year social chasm between herself and her mother (chaps. 2, 3).
Tess can express the country fatalism at Prince's death—that she
lives on a "blighted" star (chap. 4)—and yet in contradiction to
that fatalism, she cannot absolve herself of responsibility for what
happened—"Nobody blamed Tess as she blamed herself" (chap.
4). She bitterly castigates herself for her liaison with Alec, refusing
country fatalism but nonetheless fatalistically accepts Angel's rejection: "It was to be." Tess's own nature holds the complexity of

changing social attitudes, and she is destroyed by a combination of rural inertia and passivity and modern responsibility and self-determination. It is not merely amusing that Tess "felt quite a Malthusian towards her mother for thoughtlessly giving her so many little brothers and sisters." Such attitudes are a consequence of Tess's having "passed the Sixth Standard in the National School under a London-trained mistress" (chap. 3). Tess accepts both the values by which her parents live and another, contradictory set of values by which she has been educated. She never reconciles the two. When Tess wishes to marry Angel, she writes her mother for advice. Mrs. Durbeyfield characteristically counsels silence: "No girl would be such a Fool, specially as it is so long ago, and not your Fault at all." But Tess confesses because "Her mother did not see life as Tess saw it" (chap. 31).

The conflict in Angel is marked by a similar tension between received attitudes and educated ideas. The external and internal dimensions of society merge forcibly in Hardy's depiction of Angel Clare, whose personality expresses conflicts similar to Tess's and whose actions precipitate her destruction. Dairyman Crick's household provides a social environment that initially masks these conflicts and enables Tess and Angel temporarily to transcend the social determinants of their lives and natures. Immersion in this "natural world" enhances Tess's beauty and elemental purity, both paradoxically deepened by her experiences, what the narrator calls her "liberal education." Further, the household itself enjoys "perhaps the happiest of all positions in the social scale, being above the line at which neediness ends, and below the line at which the *convenances* begin to cramp natural feeling, and the stress of threadbare modishness makes too little of enough" (chap. 20). This social context frees Tess and Angel for an interaction impossible in any other environment, and its ideality masks the deep social chasms that will soon divide them.

The conflicts are evident but suppressed. Tess quickly discovers that her "supposed untraditional newness . . . had won interest in [Clare's] eyes" and so holds her tongue "about the d'Urberville vault" (chap. 19). Yet later Angel seizes on Tess's lineage as a great value in winning his parents' approval of her, and Angel selects the former d'Urberville mansion as their honeymoon site. Clare apotheosizes her as a "pure, and virginal daughter of nature," yet the qualities that attract him stem from her past experiences and loss of virginity: "her passing corporeal blight had been her mental harvest" (chap. 19). So bound up is Angel in mythological images and ideas of Tess's purity—a kind of deified virginity—that he fails to see, as Tess later pleads, that she, the fallen woman, is, in fact, the woman he loves.

All of Angel's liberal notions are checked by traditional attitudes when Tess reveals her past with Alec. The narrator makes abundantly clear that Angel's are not biblical standards transcending particular social attitudes: "No prophet had told him, and he was not prophet enough to tell himself, that essentially this young wife of his was as deserving of the praise of King Lemuel as any other woman endowed with the same dislike of evil, her moral value having to be reckoned not by achievement, but by tendency." They are, instead, particular received social values, which form and inform his nature: "But over them both there hung a deeper shade than the shade which Angel Clare perceived, namely, the shade of his own limitations. With all his attempted independence of judgment this advanced and well-meaning young man, a sample product of the last five-and-twenty years, was yet the slave to custom and conventionality when surprised back into his early teachings" (chap. 39).

The novel's conclusion plays out these tensions. Tess herself begins to evaluate the pressures that have coerced and threatened her and discovers they have been produced by an "arbitrary law of society which had no foundation in Nature" (chap. 41). Under duress, both she and Angel grow. What traveling to Brazil accomplishes for Angel—a broadening of his perspectives, a liberation from the constraints of received values—suffering accomplishes for Tess. Indeed, Tess gains sufficient understanding to castigate Angel—"O why have you treated me so monstrously. . . . It is all injustice I have received at your hands" (chap. 51)—just when Angel has come to understand the shade of his own limitations: "His own parochialism made him ashamed. . . . His inconsistencies rushed upon him in a flood" (chap. 49).

Tess succumbs to Alex only temporarily; in killing him she asserts herself and overcomes the passive acquiescence that has crippled her. She is given one idyllic week with Angel in whom "tenderness was absolutely dominant . . . at last" (chap. 57). It constitutes fulfillment for her, a tragic fulfillment in which her self-realization and self-determination lead to her destruction. She can accept her destruction and say, "I am ready" (chap. 58), now that she has understood her antagonist, not only as something external to her, but as deeply wrought into her own nature, wrought into the nature of her existence. Such an understanding helps explain her insistence that Angel marry Liza Lu: "She has all the best of me without the bad of me" (chap. 58), and her reiterated final comment to Angel: "It is as it should be. . . . I am almost glad . . . now I shall not live for you to despise me!" (chap. 58). To Tess, her own nature holds the corruption that has destroyed her. Tess achieves tragic stature in her understanding and acceptance of responsibility.

Jude the Obscure expresses, perhaps, a darker vision since Jude is not allowed a tragic fulfillment similar to Tess's at Stonehenge, but the final fourth of this novel presents an extended fulfillment for him marked by an increasing awareness of his own complicity in Sue's and his failures. Despite Jude's remarrying Arabella, an action that expresses conventional notions of duty—"I said I'd do anything to save a woman's honor . . . and I have"—Jude seems capable of a new self-irony in that statement. He has come to some understanding of the forces that have shaped his life and the attitudes from which he has never completely freed himself, and in that understanding he finds his tragic fulfillment.

Hardy's *Tess of the D'Urbervilles* depicts the two ways in which society increasingly oppresses individuals. As a fabric of opinion, it cripples the ability of distinctive individuals to realize their best selves, and, as a context in which to act, it bars the expression of individual goodness by insisting on the letter of the law. Though clearly once a structure of support, community has become a potential prison. But the spirit of meaningful human community still breathes through Hardy's novels and is manifest in the protagonists' understanding and embracing their individual responsibilities. Individual responsibility, in Hardy as in George Eliot, begets freedom, and out of freedom grows the potential for real community.

In contrast stands Gustave Flaubert's bourgeois tragedy, *Madame Bovary*. Emma, like Tess, struggles against a milieu with an inadequate "self," a self in Emma's case largely shaped by that milieu. Where George Eliot and Thomas Hardy postulate a core of self distinct from social conditioning and capable of ultimate moral superiority to it, self is a pastiche of social conditioning and social opinion in Flaubert. The superior self in Eliot and Hardy is capable of accepting responsibility for his or her fate and ultimately capable of sharing a narrator's vision of community; Emma Bovary will never share any perspective with her narrator. She will never achieve the heights that enable him to evaluate her and her fate. She will never see her fate as he does. Eliot's Dorothea and Hardy's Tess can aspire to those heights. That absolute distance between protagonist and narrator distinguishes Flaubert from Eliot and Hardy and extinguishes the location of positive values within social organization. Hardy and Eliot offer garrulous narrators compared to Flaubert's; but they are made talkative partly to give scope to the conviction that beauty can reside in human life within society, and that significant meaning can be discovered in an individual's relationship to society.

In *Madame Bovary*, the "myth" of objectivity allows Flaubert to leave his protagonist as unredeemed at the end as she was at the beginning. She fails to understand the laws of her world. It is no surprise that Flaubert has been termed more "naturalistic" than the naturalistic novelists. He sees self as so entirely shaped by society that it never glimpses the force of that conditioning. Flaubert dispenses with the assumption that beauty can reside in human life for the conviction that true beauty is to be found in aesthetic objects. Indeed, the beauty of *Madame Bovary* resides in its craft as a novel: it is the beauty of art, the beauty of a wrought object.

Flaubert anticipates one direction in which the novel will go, that is, toward a subtle exploration of itself as artifice. D. H. Lawrence, to whom I turn next, charts another direction, which continues the emphases of a George Eliot or a Thomas Hardy. Lawrence, too, recognizes value in the idea of community, but he recognizes the increasing destructiveness of society and moves toward fates in which one's accommodation to society is marked by an achieved internal state, rather than by some change in external condition. It is true, of course, that no novelist makes achieved social status an end in itself; nonetheless the success of characters in earlier novels was often reflected in some external change. In *Pride and Prejudice*, for instance, although marriage per se does not define Darcy's and Elizabeth's fulfillment, the social fate of a good marriage reflects the personal growth of both protagonists. In *Tom Jones*, Tom wins Sophia; in Dickens's novels, Esther gets Woodcourt, Eugene wins Lizzy; even Eliot's Dorothea wins Will Ladislaw.

In the modern novel, authors began experimenting with fulfillments that were not tragic, yet which resulted in some loss of social station or in an inability to discover one's place in society. Lawrence, especially in the figure of Ursula Brangwen, depicts a fate that we do not interpret as tragic, a fate in which society plays a significant role and yet a character's fulfillment is not expressed by some tangible achievement or success within the society.

Society as Other in *The Rainbow*

In often-quoted lines from "Morality and the Novel," D. H. Lawrence claims that immorality results from the author's "thumb in the scale" pulling down the balance "to his own predilection." The "delicate, for ever trembling and changing *balance*," which a writer must not violate, is that "between me and my circumambient universe, which precedes and accompanies a true relatedness."[26] Lawrence's novels depict quests after that true relatedness to another person, people, a nation, a race of men, animals, trees, flowers, earth, skies, sun, stars, and the moon. On the one hand, that relatedness suggests society, on the other, the natural world and cosmos. This "circumambient universe" conscribes the complex medium for character definition; the trembling instability of the balance determines the morality of the whole. Although relationship with the natural world is not automatic, it is more immediate for the Laurentian protagonist than his relationship with society. Indeed, an ability to respond fully and sensuously to nature and natural process distinguishes the Laurentian hero from others around him and provides the energy for his struggle with restricting and inimical social forms, a struggle central to the novel.

Lawrence's concept of "pure relatedness" accompanies that of transcending "the old, stable ego." He wants to avoid the "old-fashioned human element—which causes one to conceive character in a certain moral scheme and make him consistent."[27] Since characterization and the representation of society are related, to go beyond the old, stable ego, Lawrence necessarily must alter his representation of society. What has been a constant aspect of represented society in a large group of novels, shared values and norms that shape individual psychology, Lawrence, in effect, denies and abandons; Lawrence no longer conceives society as a context for ethical behavior. He is not interested in social ethics, in how individuals get along in societies. Characters are judged primarily for their failures of responsibility to self not to others. Perhaps surprisingly, then, Lawrence is very interested in community and the possibility of a human community beyond the existing, deadening forms.

This interest and possibility develop because Lawrence, like George Eliot and Hardy, conceives of society as a series of relations or possibilities for true relatedness. While he denies the ethical values that Eliot and Hardy place on those relationships, Lawrence insists on a new morality based on balance between self and other. Just as in Eliot and Hardy, the nature of society as other, as it threatens to upset equilibrium and threatens to limit or destroy individuality, poses a danger to characters. The vocabulary has changed; the formal understanding of how society, in general, relates to individuals has not. Society in all of the novels considered in this chapter both stimulates and threatens individual growth and self-realization. Society cannot be ignored; neither can it be assimilated automatically. From the protagonists' struggles to accommodate medium and self evolve complex issues of individual morality and its relation to social forms. Although these issues of accommodation are acute in *The Rainbow*, community is still possible. In *Women in Love*, Lawrence's next novel, the possibility of a "community" of more than two becomes increasingly remote. Ursula and Birkin achieve "mystic otherness of being" with each other, and Birkin wants that same communion with Gerald Critch, but the possibility of any meaningful community of individuals has disappeared. *Women in Love* expresses the tension born of a longing for community and a sense that larger communities are impossible.

Fictional society in *The Rainbow* is a fluid medium whose meaning changes over time as well as from individual to individual. What Tom Brangwen sees as society will not be the same as what his brother Alfred experiences; his vision will correspond to the possibilities in himself. Society relates organically to the elemental in Lawrence's protagonists. Because true relatedness is individual and unique, society consists of whatever an individual needs to assimilate from the wider world of men and experience. At the same time, it has recognizable external forms: for example, the world of work or the world of industrialization in Ursula's generation. Society is, however, something to be integrated with the "in-human will."

Julian Moynaham summarizes the reader's dilemma in attempting to explain the relation between society and self: "it is certainly true that Lawrence did not fully succeed at the enormously difficult task of clarifying the relation of his 'inhuman selves' to social roles on the one hand, and to vital forces on the other."[28] One might add that Lawrence cannot clarify because the relation is fluid, unstable, and above all individual. In other novels, all characters confront a similar society: that is, its values, attitudes, and beliefs are experienced by everyone in roughly the same way. Dorothea and Lydgate share the same "society" as do Angel and Tess. In *The Rainbow*, however, society even for two characters of the same generation has different manifestations.

Lawrence's novels stand on assumptions about the representation and role of society that have grown up out of the nineteenth century. The group of literati, who gathered to "honor" Lawrence on the occasion of the fiftieth anniversary of his death, did him an injustice when they sought to define his influence on the novel in terms of later novelists and concluded, "He didn't have any."[29] Lawrence is more important for his ability to conceive old assumptions in new ways, and he took those old assumptions as far as they can go. Society is not an illusion for Lawrence, as it would be for some modern novelists, not simply a projection of an individual psychology, but real and autonomous. Characters must either fit its presence into their lives or assimilate it in order to transcend it, but it cannot be ignored. Lawrence insists on locating his characters' meaning in the worlds of other individuals.

A closer look at fictional society in *The Rainbow*—both what it includes and what it excludes—helps clarify its role. That representation depends initially on a dichotomy between the inward life of nature, natural forces, and "blood intimacy" and the outward world emblematized by the "active scope of men." While the early Brangwen men face "inwards to the teeming life of creation," the women look to the world beyond, to a society that comprehends education, experience, formal knowledge, power, refinement, culture.[30] The vicar, his wife, and Lord William represent that world for the early Brangwens. The particular comprehensive scope of society in this novel is unusual: it includes all that does not belong to natural forces and the processes of generation, birth, fruition, and death; that is, society in large measure achieves its definition in opposition to nature.

Despite this general inclusiveness, Lawrence's fictional society excludes much of what generally characterizes society in the novel. Graham Hough has observed that what might ordinarily be considered the province of any represented society, the manners and customs of daily living, is largely absent, and he criticizes this absence as a fault in the novel: "Dr Leavis has rightly emphasized the range and grasp of Lawrence's picture of twentieth-century England; but this is continually vitiated by presenting it as a place of vile tempers and no manners at all. And this is only part of a growing inability or unwillingness to render the texture of ordinary life, of unimpassioned daily living."[31] As far as Hough's observation goes, it is correct. However, in choosing to depict society as he does, Lawrence emphasizes society's role as other, a realm outside the characters' experience and mastery.

Sometimes Lawrence does not exclude a traditional aspect of society. He simply gives it a new dimension consonant with his formal ends. It should not surprise us, then, that for Lawrence the value of society no longer resides in the community's regulation of ethical behavior. In fact, his definitions of moral and immoral behavior run counter to common social ethics. For example, Alfred, Tom, and Will Brangwen are all adulterers or potential adulterers, but their impulse toward adultery is defined as a fear to meet a challenge to themselves. In the first generation, when Tom turns from Lydia toward another woman, Lydia confronts him for his resistance to her and what he needs to assimilate of her otherness. He turns back to Lydia and accepts the challenge. A social ethic is not in question here, rather a special Laurentian ethic predicated on equilibrium between self and otherness.[32]

Finally, F. R. Leavis has noted that Lawrence reveals little "of class feeling in the ordinary sense." Superior social rank is not merely an accident of birth; it reflects real achievement. Leavis elucidates this point: "The imaginative values enjoyed by the women cannot be reduced to snobbery, and the superiorities they see, with substantial truth, as associated with class-differences are real."[33] As we shall see, Lawrence uses class hierarchy to stimulate his characters to seek knowledge beyond themselves, a search at the heart of the Laurentian ethic.

Knowledge of a literal "beyond" suggests contact with a metaphoric "beyond," beyond the self. Lawrence establishes this relationship of society to self in *The Rainbow*'s first chapter: "And the Brangwen wife of the Marsh aspired beyond herself, towards the further life of the finer woman [the wife of the vicar], towards the extended being she revealed, as a traveller in his self-contained manner reveals far-off countries present in himself. But why should a knowledge of far-off countries make a man's life a different thing, finer, bigger? And why is a man more than the beast and the cattle that serve him? It is the same thing" (chap. 1). The vocabulary of "extended being," the image of a traveler, and the contrast with instinctual beasts capture the heart of what society, embodied in the vicar's wife, means to the Brangwen women: a finer, bigger life. The narrator endorses their perspective and its importance in shaping lives otherwise so limited that "they would have been heavy and uninspired and inclined to hate. So long as the wonder of the beyond was before them, they could get along, whatever their lot" (chap. 1). The idea of a larger community of values humanizes; it distinguishes men from beasts.

Each individual must meet the challenge in that beyond; the danger is that he will succumb to the merely mechanical in his meeting with society. The danger of failing to transcend particular customs is always there for Lawrence's characters, as it is for Eliot's or Hardy's. This fate meets Tom Brangwen's brothers, for example, in the first generation and Will and Anna Brangwen in the second; both groups succumb to limited realization within prescribed and safe social roles. Despite Lawrence's new conception of character, his individuals still meet the pressure of being socially safe. Society is, as we have found it earlier, both a challenge to growth and an excuse for failure. Lawrence's narrator may speak of Alfred Brangwen's "crushing the bowels" within him or describe Will as possessing "folded centres of darkness which would never develop and unfold whilst he was alive in the body" (chaps. 1, 7), capturing in his unique imagery and language a sense of something essential that has been destroyed or lost, but he is still speaking of individual potential meeting an agent of limitation or destruction which is society. Represented society in Lawrence's novel is less obviously a set of opinions that limit the characters; it is broadly, and increasingly as time passes, a set of narrow possibilities within whose limitations individuals are trapped and crushed, a capitulation of self to other. Lawrence shares a surprising commonality with George Eliot and Thomas Hardy in that individuals' encounters with convention and expectation in fact force them either to acknowledge their own participation in that limitation and transcend it or to stifle further desires for self and accept personal limitation. Lawrence speaks of character "passing, as it were, through allotropic states," a metaphor that suggests a process of assimilating the meaning of each new surface in order to probe still further to the core or essence, Lawrence's "carbon."[34] Although his language differs substantially, Lawrence's metaphors yield themselves to an understanding of individual and society congenial to Eliot and Hardy.

Fulfillment for each member of Brangwen generations depends on his or her ability to participate in the outward social world in order to assimilate its meaning and relation. That assimilation, however, increasingly dictates transcendence of the particular outward forms, which become prisons stifling the vital forces. This struggle to assimilate the outward is made more difficult because it must not sacrifice the individual's communion with the natural world. A connectedness with nature provides the vigor for that higher struggle, but at the same time, the higher struggle threatens to dissociate the individual from natural processes. With each generation the problems become more difficult, but the resulting fulfillment is richer because more comprehensive.[35]

As we have seen, incorporation of the outward world is positive and direct for the early Brangwens because each individual is still nourished by nature and its cycles. The outward—society and culture—means a finer, bigger life. For Tom Brangwen, empathy with the natural world is almost automatic. The Marsh farm, the family homestead, stands as the physical embodiment of his roots in the land: "The homestead was just on the safe side of civilisation, outside the gate" (chap. 1). It cannot withstand the forces of industrialization, however, and a flood, caused by a breakdown of the railway embankment, destroys both the resource of Tom Brangwen and the Marsh farm for Ursula in the third generation. Before this happens, Will's and Anna's moves to Cossethay and later to suburban Beldover express the increasing urbanization of the society and difficulty of access to those old resources available at the Marsh farm.

To satisfy his spiritual yearnings, the demand of his nature that he incorporate the outside world, Tom marries Lydia Lensky, a

Polish woman, who as a traveler with a "knowledge of far-off countries [makes his] life a different thing, finer, bigger." Tom, in his earlier contact with a foreign gentleman had discovered that "it was the gracious manner, the fine contact that was all" (chap. 1). By marrying a part of that foreignness and bringing it to the Marsh farm, Tom enlarges his life and becomes himself a traveler, but he cannot appropriate that foreignness without destroying the life it represents. Lydia Lensky remains in life-giving opposition to him and that vitality of the other provides the necessary stimulus for growth of both. Tom is able finally to discover the richness and splendor of his own life, seeing himself and his wife as "two children camping in the plains." They are the eternal travelers: "there was no end, no finish, only this roaring vast space" (chap. 5).

In the next generation, neither Will nor Anna is able to achieve Tom's synthesis of the sensual and spiritual represented in the world beyond, because the outer life, society and culture, can no longer be integrated directly. The forms have become subtle traps that fragment individuals. For example, Anna and Will want to be "like other people, decently satisfied," but Anna is frustrated: "Everything seemed to be merely a matter of social duty, and never of her *self*" (chap. 6). She satisfies herself through childbearing, through the body; "If her soul had found no utterance, her womb had" (chap. 7). The difficulty, of course, is to give utterance to the soul. Denied Anna's fulfillment, however limited, Will turns to the church for meaning and becomes entrapped in "an enclosed circle," whose only fulfillment lies through fragmentation of body and soul. Finally the pursuit of sensual activity satisfies Will's body and frees his social self: "He had at length, from his profound sensual activity, developed a real purposive self" (chap. 8). Although he develops a "new public spirit," he has embraced empty form. He lives a dichotomized life: on the one hand, a dark, sensual self, on the other, a social, purposive being. Neither satisfies the soul.

Ursula, who inherits her parents' struggles, must meet not only their challenges but also those posed by a more complex society. Like her grandfather, Ursula is a "traveller on the face of the earth, and . . . she must go on and on, seeking the goal that she knew she did draw nearer to" (chap. 14). In the third generation, certain patterns become clear. First, whereas accommodation of the social and natural worlds had been possible for Tom, fragmentation and dichotomy have characterized the experience of Anna and Will. For

Ursula fulfillment must lie in assimilation and transcendence. This aspect of Ursula Brangwen's experience in *The Rainbow* bears a marked similarity to that of Birkin and Ursula in *Women in Love*. The rich satisfactions of her grandfather's environment are not immediately available to Ursula, and yet she cannot ignore the enlarging experience of participation in the outward world. She participates to assimilate and transcend. At each stage, she has peers who fail to meet the challenges and so provide a standard by which to measure her achievement.

Second, she inherits from the previous generation, as had Anna and Will before her, what remains unresolved and unassimilated in her parents' lives. By continuing instabilities from generation to generation, Lawrence creates continuity in his world, the sense of organic growth and change, while revealing the increasing difficulty of fulfillment in that world. Ursula must assimilate much more than confronted her grandfather, Tom, and she has no center of nurturance to rely on.

Finally, in the context of three generations, Lawrence's valuing of social/public life—with all its implications of "extended being," of a larger finer life—has its full exploration. Not only Tom, who is immersed in the natural world, but also Ursula, who has largely lost the natural world as resource and is confronted daily with deadening social form, must move outward. Ursula, like Birkin in *Women in Love*, has, however, an immediate relation to the natural (cosmic, vegetable, and animal), which other characters like Anton Skrebensky have lost, and her contact with the natural world provides a stimulus to the larger struggle. Connection with the natural does not, however, stimulate growth outward. That is society's role. Thus society in Lawrence's novel is not simply corrosive and destructive of human life, and even when it largely frustrates, limits, or destroys, the only way to Laurentian salvation is through society, which enlarges those who have the strength to meet it.[36]

To answer her longings, Ursula first turns where her father had turned before her: to the church. She then quickly revolts from it because Christ's resurrection separated him from the people whom he should have joined in human community: "Can I not eat with my brother happily, and with joy kiss my beloved, after my resurrection, celebrate my marriage in the flesh with feastings, go about my business eagerly, in the joy of my fellows? . . . Is the flesh which was crucified become as poison to the crowds in the street, or is it a strong gladness and hope to them, as the first flower blossoming out of the earth's humus?" (chap. 10). Ursula, in this first rejection, glimpses the narrator's vision of community, a religion in the flesh, a vision uniting men not only with one another but with the whole circumambient universe.

Ursula's movement to integrate both sensual and spiritual selves gets its impetus from a desire for this social communion. Having rejected spirituality alone, she now plunges into sensuality with Anton Skrebensky, where, however, she is blocked by the same sense of limitation, of failed communion, because such passion culminates for each individual in a "sense of his or of her own maximum self, in contradistinction to all the rest of life" (chap. 11). Fulfillment for Lawrence's protagonists demands an inclusiveness that eludes Ursula.

Finding the spirit and the flesh insufficient as separate answers, Ursula turns for answers to the particular forms of self-definition offered by her milieu. The great machine of the colliery, "which has taken us all captives" (chap. 12), offers Ursula a vision of community that temporarily seduces her, but she rebels at a community born of slavery not of freedom. In teaching, too, the world of work, Ursula expects to find freedom of financial independence, but the narrator's metaphor of a filly being "broken into the shafts" suggests another form of slavery. Ultimately Ursula rejects this world, yet only after she has embraced it and submitted to it for a time. To fail to so do would be to fail to "free herself of the man's world . . . of the great world of responsible work" (chap. 13). Higher education, Ursula's next avenue, seemingly offers freedom of the mind, yet she finds it another form of enslavement, "a little apprentice-shop where one was further equipped for making money" (chap. 15). She turns back to Anton, and pregnancy seems to provide an avenue of escape from her dilemma. Ursula has the opportunity to choose the avenue her mother, Anna, has taken before her and momentarily rejects as wrong that other thing, "that fantastic freedom, that illusory, conceited fulfillment" (chap. 16). Ursula, of course, is not wrong; she must pursue that fantastic fulfillment, and her subsequent miscarriage and sickness—a final process of breaking down the old—brings her to an affirmation of the fulfillment she seeks: "She was the naked, clear kernel thrusting forth the clear, powerful shoot, and the world was a bygone winter, discarded, her mother and father and Anton, and college and all her friends, all cast off like a year that has gone by, whilst the kernel was free and naked and striving to take new root, to create a new knowledge of Eternity in the flux of Time" (chap. 16). Ursula has finally found that kernel of self by stripping off, or breaking through, the husks of her existence. This process of affirmation/negation, acceptance/rejection—what Lawrence, speaking of language in *Women in Love*, would call a "frictional to-and-fro"—moves her steadily toward the essential, the kernel from which new life is possible.

Ursula's final vision of a positive community has not fully persuaded critics.[37] However, that vision is not one of a brave new world "acoming in" but one of personal transcendence for Ursula:

> And the rainbow stood on the earth. She knew that the sordid people who crept hard-scaled and separate on the face of the world's corruption were living still, that the rainbow was arched in their blood and would quiver to life in their spirit, that they would cast off their horny covering of disintegration, that new, clean, naked bodies would issue to a new germination, to a new growth, rising to the light and the wind and the clean rain of heaven. She saw in the rainbow the earth's new architecture, the old, brittle corruption of houses and factories swept away, the world built up in a living fabric of Truth, fitting to the over-arching heaven [chap. 16].

The measure of Lawrence's achievement lies in the seriousness with which we take Ursula's final vision. Whatever the limitations of society, we have watched her confront it and struggle to a new self-awareness that expresses a meaningful connection with that outer world. In these final passages, Lawrence does not seem to be making a significant judgment of society as much as using society and its realized limitations to make the significant judgment of Ursula and her fulfillment. Society, then, is essential to a definition of character and of individual morality, for in a character's confronting real limitations within a society, significant development occurs, true morality is revealed. The emotional power of this novel, like that of Eliot's and Hardy's, depends on our both recognizing the binding limits of the social milieu and perceiving the struggles of individuals to fulfill their potential within the limitations. The power of *The Rainbow* resides in our having appreciated to the fullest extent both the ability of society to limit Ursula and her discovery—through a developed spiritual awareness—of a mode of confronting those limitations without submitting to them. Her final vision can thus speak not only of herself but of humanity as a whole.

The individual must participate in society, whatever its limitations. No significant fulfillment exists in turning back to the blood intimacy and connection with the soil of the early Brangwen men. The inward life must be fused with a developed spiritual awareness born of participation in the outward social world of men, knowledge, culture, and power. In *The Rainbow* each confrontation with the external world defines for us a significant internal movement, culminating in the revelation of a fulfillment for the last generation that is an achieved internal state.[38]

Lawrence wrote of George Eliot that it was she "who started it all. It was she who started putting all the action inside."[39] His comment pinpoints Eliot's tendency to make the social medium revelatory of character and individual psychology rather than letting characters, who serve as emblems or types, define the medium or society. With the action located inside, fulfillment for Eliot's, Hardy's, and Lawrence's characters rests largely on an achieved internal state: Dorothea's and Ursula's vision of community, Tess's understanding of her fate. That fulfillment is no longer mirrored in some outward social success: an ideal marriage, social prestige, fortune, or political power. That internal fulfillment, however, does not deny the value of society and social forms. Although the protagonists do not readily find an enabling community, these novels always acknowledge the value of communal experience.

Henry James's Social Aesthetic

Henry James's novels also participate in this movement inward that was inherited from George Eliot. In *The Ambassadors*, for example, Lambert Strether, a product of American values, beliefs, and expectations, enters European society. The resulting conflict of social norms generates Strether's liberation. He begins by envying his friend Waymarsh, but it is he who finally exhorts Waymarsh, in whom he hears the "conscience of Milrose": "*Let* yourself, on the contrary, go—in all agreeable directions."[40] European and American social norms serve as perspectives on each other. For Strether, "seeing" entails experiencing the limitations of each frame.

James's characters, when they succeed, see beyond a particular socially determined correctness, to a larger "rightness"—a freedom from the weave of social value and expectation, an internal growth that waits on social experience for its maturation. Strether is more fortunate than Winterbourne of *Daisy Miller* who only glimpses the alternative social values by which a Daisy acts. Locked into his social categories of right and wrong, values exemplified by Mrs. Costello and Mrs. Walker, he is "booked to make a mistake."[41] He is incapable of seeing, incapable of "being right."

James's novels play with this conflict of values: one a social morality, the other what may with justice be called a social aesthetic. The former accepts codes, values, and norms of behavior implicit in a certain society. A person is defined by his or her behavior, for how he or she conforms to common expectation. A social aesthetic is also shared, but it prizes things purely for their own sakes: an ethos derived from G. E. Moore's *Principia Ethica*. "By far the most valuable things, which we know or can imagine, are certain states of consciousness, which may be roughly described as the pleasures of human intercourse, and the enjoyment of beautiful objects."[42] This attitude—an appreciation for beauty, elegance, tone—constitutes a "social aesthetic" in James's novels, and it is shared by his characters.

In *Portrait of a Lady*, common aesthetic ideals allow Madame Merle and Osmond to regard Isabel Archer as an elegant object. W. J. Harvey has explored the precarious balance "between aesthetic vehicle and moral tenor" in James's novels, finding a perversion in Osmond's case because he uses the aesthetic object instead of merely appreciating it.[43] Susceptibility to the aesthetic marks the Jamesian protagonist, but difficulties begin when appreciation leads to appropriation. In negotiating that difficult territory, Strether remains "right" in *The Ambassadors* because he recognizes that he must "not, out of the whole affair, to have got anything for [himself]."[44] Maggie Verver's fate in *The Golden Bowl* is much more ambiguous because she has, in one sense, appropriated the prince, supposedly out of higher motives than those of Osmond in *Portrait*. However, Maggie's social propriety merges uneasily with her aesthetic sense; she does not transcend both categories, as does Strether, by getting nothing but his "wonderful impressions."

As we look back to George Eliot's novels, we discover worlds dense with objects, objects that help reveal character. Dorothea Brooke's spontaneous pleasure at the light through her mother's gems develops an important aspect of her personality, one substantiated by her love of horseback riding. The objects here signify Dorothea's unacknowledged sensuality. By the time James writes, aesthetic objects can have an equivalence to human beings, and people can be converted into aesthetic objects. Alienation from increasingly narrow social ethics has made art its own justification, and moral value is found in aesthetic value.

George Eliot's Dorothea Brooke is pardoned for her resistance to, even revulsion from, "the weight of unintelligible Rome," which the narrator points out "might lie easily on bright nymphs to whom it formed a background for the brilliant picnic of Anglo-foreign society." This historical-aesthetic appeal of Rome becomes for Dorothea, however, a "vast wreck of ambitious ideals, sensuous and spiritual," images that in later years afflict her like "a disease of the retina" (chap. 20). Henry James's Strether, on the contrary, is alive to aesthetic, sensual beauty. He experiences his uneasiness from an altogether different source, lest "any acceptance of Paris might give one's authority away. It hung before him this morning, the vast bright Babylon, like some huge iridescent object, a jewel brilliant and hard, in which parts were not to be discriminated nor differences comfortably marked."[45] Dorothea cannot appreciate the aesthetic for its own sake. Lacking the historical perspective, she lacks means of aesthetic appreciation that to James's Strether are immediate and persuasive. The social bias that dominates her ethics is, however, celebrated not in its narrow manifestations but as an ideal of human community and commitment to others. James's emphasis celebrates "wonderful impressions" and their value to an individual. Community is less important.

James's novels, like Lawrence's, may be seen as pivotal in the development of form in the novel but for a different reason. Where Lawrence's characters fight to define themselves within the natural and social worlds, struggling to attain a difficult assimilation and transcendence of concrete society in a larger social vision, James's protagonists hover uneasily between moral and aesthetic social values, and, in some instances, the moral becomes identical with the aesthetic. James's vision leads to an increasing emphasis on self over community, a morality and a world defined in personal rather than in communal terms.

Society in the Light of History

One way to illuminate these several novelists' achievements is to contrast them with that of another great nineteenth-century novelist, Leo Tolstoy. A comparison between *War and Peace* and the novels discussed here clarifies general theoretical issues and summarizes from a different perspective this chapter's central understanding of one formal possibility for represented society in the novel.

Society is given a different value in Tolstoy's *War and Peace* than it has in *Middlemarch* or *Tess* or *The Rainbow*. Whereas the narrator of *Middlemarch*, for example, is concerned with articulating an abstract notion of society, Tolstoy's narrator articulates an abstract idea of history. The characters of both novels are fully and convincingly enmeshed in a social medium. For George Eliot that represented medium is Middlemarch, a piece of the whole of English society. For Tolstoy, whose novel ranges over Russia and Europe, that medium is represented by the salon—itself largely dominated by women—by the army, government, and politics—largely dominated by men—by the estate with its emphasis on class structure, and by religion and freemasonry with their emphasis on the spiritual. All are systems with rules, priorities, and values. In Eliot's *Middlemarch*, the major movement is toward transcending particular circumstances to participate in a social ideal of fellowship. In Tolstoy's *War and Peace*, our dominant sense is of disruption of those social systems by the force of historical events.

Tolstoy establishes this pattern in chapter 1 when Pierre Bezuhov blunders into Anna Scherer's salon. The anxiety his presence produces is comic. The fact that Pierre does not intend to disrupt the salon accords with Tolstoy's idea of history. True history, he felt, is not an examination of the actions of great men but an explanation of the impersonal logic of events. Pierre, rather than being expelled from the salon as a buffoon, is more firmly installed there by a natural event: the death of his father, the Count Bezuhov.

Pierre's presence on the battlefield at Borodino underscores the impersonal logic Tolstoy sees in events. To Pierre all is chaos; he blunders into the conflict and finds himself unwittingly at the center of the action. It is the center not by any plan; only the logic of events has determined its centricity and Pierre's participation in it. Pierre's presence on the battlefield as in the drawing room underlines the fatuities, the incoherence of social systems by which people live, and it exposes their inability to order events and to confer real meaning. For example, the army initially offers security for someone like Rostov because he sees it as ordered, rational, and predictable. Prince Andrei sees government that way; Pierre looks for order and meaning in freemasonry. While the characters seek meaning in social organizations, their lives are really being determined by historical events over which no one has any control.

Pierre figures in all the major events of the novel yet remains at their periphery. His peripheral presence, however, makes him central to the novel's vision of significance, which finds Napoleon a buffoon and Pierre a "typical" hero.[46] Georg Lukács's term describes Pierre's part: Pierre embodies the tensions endemic to his world; he is a figure of exceptional qualities who mirrors all the essential aspects of a particular stage of development.

Tolstoy's historical perspective prevents his serving up his characters with a sauce of morality: "He shows the objective dialectic of their rise or fall, always motivating both by the total sum of their own natures and the mutual interaction of this their nature with the total sum of objective circumstances, never by any isolated value-judgement of their 'good' and 'bad' qualities."[47] So Lukács speaks of Balzac and Stendhal, but his comments apply equally well to Tolstoy, another writer whom Lukács identifies as a "realist." Morality, or value-judgment, as Lukács has defined it, depends on assessing a character's behavior in a social situation and on finding that his behavior defines his nature, whether good or bad. Tolstoy's narrator is not interested, however, in passing judgment on characters in their limited social circumstances; he wants to capture a process, to provide a full treatment of individual nature and objective circumstance. Meaning, hence morality, depends on the evolution of that process.

The protagonists wait to discover the meaning of their lives in those larger events. For them, meaning does not reside in a fatuous

daily social round. Pierre, after his duel with Dolohov treads end-
lessly the same unfruitful ground: "What is wrong? What is right?
. . . What is life for, and what am I? What is life?"[48] He can find no
satisfying answer to explain his marriage to Hélène, because every
answer he can articulate focuses on social formulae. Just as meaning cannot be answered in social terms, morality cannot be explained in social relationships. Pierre's marriage to Hélène does not
reflect on him the way Lydgate's marriage to Rosamond does on
him. We recall that Lydgate is "spotted with commoness"; Pierre is
simply caught up in the moment. Likewise Pierre's participation in
a Moscow life of dissipation is an inevitable part of a social process:
"Pierre was one of those retired gentlemen-in-waiting, of whom
there were hundreds, good-humouredly ending their days in Moscow.

"How horrified he would have been seven years before, when he
first arrived back from abroad, if anyone had told him there was
no need for him to look about and make plans, that his track had
long ago been shaped for him and marked out before all eternity,
and that, wriggle as he might, he would be what everyone in his
position was doomed to be."[49] When Tolstoy wants to convey the
moral turpitude and corruption of particular individuals, for example, Anatole and Hélène Kuragin, he uses a broad social taboo,
their implied incest, but the broad nature of the taboo suggests
how far Tolstoy is from using particular social norms, values, and
beliefs as a context for moral judgment.

A comparison of Tolstoy's Lise Bolkonsky with Eliot's Rosamond
Vincy further illustrates the point. Lise—inane, pretty, superficial
social butterfly—lies dead in childbirth, an image of innocence and
lack of understanding. "I love you all and have done no one any
harm. . . . oh, what have you done to me?"[50] her face seems to say.
Lise, like Rosamond, is incapable of any understanding of herself
and her fate. Rosamond is judged and condemned by Eliot's narrator; Tolstoy's narrator, who sees this moment as part of a larger
evolution, exculpates Lise. He asks that we see her as a function of
an historical moment. In this larger process, she is not wholly responsible for her fate.

Tolstoy imbeds his idea of society in history; George Eliot imbeds her idea of history in society. For Eliot history is the evolution
of an ideal of community. It is the ideal that the narrator affirms

and toward which her protagonists tend. History, to think of the Reform Bill in *Middlemarch*, is understood as a movement toward social justice and social harmony. Each character, then, in George Eliot's novels is held morally accountable for society's tendency toward good or evil: the philosophical end of social existence is the "growing good" of mankind.

Tolstoy imbeds his idea of society in history, stressing historical evolution, a logic of impersonal events in which social change occurs seemingly unwilled. Napoleon cannot control what happens during his invasion of, and retreat from, Russia: events control him. It is in this light that Tolstoy's narrator can regard kings and generals to be most complete slaves of history.

Tolstoy makes sense of human experience in a historical context; Eliot makes sense of human experience in a social context. Both raise questions about the meaning of existence in a social medium, but Pierre's questions are not answered in his conscious search for answers within society—through penetrating high society, through marriage, or through freemasonry—but rather through his participation in cataclysmic historical change. Growth is largely unconscious; through participating in change, meaning is revealed. So we see Rostov in 1807 defending himself fom the obvious lessons of his experience; in 1812 he is no longer defensive; he accepts the wisdom and logic of his experiences.

George Eliot's characters also pursue the meaning of life and the locus of value, but that pursuit defines morality in terms of one's responsibility to society and community. Eliot's epistemology stems from a conception of man as social being. Both morality and epistemology focus on man's egotism, his tendency to see events as organized around himself and to become himself the ordering principle in the universe. The solipcism that results destroys community. For Eliot, true morality and knowledge demand transcending that egotism, seeing that others have an "equivalent centre of self, whence the lights and shadows must always fall with a certain difference" (chap. 21). Growth and knowledge are thus self-conscious efforts to see beyond the limitations imposed by personality and egotism.

George Eliot, however, has been criticized for failing to see society in a larger historical context, in short, for failing to do what Tolstoy carries to some extreme:

The English novel is so much the richer for George Eliot's contributions that one may be tempted into scolding her for not doing what no English novelist of the century did: for not taking possession of the great world. Her sense of community, her finely modulated articulation of passion and idea, the clarity and firmness of her characterization—these things alone justify Virginia Woolf's remark that *Middlemarch* was one of the few English novels written for grown-up people. Since the grown-up perspective includes Flaubert and Tolstoy, we are of course conscious that George Eliot did not share their power to incarnate the great world in the lesser one, to make the novel an instrument which can register the fate of a society in the perspective of history and heroic achievement. To exercise this power she would have had to take her own splendid powers for granted, and this she could not do.[51]

Quentin Anderson here speaks of inferiority or superiority, but the issue is really one of different choices. George Eliot could not have explored society and questions of individual morality with the complexity she did had she put the whole in the context of historical change. A general rule of exclusion operates. When history is the medium in which we see individual lives, then individual choice and individual morality will not have the significance and urgency they have in novels in which society is that medium. When history is that context, then society in its various stages shapes and largely extenuates individual behavior. Pierre concludes he has been brought to his position by the "force of circumstances, by conditions of society and birth—that elemental force against which man is powerless."[32]

In George Eliot's novels, in contrast, conflict exists between individuals and society. Individuals are, Eliot recognizes, shaped by social attitudes in deep and subtle ways, but the possibility exists that through their own efforts, not through a large, impersonal process, they might transcend the limitations of a particular society in a positive vision of community. Each individual is morally accountable. *Middlemarch* offers a moving depiction of that struggle in which an individual fights to transcend her socially determined and limited self in an inimical world and to assert her individuality and the possibility of real community. Terry Eagleton's Marxist analysis of George Eliot reaches a conclusion similar to mine but by another route and with a different emphasis. Eagleton explains that

> *Middlemarch* projects back onto the past its sense of contemporary stalemate, and since the upshot of this is a radical distrust of "real" history, that history is effectively displaced into ethical, and so "timeless," terms. Yet such displacement thereby provides Eliot with an ideological solution: for what cannot be resolved in "historical" terms can be accommodated by a moralising of the issues at stake. This, indeed, is a mystification inherent in the very forms of realist fiction, which by casting objective social reality into interpersonal terms, constantly hold open the possibility of reducing the one to the other. . . . The suffering abnegation of the ego offers itself as an answer to the riddle of history.
> Yet such a solution is ideologically insufficient.[53]

Eagleton looks at the novel's production of an ideology and finds Eliot's solution—casting "objective social reality into interpersonal terms" and "making the suffering abnegation of the ego . . . an answer to the riddle of history"—ideologically insufficient. In contrast, I look at the novel's expression of value and see that the "solution" clearly permits a rich exploration of the importance of individual action. Our joint interest in values and society, despite very different emphases, allows both of us to discover Eliot's diminishment of history's significance.

It is worthwhile pausing here since the English tradition in the novel has at times been faulted for not matching the achievements of the continental or Russian novel. The comparison between *Middlemarch* and *War and Peace* enables us to get beyond some critical truisms. While readers of these novels generally proceed from the assumption that there is a formal relationship between character and medium, they tend to ignore the consequences of that formal relationship. Authorial decisions about the medium inevitably shape a narrative's presentation and evaluation of character. A particular representation of medium can preclude a close examination of individual morality and responsibility. George Eliot, Thomas Hardy, and D. H. Lawrence, however, are keenly interested in questions of a milieu's effect on character, and their careful attention to the representation of society—especially in terms of community, values, attitudes, opinions, and beliefs—yields a complex vision of society's power and individual potential. They present the poignant recognition that humans need to define themselves in a community, even if those social definitions threaten to limit or destroy individual potential. They give us the triumph and validation possible only when individuals can, in part, transcend their immediate environment. The idea of community exists as a worthwhile goal for individuals to pursue even if its realization is precarious or remote. This special understanding of individual and social interrelationship makes the British tradition the best example of that formal paradigm depicting society as a context that both defines and limits characters, a context in which individual merit is both tested and judged.

The next chapter will look at novels that mark one inheritance from both Tolstoy and Eliot: the naturalistic/sociological novels. Lukács complained of Émile Zola, a major proponent of the naturalistic novel, that he had lost the "typical hero"; his novels no longer articulate the historical dialectic. Zola and the sociological novelists in England and America do fulfill the tendency to see nature and nurture as determinative of individual fate. These writers use their novels as vehicles to explore the inevitably destructive effect of existing social orders on individual life.

The Art of Sociological Naturalism in Zola and Dreiser

Man is not alone but exists in society, in a social environment, and so far as we novelists are concerned, this environment is constantly modifying events.
—Émile Zola, "The Experimental Novel"

They accuse us of immorality, we writers of the naturalist school; and they are right: we lack the morality of mere words. . . . We are looking for the causes of social evil; we study the anatomy of classes and individuals to explain the derangements which are produced in society and in man.
—Émile Zola, "A Letter to the Young People of France"

I had long brooded upon the story [of An American Tragedy*], for it seemed to me not only to include every phase of our national life—politics, society, religion, business, sex—but it was a story so common to every boy reared in the smaller towns of America. It seemed so truly a story of what life does to the individual—of how impotent the individual is against such forces.*
—Theodore Dreiser, letter to Jack Wilgus, 20 April 1927

No great writer celebrates the established social order. All evince awareness of its potentially limiting or destructive nature; all recognize the ways in which society shapes individual fates, but focus falls on the individual rather than on society. He is explored; society is the medium in which he acts and defines himself. The primary purpose of most novels is not to expose society but to explore the individual.

It did not take great vision, however, to see the novel's potential as vehicle for social criticism. Society remains a medium; character and individual experience, however, reveal social values, and these novels' conclusions stress a logic of society rather than the fulfillment of an individual; that is, this kind of novel, in general, finds society increasingly inimical to individual aspirations. Flaubert's *Madame Bovary*, for example, has been praised for containing the seeds of the naturalistic novel. Flaubert's novel presents, in one light, a close study of the destructive effects of environment on character. Ultimately, however, Flaubert's artistry, his conception of his novel as a wrought artistic object—a function of the narrative perspective which sees and presents—creates the terms in which we evaluate the whole. Much as Flaubert reveals about the effects of social environment on character, he is primarily interested in his characters and world as an aesthetic object; his principal concern is with the artistic presentation of this object.

Other novelists, however, were then, and had been earlier, interested in the social issues inherent in the object. Their purpose was not simply to shape the novel for aesthetic contemplation but to arouse the social conscience and inculcate a social moral. Thus was born the "social novel" of England's 1840s, as written by Mrs. Gaskell, Benjamin Disraeli, and Charles Kingsley, the later naturalistic novel whose most articulate proponent is Émile Zola, and the American sociological novel of the 1920s dominated by Theodore Dreiser. The public's quarrel with these novelists centered on an aesthetic issue. These writers were accused of using the novel's popular appeal to reach a wider audience for their propaganda, of sacrificing the artistry of the novel, and of reducing characters to mechanisms in order to promulgate a social theory.

While it is true that some social novelists simply superimpose a story on a political tract—disguising the strictly utile with an appearance of dulce—others have pursued their aims with greater artistry. Novels of these latter writers outlive the contemporaneous issues that prompted them, first because they attack not a specific set of social conditions but the principles that govern a whole society. Second, and more important to artistic success, these novelists do not simply dress up a tract in a garment of fiction; they discovered techniques to make the novel a vehicle to explore the nature of a society rather than of individuals.

Those social or naturalistic novels that critics have been reluctant to relegate to the category of "social novel" present the most interesting study here. This chapter looks at two novels: Émile Zola's *Germinal* and Theodore Dreiser's *An American Tragedy*. In depicting the destructive nature of corrupting social orders, these novels share a formal role for society. Zola and Dreiser exemplify that destructiveness in their characters' lives, and their narrators stress the idea that individual morality has a social and economic base. Thus, these fictions' major centers of value—character, medium, and narrator—all emphasize society's inescapable influence. We discover that in sociological/naturalistic narratives, like those of Zola and Dreiser, society is not only the medium in which characters live, it is also the subject matter of the novels, a locus for each story's major themes. Any discussion of formal issues leads inevitably into thematic ones, so that in *An American Tragedy* and *Germinal*, our consideration of formal questions has immediate thematic implications. Both novels are about society.

But *Germinal* and *An American Tragedy* are also significantly different in their approach to society as subject. Zola is interested in exploring a social dialectic—the historical evolution of a society—and his particular representational techniques conduce to social process. Dreiser, on the other hand, anatomizes society. His techniques clarify the extent to which social values and expectations pervade all aspects of human existence.

The Social Dialectic in *Germinal*

Émile Zola developed and propounded a whole theory that saw the novel as a laboratory for testing hypotheses about man in society. Through the experiment of a novel, one can possess "knowledge of the man, scientific knowledge of him, in both his individual and social relations."[1] Such scientific knowledge is, of course, predicated on the notion that general, deducible rules govern humans and human behavior, societies and social behavior, just as they govern the physical world.

Zola uses, as a starting point for his theory of the novel, Claude

Bernard's "Introduction à l'Étude de la Medicine Expérimentale."
Bernard was espousing the application of the experimental method
to medicine as it had formerly been used in chemistry, in order to
make medicine a science rather than an art. Zola wants to carry
the process one step further and, by using the experimental
method in literature, to make novel writing into a science, a science for studying the workings of man and society. Zola claimed:
"That is just where our real task lies, in studying the interaction of
society on the individual and of the individual on society." The
experimental method "consists in finding the relations which unite
a phenomenon of any kind to its nearest cause."[2] Zola argues that
formerly novelists depended solely on observations. The new ex-
perimentalists, like himself, would derive testable hypotheses and
arrive at general laws.

Of course, many of Zola's novels predate his theory; *Germinal,*
examined here, is one. We need to examine not the adequacy of
Zola's theory of the novel or the fidelity of his novels to it, but
rather its consequence of inevitably leading Zola to propound a
social or political theory of human evolution.

Germinal explores the relationship of workers and masters at Le
Voreux mine during a crisis provoked by a disguised wage cut.
Although society is focused in a particular place, that place is seen
as paradigmatic of the larger world. This society is characterized
by class divisions, which are represented as economic in nature;
that is, *Germinal,* like other sociological novels, depicts society as a
set of class relationships determined almost exclusively by wealth.
Political systems reflect the economic structure. There exist rich
and poor, workers and masters, the governors and the governed.
The action of the novel revolves around class conflicts. The novel,
in its structure and action, argues for social determinism and for
the economic base of human relationships. This is the "reality"
Zola wanted to stress, not an historical reality but a scientific one.
He claims not to be writing a story about people who really existed
but to be deriving true, general hypotheses about the behavior
of human beings under certain conditions. By stressing the interdependence of individuals and environment, he is making social
change a prerequisite to individual development.

Characters thus act by determinable laws. In characterization,
then, the promptings of human hearts and souls are not represented. Whereas the narrator in Tolstoy's *War and Peace* can say of

Sonya's decision to tell Natasha that the wounded Prince Andrei is traveling with them, "Sonya, to the surprise and annoyance of the countess, had *for some unaccountable reason* found it necessary to tell Natasha that Prince Andrei was among the wounded travelling with them"[3] [emphasis added], the social novelist consistently explains actions in terms of heredity and environment. We can find good reasons for Sonya's behavior—a wish to restore relations between Natasha and Andrei in order to break off those between Nikolai and Princess Maria—but these are only partial promptings of her complex spirit and situation. Although most novelists do trace behavior at least partly to heredity and environment, they often assume there exists some larger motive or cause. Indeed, in many cases, characters ennoble themselves by transcending their heredity and environment. D. H. Lawrence tried to give this larger motive a name—"inhuman will"—and although his articulation of this concept was new, the belief in it was not. There is something more to character than inherited nature and nurture. We never worry that Elizabeth Bennet differs so dramatically from her sister Lydia, or that Dorothea and Celia Brooke share little except a last name, and the difference between Tom Jones and Blifil is not satisfactorily explained by tracing the paternity of the former to Summer and that of the latter to Captain Blifil. The naturalistic novelist, in contrast, concentrates on determinism by heredity and environment in order to make social reform an issue, in order to harry the social conscience. Since an individual cannot transcend his inherited nature, then it becomes imperative to alter his social environment. Only through social change can individuals grow.

In this logic, of course, morality is relative and must be seen as socially or hereditarily determined, rather than as an absolute expression of individuality and personal integrity. Moral absolutes interfere with a full revelation of the compulsion that social environment exerts on individuals. Moral behavior, rather than being a matter of social conscience, becomes a matter of social status, largely determined by material well-being. For example, in *Germinal*, La Mouquette is described as "an eighteen-year-old haulage girl. She was a strapping wench, with a bosom and buttocks that almost split her vest and breeches."[4] A free and easy sexuality accompanies this physical endowment, but we, as readers, are not encouraged to judge or blame her for her promiscuity. In fact, her generous sexual nature is complemented by a very likable generosity in all other matters, both are simply an expression of heredity that is manifest physically. She even dies cheerfully, having shielded Catherine from bullets, but we do not see this act as a moral choice or as a complex psychological decision, a perception that would lend her character dignity. Her behavior is physiologically and socially determined.

Class and economic status also determine morality. No individual moral norms are absolute; they can shift as rapidly as social conditions shift. Until the strike at Le Voreux mine and the subsequent starvation, La Maheude violently opposes begging. Suddenly we learn that "neither Lénore nor Henri had come back from tramping the streets with Jeanlin, begging for coppers" (6, chap. 2). Étienne Lantier, the novel's protagonist, learns of this behavior "with aching heart. She used to threaten to kill them if they begged in the street. Now it was she who sent them out" (6, chap. 2). People will adopt whatever morality a situation demands. A great objection lodged against social or naturalistic novels is that they make character into mere mechanism. Stuart Sherman, examining Dreiser's naturalism, concludes: "it is a representation based upon a theory of animal behavior. Since a theory of animal behavior can never be an adequate basis for a representation of the life of man in contemporary society, such a representation is an artistic blunder."[5] The social novelist faces the difficult task of coupling stature and significance for his protagonists with social determinism. Zola's characters gain stature through their resentment; their moral flexibility does not prevent their bitterly resenting their subjugation and degradation. Individuals are aware of moral alternatives largely by contrast with a more dignified past. They are, after all, reflective beings, and their acute sense of degradation redeems in part their swift, amoral adjustment to new social conditions and their debasement within those conditions.

Because Zola is interested in art as well as social reform, he uses the resources of novelistic art to enhance his novel's examination of social process. In *Germinal*, Zola found the means to shape his work artistically—to create its beginning, middle, and end—without falsifying social reality. To do so, he conceived character and scene both metaphorically and objectively, and he conceived the action both in personal and in social/political terms. The novel thus has two complementary narratives.

We turn first to Zola's metaphoric conception of character. Although Zola binds most of his characters by heredity, environment, and the probabilities of the two, he also introduces various symbolic characters whose personalities and fates express the logic of his represented society. In this light, La Maheude and Maheu, with their larger concerns for justice and morality, are the matriarch and patriarch of the society. Their individual degradation charts for readers the larger degradation of society. Writers have difficulty in making readers identify with such an abstraction as society. When a fiction asks us to identify with individuals, its writer usually illustrates society's values in minor characters. Since the naturalistic novel's principal purpose is to reveal the nature of a particular society, even major characters are subsumed to that purpose. Personal development is subordinated to a desire to reveal flaws and limitations in society. For example, the patriarch Maheu —kind, considerate, and judicious—wins our sympathy through his concerned interest in Étienne and his unselfish desire to share what little meat he has with his children. As the strike progresses, Maheu fades further and further into the background. Suddenly he is shot down by the soldiers. We know little of his motives for being in the front lines except that La Maheude has goaded him on. When Maheu is killed, it is hard to feel the sympathy one would expect for such a likable character. It seems that the traits characterizing him neither explain why he is where he is nor do they provide sufficient psychological insight into his emotions at the moment. Zola distances us from him deliberately so that Maheu's experience can represent something outside himself. The system of symbolic structures—the use of red, of anger, of violence—suggests that Maheu, from a metaphorical standpoint, is consumed just as the society is consuming itself. We focus not on the loss of one sympathetic character but on a didactic point: society structured in this way will lead to senseless bloodshed and so destroy itself.

Other writers employ an artifice similar to Zola's but with a different emphasis. For example, Gustave Flaubert, embedding Emma's romance with Rodolphe in the proceedings of the agricultural show, permits us to see the large in the small, the social process in the individual life. We feel the pathos of Emma's soul stirring under such banal conditions, but the focus is on character. In Zola, the emphasis is on social process; our involvement even with major individuals is limited.

Maheu, then, dramatizes one immediate end of social process.

Zola employs other characters—Jeanlin, Bonnemort, and Cécile—
to dramatize the ultimate end of this process. Bonnemort and Cécile, although very much products of heredity and environment,
also represent a final confrontation between an overfed bourgeoisie
and a starved working class: "They gazed at each other in fascination, she, buxom, plump, and pink from the days of well-fed idleness of her race, he blown out with dropsy, hideous and pathetic
like some broken-down animal, ravaged by a century of toil and
hunger passed down from father to son" (7, chap. 4). Bonnemort,
a figure out of the past, the paradigmatic victim of social injustice,
wreaks his vengeance on the flower of the bourgeoisie, Cécile.

Jeanlin, the other symbolic character, is first described as possessing a "face, like a small, frizzy-haired monkey's, with its green
eyes and big ears" (1, chap. 2). The evolutionary implications of
this description follow later: "Unhealthily precocious, he seemed to
have the mysterious intelligence and bodily skill of a human foetus
reverting to its animal origins" (3, chap. 5), and later: "[Étienne]
contemplated this child, who, with his pointed muzzle, green eyes,
long ears, resembled some degenerate with the instinctive intelligence and craftiness of a savage, gradually reverting to man's animal origins. The pit had made him what he was, and the pit had
finished the job by breaking his legs" (4, chap. 6). In the last
sentence Jeanlin's character is attributed to the pit, but he represents the end of a process that has been going on, a reduction of
man to his animal instincts, a reversion back to his animal origins.
We are to conclude that the ultimate effect of social determinism
here is the dehumanization of man. Society, which is intended to
humanize, becomes an agent to destroy him. Zola makes a powerful didactic point through this character; if society does not destroy
itself, in perpetuating itself in its present form, it will destroy humanity.

Zola's strongest social criticism and his only social optimism—
his vision of a new society—emerge through the structure of his
novel: a paralleling of metaphor with fact, of personal experience
with social experience. The novel opens at night when Étienne
Lantier arrives at Le Voreux mine. The narrator describes the mine
both as an evil beast and as an objective thing:

> While Étienne lingered by the fire warming his poor raw
> hands, Le Voreux began to emerge as from a dream. He

could now pick out each part of the works: the tarpaulin-covered screening shed, the headgear, the huge winding-house, the square tower of the drainage pump. With its squat brick buildings huddled in a valley, and the chimney sticking up like a menacing horn, the pit was evil-looking, a voracious beast crouching ready to devour the world. . . .

Le Voreux struck fear into him . . . and, huddled in its lair like some evil beast, Le Voreux crouched even lower and its breath came in longer and deeper gasps, as though it were struggling to digest its meal of human flesh [1, chap. 1].

The first sentence personifies the mine. A literal description of the works follows, and the last sentences once again personify the mine, now as an evil beast. This metaphor makes us expect and fear certain events and desire alternative ones; it makes us feel the inevitability of destruction at this point. It allows us to anticipate the developing conflict. In short, it shapes Zola's objective presentation of society in novelistic ways. More important, in this juxtaposition of metaphor and fact, Zola remains faithful to the objective reality of the world he depicts. Part of the naturalistic novelist's effect depends on persuading readers to accept the fidelity of his vision of society. Implicit in Zola's theory of the novel lies a desire *not* to be seen as tampering with social conditions and represented society in the effort to suit larger artistic ends. Hence Zola insists that the novelist sets up his experiment and lets it run by itself; he does not prejudge the results.[6] Zola's talent as artist, however, enabled him to discover means to shape events without falsifying social reality.

In addition to conceiving character and scene both metaphorically and objectively, Zola also conceives the action in two dimensions. *Germinal* entwines complementary narratives: a personal one, which focuses on the relationship between Étienne and Catherine and is resolved in their sexual consummation, and a social one, which depicts the larger class struggle and cannot realistically be resolved since that resolution would dictate the dawn of a new era based on general equality. Unlike Thackeray's *Vanity Fair*, whose two narratives create conflicting social realities and therefore prevent the reader from arriving at a coherent set of social expectations, Zola's *Germinal* makes its two narratives share a social reality so that the expectations that shape one narrative can, by analogy, suggest a shaping to the other. The effect, then, of this intermingling of stories is that Étienne and Catherine's relationship shapes our expectations for society and ultimately allows us to anticipate another, better social reality that has its seeds in the destruction of the present one, although, in fact and realistically, society cannot change so quickly and dramatically, and our optimism is unwarranted.

Germinal begins with Étienne's arrival at Montsou. He almost decides to leave after one day in the mines, but two things detain him: "Suddenly Étienne made up his mind. Maybe he thought he saw Catherine's pale eyes up yonder, where the village began. Or perhaps it was some wind of revolt blowing from Le Voreux. He could not tell. But he wanted to go down the mine again to suffer and to fight" (1, chap. 6). He is attracted by a woman and a social situation. First he pursues Catherine, but, losing her to Chaval, he becomes interested in the political situation at the mines. He comes closer to Catherine for a while when he moves in with the Maheus, but she moves out to join Chaval, and her rupture with her family is mirrored by the miners' strike. Étienne becomes wholly involved in the strike, but love is also a factor in his political ambition. At the meeting in the woods, Etienne is spurred on by the thought of Catherine: "He had recognized Chaval among his friends in the front row, and the thought that Catherine must be there too had put new fire into him, and a desire to be applauded in front of her" (4, chap. 7). By this parallel structure, Zola has identified the romantic situation with the political one, a very important identification in the final effect of the novel.

The parallels continue. The miners seek violent retribution for injustice; Chaval and Étienne immediately thereafter come to blows over Catherine. The miners protest the importation of workers from Belgium and are shot. Catherine, too, is bloodied, but "it was the pent-up flood of her puberty released at last by the shock of that dreadful day" (7, chap. 1). Catherine's physical maturation suggests a maturity in the consciousness of the workers. The seeds now planted will grow to fruition. Finally, Étienne decides to return to the mine with Catherine. His love is at least a partial motive. Souvarine speculates, "When a man's heart was tied up with a woman he was finished and might as well die" (7, chap. 2). Étienne and Catherine have their consummation: he plants his seed in her womb in the bowels of the earth, a larger womb.

Although the workers return to work with seemingly no gains, we do not feel that *Germinal* is a pessimistic novel. The seed has been planted and will burst through the earth: "Men were springing up, a black avenging host was slowly germinating in the furrows, thrusting upwards for the harvests of future ages. And very soon their germination would crack the earth asunder" (7, chap. 6). Étienne's hopeful lyrical speculations on society would be unwarranted without the parallel love situation and its powerful consummation. In other words, our reaction to the novel has been precisely determined by the complex interrelationship between a personal situation and a social one.

Zola lays a social situation before us in great complexity, and he refuses to resolve it except by means of this parallel relationship between Étienne and Catherine described above. In a sense there are two resolutions in *Germinal*: a personal one and a social one. The personal one is resolved in the bowels of the earth; the social is actually never resolved. The workers return to work. We would like them, after all their suffering, to win their demands, but they do not, and to this extent we feel that we are in touch with the way things happen in the real world. Zola has, in short, enhanced his didactic ends; he affirms social determinism; he illuminates the inevitable consequences of class divisions in a capitalist society. Yet, at the same time, he has used parallel structures to achieve the power of resolution in anticipated social change without warping the social reality he wants to depict. As a result, Zola has created no simple social document but a novel with a strong element of reality that propounds a social theory and urges social change and that does so by engaging us with characters for whom we deeply care.

Society Anatomized in *An American Tragedy*

Dreiser's naturalism, unlike Zola's, expresses little social optimism.[7] Rather than presenting us with images of germination and imminent birth, Dreiser concludes *An American Tragedy* with the same scene that began it—except that the boy Clyde has been replaced by his sister's illegitimate son, Russell. The repetition of scene, "Dusk—of a summer night," "up the broad street, now comparatively hushed"; the repetition of experience, "As they sang, this nondescript and indifferent street audience gazed, held by the peculiarity of such an unimportant-looking family publicly raising its collective voice against the vast skepticism and apathy of life"; and the repetition of character, "Of the group the mother alone stood out as having that force and determination which, however blind or erroneous, makes for self-preservation, if not success in life"—all these suggest that Clyde Griffith's tragedy will be repeated in the next generation, that the experience will repeat itself indefinitely because it expresses American life and values.[8]

Zola and Dreiser present an important contrast because they both seek to illuminate the force of society in shaping individual lives, but in this illumination Zola finds cause for hope and Dreiser finds only repetition and defeat. Zola's stress on process and his optimism are achieved by his presenting society as a particular, paradigmatic place. Society, so defined, can become a concrete locus for change. Dreiser prefers to analyze a whole social world.

The scope of Dreiser's fictional society, by comparison, is enormous. Dreiser ranges in locale from West to Midwest to East; from large city to small city, from town to countryside, from impoverished farm to lavish resort. He depicts foreign immigrants, the lower classes, and lower-middle classes from which Clyde comes. He recognizes a distinction between the new rich, like the Finchleys and Cranstons, and the established rich like the Samuel Griffiths. The scope of religious experience ranges from the street preaching of Clyde's youth to the church social functions Clyde attends in Lycurgus. There seems to be no element of society that Dreiser cannot or does not portray. Perhaps his depiction of Lycurgus's frivolous social set includes some falsity of tone, but in this novel that falsity contributes to the sense of unreality and idealism that Clyde himself brings to the upper classes.[9]

Dreiser's society includes not only a broad geography and a sound understanding of class distinctions but also a full depiction of American institutions, businesses, finance, and politics. Irving Howe has observed that Dreiser's books are "crowded with exact observation . . . about the customs and class structure of American society in the phase of early finance capitalism. No other novelist has absorbed into his work as much knowledge as Dreiser had about American institutions: the mechanisms of business, the stifling rhythms of the factory, the inner hierarchy of a large hotel, the chicaneries of city politics, the status arrangement of rulers and ruled."[10]

Dreiser presents a whole society at a particular period. What unifies these diverse scenes and social classes are common ideals fostered by this society and shared by all its members. These common ideals are expressed in the gaudiness of the Green-Davidson Hotel and reflected, with greater sophistication, in the home of Samuel Griffiths. They can best be summarized as a respect for wealth and all of its manifestations: material success becomes man's highest goal. Clyde's material ambitions not only express the collective aspirations of his society, but they are also sanctioned by all its norms and customs. The religious vocation of Clyde's parents arouses only the contempt and pity of those whom it intends to succor, and it arouses contempt because the Griffiths are obviously financial failures—failures on the one scale of values that confers meaning in this society. Even Clyde's mother, of unquestioned religious integrity and faith, shares her son's hope for some financial assistance from his rich uncle. Later, Roberta Allen, the woman Clyde murders, finds Clyde attractive because he is a "Lycurgus Griffiths." Society, then, in *An American Tragedy* more than in any other novel encountered thus far, depends on the shared materialistic goals and values of a world widely disparate in experience, class, and geography.

Although class relationships in both *An American Tragedy* and *Germinal* are determined by economic factors, there are differences. Clyde Griffiths seeks money. He wants to join those at the top and is willing to trample on those below to get there. The protagonists of *Germinal* do not seek simply more money, they seek justice, which for the nontheoretical becomes "A day's pay for a day's work." They do not want to be masters to tyrannize over other men; they want a more equitable system, and they are capable of envisioning such a system. Dreiser's protagonists are not. This is a consequence of Zola's emphasis on social process and Dreiser's concentration on anatomizing society at a particular period.

Implicit in *Germinal*, in contrast to *An American Tragedy*, is a distinction between humans and beasts. The protagonists of the former novel face starvation and the attendant degradation of desperate people. Their situation reduces them to bestial behavior, a behavior which, however necessary, as I have pointed out, is bitterly resented. Their social situation has deprived them of human dignity. The lesson of Zola's Jeanlin is precisely that of man reduced by a social system to his bestial origins.

Dreiser's protagonist never faces starvation. American capitalism allows subsistence for all, but at the same time it has entrenched the gaps between rich and poor. The poor will not starve, but neither will they be allowed to move out of poverty. When Zola makes the social situation of a particular locale a paradigm for society as a whole, he creates the breadth of criticism he wants, yet has a specific locus for conflict and resolution, actual or potential. Dreiser's expanded society provides no locus for challenge, conflict, and change. The protagonist's plight is more desperate in one sense because more amorphous and less remediable.

Poverty has become a source for a kind of humiliation other than that born of the degradation we saw in *Germinal*. Although Dreiser reveals the injustices of the social system and the ways in which those injustices are perpetuated, to the characters themselves, poverty means moral failure. Those who are poor are so because they deserve to be not because of the social system. In that world's perspectives, the genuinely meritorious will succeed, a perspective born of confusing a business ethic with Christianity, a confusion characteristic of American morality. It seems that Dreiser gives Clyde's parents a religious vocation to show the failure of moral absolutes in affecting the community at large. His parents earn contempt for their indigence rather than respect for their devotion.

This confusion of morality and wealth existed in *Germinal*. It usually plays a role in sociological/naturalistic novels. From the wealthy characters' perspectives, their "superior" morality antedated their wealth; indeed, their wealth, as they see it, is a consequence of superior morality. In the narrator's eyes, however, that morality is made possible by social standing, not the other way around. Morality, then, is a luxury; the richer one is the more one can afford it. This issue becomes acute in Dreiser's novel because his protagonist is not starving or suffering physically, yet he murders to improve his social position. Can he be a victim of society when he is not suffering obvious degradation and horror?

The larger question asks whether Clyde's is the act of a depraved individual or the consequence of a social system's values and priorities. Dreiser's *An American Tragedy* began with that question, a question provoked by the real events that gave rise to this novel. A young man murdered his pregnant girlfriend in order to marry a wealthy woman. Although the American press, courts, and public of his day saw the case as resulting from the aberration of an unstable nature, Dreiser found in it a prototype for our social experience, the logic of our society's values.

Dreiser, then, finally explores a social logic not an individual morality. His indictment is of a society not of an individual. In order to make Clyde Griffiths sympathetic, Dreiser has created and developed his personality and fate in such a way that we become acutely conscious of the social forces that have produced him and that limit him.

The novel's initial scenes survey the characters or "street-preachers" impersonally and objectively, referring to them as "a man," "a woman," "a small boy," "a girl of fifteen." The absence of verbs in the main clauses suggests a timelessness to these events reminiscent of the more famous opening lines of Dickens's *Bleak House*. The narrator gradually focuses on the boy, first speculatively, "he seemed more keenly observant and decidedly more sensitive than most of the others—appeared indeed to resent and even suffer from the position in which he found himself," then authoritatively, "plainly pagan, rather than religious, life interested him, although as yet he was not fully aware of this" (1, chap. 1). This technique encourages us to see the character as a product of a preexisting social situation.

Of greater consequence to Dreiser's achievement in *An American Tragedy* is his ability to make the novel's conflict derive immediately from tensions in Clyde's social situation: the tawdriness of his family's religious life versus the seductive glamor of money. To Clyde, "his parents looked foolish and less than normal—'cheap' was the word he would have used if he could have brought himself to express his full measure of resentment" (1, chap. 1). Clyde is relegated to one sphere of society; he wants to participate in another. In other novels, those of George Eliot, for example, the protagonist's nature conflicts with dominant values in his society. Dorothea Brooke has qualities that prevent her fate from being decided merely according to custom and "canine affection." Clyde Griffiths's desires, on the contrary, harmonize with society's dominant material values. Appropriately, his parents seem "cheap," a word connoting both tawdriness and insignificant monetary value. He wants to experience the superior life of wealth. He is in conflict with his current position, but he is in harmony with the values of his world.

Dreiser does not pretend that society bears the entire blame for what happens to Clyde. The boy's nature is seriously flawed. His mother early sees that he is "not any too powerful physically or rock-ribbed morally or mentally" (1, chap. 16). The narrator confirms that "he lacked decidedly that mental clarity and inner directing application" (2, chap. 3). The boy possesses a "naturally selfish and ambitious and seeking disposition" and "a temperament that was as fluid and unstable as water" (2, chap. 24). Part of Dreiser's aim, like Zola's, is to use individual weakness to demonstrate the need for social change. Since individuals are already hereditarily determined, the only way to improve humanity is through change in the other determining factor: society.

In light of Clyde's personality, it may surprise us that his life arouses as much sympathy and forestalls as much condemnation as it does. This achievement depends on Dreiser's understanding of character in society, an understanding that parallels Zola's. Clyde's society not only compounds his personal weaknesses, but, more seriously, it perverts his personal strength. Usually, in the novel, a character's strengths will help him fight the spurious in his society. In *An American Tragedy* not only do Clyde's weak qualities leave him vulnerable to social determinants, but his strengths—his eager determination, his sensitivity, his keen powers of observation—increase his vulnerability. Other characters remain invulnerable, not because they are represented as superior, but because they neither experienced the pain of Clyde's childhood nor shared his vision. We learn that a minor character, Governor Waltham, who must help decide Clyde's fate, was "a tall, sober and somewhat somber man who, never in all his life had even so much as sensed the fevers or fires that Clyde had known" (3, chap. 34). The Reverend McMillan recognizes that "[Clyde's] hot, restless heart which plainly for the lack of so many things which he, the Reverend McMillan, had never wanted for, had rebelled" (3, chap. 33).

An American Tragedy works to make Clyde sympathetic precisely because of his greater sensibilities and his desires to attain what is represented in the novel as a better, because it is a more gracious, way of life. As opposed to Clyde, his sister, Esta "appeared not so much to mind, as to enjoy the attention and comment her presence and singing evoked" during the street preaching (1, chap. 1). She exhibits a coarser strain of vanity than does Clyde. And Clyde's bellhop friends at the Green-Davidson are safer from the lures than Clyde because they are more limited: "Hegglund, as he could see, was vain and noisy and foolish—a person who could be taken in and conciliated by a little flattery. And Higby and Kinsella, interesting and attractive boys both, were still vain of things he could not be proud of—Higby of knowing a little something about automobiles . . . Kinsella of gambling, rolling dice even" (1, chap. 9).

Not only does Clyde emerge as more sympathetic than these youths, but, perhaps more important, no other character in Dreiser's world arouses greater sympathy. Some characters are, of course, superior to others. Clyde's mother certainly wins our admiration for her devotion, dedication, and resourcefulness, but in that milieu much of her effort is futile. She fails to comprehend either her position in that world or the forces crucially affecting and defining her family. Her good qualities lead only to self-preservation, not success in life (1, chap. 1). Her inadequate response to Clyde's tragedy is to try with young Russell to "be kind to him, more liberal with him, not restrain him too much, as maybe, maybe, she had [Clyde]" (Souvenir).

Further to insure sympathy for Clyde as a victim of society, Dreiser early establishes a pattern of description and evaluation that operates throughout. Whenever Clyde is confronted by one of a series of crucial decisions, a particular process is enacted. In the first book, these decisions range from the proposed visit to the house of prostitution, to his mother's request for the money he needs to finance Hortense's fur coat, to the proposed excursion in the stolen car, to the accident culminating in Clyde's flight. First Clyde becomes sympathetic (as opposed to his peers) by experiencing some conflict over the proposed course of action. For example, when the bellhops urge Sparser to take his employer's car for their personal use, we learn that "the only one, apart from Sparser [who fears his employer's imminent return], who suffered any qualms in connection with all this was Clyde himself." What at first seems to be a moral dilemma, that of "taking anything that belonged to any one else," is quickly translated into a dilemma born of potential personal consequences in that society, "They might be found out." The social consequences become even more cogent to Clyde; "he might lose his job through a thing like this" (1, chap. 17). These reflections conclude Clyde's thoughts, and in this way the author keeps us within a frame of judgments more sensitive to social consequences than to any moral imperatives.

Although we appreciate Clyde's vulnerable social position, it is also possible that we might condemn him for his moral inadequacies. Dreiser's decision to leave this episode without stressing any moral inadequacies in Clyde invites our condemnation of the social values that shape his reaction. In fact, it would seem that Dreiser must preclude certain types of moral judgments, or they will interfere with the revelation of an inimical social order.

George Eliot's treatment of Hetty Sorrel in *Adam Bede* presents an illuminating contrast. When Hetty has become pregnant by Arthur Donnithorne, the narrator emphasizes the social stigma threatening Hetty: " 'The parish!' You can perhaps hardly understand the effect of that word on a mind like Hetty's, brought up among people who were somewhat hard in their feelings even towards poverty, who lived among the fields, and had little pity for want and rags as a cruel inevitable fate such as they sometimes seem in cities, but held them a mark of idleness and vice—and it was idleness and vice that brought burthens on the parish. To Hetty the 'parish' was next to the prison in obloquy."[11]

Having made us feel intensely Hetty's fear of the social consequences of her action, the narrator makes us also judge her for the moral failings that precipitated her situation: "Poor wandering Hetty, with the rounded childish face, and the hard unloving despairing soul looking out of it—with the narrow heart and narrow thoughts, no room in them for any sorrows but her own, and tasting that sorrow with the more intense bitterness!"[12] This judgment of Hetty mitigates our sense of the social stigma attached to her situation and suggests that, were she less narrow and selfish an individual, she could discover understanding and forgiveness in her world. Because Dreiser never judges Clyde in this way, we neither see him as the responsible agent Hetty becomes, nor do we see any possibilities that his worst fears will not be realized. We remain impressed with the inimical nature of a social order that seems to force characters into actions without offering any clear, rewarding alternatives. In *An American Tragedy*, there exist no satisfying moral standards provided by the social milieu or by the implied author which may serve as an alternative measure of success.

Indeed, Dreiser precludes such standards in order to intensify the social pressures on Clyde. As in Zola's novel, morality is a function of social class. This phenomenon determines Clyde's shock at the suggestion that he might have had sexual relations with the wealthy Sondra Finchley. One lawyer tells another: "Once, for instance, I asked him about his relations with [Sondra]—and in spite of the fact that he's accused of seducing and killing this other girl, he looked at me as though I had said something I shouldn't have—insulted him or her. . . . He said, 'Why, no, of course not, She wouldn't allow anything like that, and besides. . . . Well, you don't want to forget who she is'" (3, chap. 15). Clyde's moral horror here is born of the social differences between Sondra and Roberta, the woman he murders. His morality takes its prerogatives and distinctions from the social system.

Roberta, too, exculpates Clyde by sharing his dream. Just as Clyde hopes to advance himself socially through marriage to Sondra, so Roberta plans to advance herself socially through marriage with Clyde: "For all [Roberta's] fears, even the bare possibility of joining her life with Clyde's was marvelous" (2, chap. 29). To the degree that Roberta shares Clyde's conception of the value of social position and prestige, we modify our condemnation of his actions. Clyde wonders, "Wasn't he of sufficient importance to move in this new world without her holding him back in this way?" (2, chap. 31). As if in response, Roberta worries that "alas, apart from this claim of [her pregnancy], what had she to offer him comparable to all he would be giving up in case he acceded to her request? Nothing" (2, chap. 40).

Sondra and her set, despite the frivolity and snobbishness of certain members, represent not only luxury, but a gracious way of life, in comparison with which the impoverished life of Roberta and the Aldens seems sordid and demeaning. Despite Roberta's worthiness, she actually emerges as inferior to Sondra, and marriage to Roberta becomes a significant failure for Clyde, because everyone in that world makes value judgments within a social framework similar to Clyde's. If they do invoke some moral imperative such as justice or moral turpitude, they seem to do so in the service of their own social well-being, or in consideration of social ends, or in ignorance of social determinants. Clyde's wealthy uncle is willing to consider the family's neglect of Clyde as a partial cause for the murder, but he concludes with Clyde's personal weaknesses. "The wretchedness of such a mind as that—the ungoverned and carnal desires!" (3, chap. 13). However, the implied author does not endorse these judgments. Unlike George Eliot's narrator, he includes no ennobling sphere for moral decisions and actions that can transcend or ignore social considerations.

Again, a comparison between the murders in two novels— Clyde's murder of Roberta and Hetty Sorrel's murder of her newborn child in *Adam Bede*—illustrates the significance of this point. In *Adam Bede*, the crime itself is not related until after the conviction. Although Hetty tells the story from her own perspective, Dinah never doubts Hetty's responsibility and guilt, an inevitable consequence of having committed the crime. In contrast, Clyde's confessor, Reverend McMillan, struggles to determine Clyde's degree of responsibility and guilt, even though he is certain Clyde murdered the woman. Hetty herself is filled with anguish and a sense of wrong-doing. She beseeches Dinah to tell her whether " 'God will take away that crying and the place in the wood, now I've told everything.' " Dinah responds with the words, "Let us pray, poor sinner: let us fall on our knees again, and pray to the God of all mercy."[13] While Clyde can finally acknowledge that "his sin was very great. Very, very terrible!" he also has a "feeling in his heart that he was not as guilty as they all seemed to think" (3, chap. 33). Whereas religion has a real sustaining effect in George Eliot's world, Clyde never can completely accept the religious solace his mother and Reverend McMillan offer.

Dreiser has depicted a character's vulnerability to the social ideals he sees about him and has used that character and his fate as a means to reveal the destructive nature of a corrupting society. Thus, the understanding Clyde achieves of the forces that determine him is a triumphant formal resolution of this novel's structure: "He was alone. He had no one who believed in him. *No one.* He had no one, whom, in any of his troubled and tortured actions before that crime saw anything but the darkest guilt apparently. And yet—and yet— . . . he had a feeling in his heart that he was not as guilty as they all seemed to think. . . . Even in the face of all the facts and as much as every one felt him to be guilty, there was something so deep within him that seemed to cry out against it, that, even now, at times, it startled him" (3, chap. 33). Clyde cannot accept his guilt because he senses extenuating circumstances, not just the accidental nature of the blow to Roberta, but the quality of his whole life. The communal denial of the social determinants only confirms more forcefully their existence and the blind subjugation of individuals to them.

So strong, in fact, are Clyde's doubts that even after he confesses his guilt on the urging of his mother and Reverend McMillan, his religious enthusiasm falters before his doubts. At the end, Clyde shakes the faith and mental peace even of the devout Reverend McMillan: "Had he done right? Had his decision before Governor Waltham been truly sound, fair or merciful? Should he have said to him—that perhaps—perhaps—there had been those other influences playing on him? . . . Was he never to have mental peace again, perhaps?" (3, chap. 34). The certainty of judgment that exists in novels like *Adam Bede* is absent in *An American Tragedy*. Dreiser offers neither the same moral imperatives for action nor the same moral bases on which to judge actions. One general result of Dreiser's technique is that the characters who are social failures appear to be moral failures as well. The two contexts for judgment are intertwined by the narrator. We may admire Mrs. Griffiths, but that admiration is compromised by the futility of her efforts "against the vast skepticism and apathy of life" (1, chap. 1). On the opposite pole, the socially brilliant Sondra, despite her triviality, never evokes any serious moral condemnation. She and all the characters remain grounded in the environment that produced them, and to this environment Dreiser attaches the heaviest blame.

Despite the fact that characters are not judged in the way a character fom George Eliot's world is judged, they do not become mere automatons. Dreiser's characters also struggle toward certain self-determined goals, and their struggles are not necessarily uninformed by moral principles. But we, as readers, lack the absolute moral principles by which we can judge each character because Dreiser has refused to supply them. Characters therefore seem to have less freedom of action and to be more determined by the dual considerations of temperament and social ideals.

The result, however, is not to turn characters into mere mechanisms or to express "a theory of animal behavior" but to realize as forcefully as possible the faults and limitations of a society by using characters who, because of both strengths and weaknesses in their constitutions, become particularly vulnerable to these social forces. While a Clyde Griffiths will never achieve the stature of a tragic hero, he can, through his struggle, evoke sufficient sympathy to render his situation tragic.[14]

Although they stress determinism, these sociological/naturalistic novels move us, not by denying free will, but by making us question the bases for our moral judgments, by representing the arbitrariness of social class and the inescapability of social determinism.

Societies that let economic factors mold their structures will find morality reduced to a commodity; either one can afford it or one cannot. In such circumstances, any pretence that morality is inherent in certain individuals is a sham. These novels expose the spuriousness of a view that sees morality as a guarantor of wealth. It is only wealth that is a guarantor of morality, often narrowly defined.

While social determinism is necessarily stressed in these novels, individuals may still explore the freedom of feeling: the freedom to resent the coercion of their situations, the freedom to doubt the justice of their worlds. Social determinism must exist in these social novels to make imperative the need for social change. Individuals are powerless to alter their worlds singlehandedly. In that view of character lies the novel's didactic end rather than in polemic and exhortation, but characters' struggles against their powerlessness partially redeem them and compel our interest in their fates. In addition, our perception that the individuals' strengths and admirable qualities leave them more vulnerable to the destructive effects of society further enhances our identification with them—and with the novel's political sympathies.

The artistic realization of this formal role for society in the novel results not in propaganda but in a profound and moving representation of the pervasive effect of society on our lives. When society functions as an inevitable determinant of individuals' lives, a determinant that thwarts or frustrates individual potential, then society cannot be ignored. Such society, which is presented as remorseless in its effects, makes an obvious thematic point; we must look to our social responsibility, because, left to their single ends, individual lives will merely fulfill the logic of the world we create and inhabit.

This chapter has explored society as subject matter of the novel —society so conceived formally that it is a focus for the novel's themes. In the next chapter we shall turn to society as protagonist, the center of a novel's instabilities.

Society as Protagonist in *Nostromo* and *Barchester Towers*

The intellectual stage of mankind being as yet in its infancy, and States, like most individuals, having but a feeble and imperfect consciousness of the worth and force of the inner life, the need of making their existence manifest to themselves is determined in the direction of physical activity.
—Joseph Conrad, "Autocracy and War"

It was only when it dawned upon me that the purloiner of the treasure need not necessarily be a confirmed rogue, that he could be even a man of character, an actor, and possibly a victim in the changing scenes of a revolution, it was only then that I had the first vision of a twilight country which was to become the province of Sulaco, with its high, shadowy sierra and its misty campo for mute witnesses of events flowing from the passions of men short-sighted in good and evil.
—Joseph Conrad, "Note" to *Nostromo*

There should be no episodes in a novel. Every sentence, every word, through all those pages, should tend to the telling of the story. . . . Though the novel which you have to write must be long, let it be all one.
—Anthony Trollope, *An Autobiography*

The novels encountered thus far have a single, or perhaps two or three protagonists, but their focus remains on individuals. Society functions as the medium in which individuals define themselves. Even in the sociological/naturalistic novels, where characters seem incapable of escaping the force of social determinism, people command the center of our interest. Their personalities and behavior may reveal the effects of social conditioning, they may seem to be almost entirely a product of that conditioning, but instabilities in their personal situations compel us; their fates are explored and resolved.

At least two novelists, Joseph Conrad in *Nostromo* and Anthony Trollope in *Barchester Towers*, have pursued another possibility: that society might function as formal protagonist of a novel. Although this claim about *Nostromo* and *Barchester Towers* sounds very like that of critics who have said that society or history or historical process is the protagonist, it is not. Their claim is a thematic one about the subject matter of the novel, speaking to the coercive force of history or society on individual lives.[1] In this loose sense, one might say that society is also the protagonist of George Eliot's *Middlemarch* or *Adam Bede*, of Thackeray's *Vanity Fair*, or of a Dickens novel like *Bleak House* or *Our Mutual Friend*.

In contrast, the claim that society acts in the narrative as a human hero would is a formal one; it explains not only the subject matter but the narrative choices in putting together the novels. It therefore has the power to illuminate aspects of both novels that have formerly puzzled or disturbed the critics who have wrestled with problems of unity in these works. By and large, these critics find both novels either marred by extraneous materials or, worse, formless.[2] Their conclusions proceed from the premise that society always plays backdrop to the realization of individual fates. By seeing society as protagonist, we also see the inevitable logic and organization of *Nostromo* and *Barchester Towers*.

To say that society is protagonist is not to claim that society is a character or has an ego analogous to that of an individual; rather it is to state that society, a set of principles or social ideals, functions in the narrative in the same way a human hero would. We are made to care about the fate of a set of principles, a society, whose movement from instability to stability compels the focus and our interest, determines the novel's unity, and resolves the series of artistic expectations established in the work.

To make society the protagonist upsets the expectations of readers: first, because the novel as a genre usually depicts the growth or change of protagonists moving from complications to stability; and second, because the novel customarily concludes in some alteration of the protagonist's external state and in some expansion of his understanding. The novel's action, in general, depicts individual change and concludes with a definitive alteration of the protagonist's state.

The writer who makes society the protagonist commits himself to engaging our primary interest in the life of an abstraction or set of principles. Here, too, action is crucial. He does not want to write a utopian novel that will focus on an idea or ideas about society. The principal end of utopian novels is to criticize or espouse a particular social order not to engage us in working out instabilities through action. In novels in which society is the protagonist, we are involved with the fate of an entire social order, and it is one about which we are made to care. The principal purpose is to present a society moving from a state of instability toward a qualitatively defined fate that is analogous to the movement of an individual hero.

To achieve this end, characters become agents through which a social order realizes its fate. This function of character entails no simple inversion of the usual relationship between individuals and society because characters can never be reduced to a backdrop the way society can, and society cannot easily achieve the particularity of definition and identity that a character can. In attempting to discover narrative terms for realizing the fate of a society, a novelist faces an enormous technical challenge. He must make us care as much about a social order as he does about a particular individual, and yet he cannot write directly about ideas; he must record the actions of humans. Because his plot will focus on no single individual but on abstract process and social hopes, he must constantly minimize individual fates and aspirations and make them clearly a function of society's larger turmoil. Our empathy must rest firmly with the social principles being threatened rather than with any single character. With this end in view, a clearly defined, circumscribed arena for action becomes necessary. Literal battles, or scenes in which battle operates as a principal metaphor, frequently appear in these novels. By bringing many of the major characters together, defining and creating allegiances, and pitting opposing social principles, such incidents of battle provide an important context for measuring the progress of those values with which we empathize.

The individuals who are principal agents by which a positive social order is to be realized may take on rather complex definition as long as the result of their complexity increases our understanding of how their personal strengths and limitations will complicate or hasten the resolution of society's instabilities. Usually, the identities of these principal agents are very clear. In fact, they often tend toward highly representative types whose personalities remain relatively static throughout the novel. Their significance resides in the fact that they embody those positive social principles being challenged or seeking realization.

Action and structure of incident must also mirror the change in focus from individual to societal protagonist. In novels in which society is protagonist, seemingly unfocused openings keep the reader from identifying with any particular individual, as the narrator chooses incidents that stress social instability over the instability of a specific person, a family, or a small social unit. Finally, the fate of the social order is enacted in a staggered resolution that, in one sense, mirrors the breadth of such novels' openings. In such endings, a sequence of resolutions to individual stories spells out the fate of a whole society.

Turning from this general account of technical demands to *Nostromo* and *Barchester Towers*, novels that exemplify society as protagonist, we see that each creates a social order or potential social order whose principles we would like to see triumphant. Through the confirmation and victory of those principles, *Barchester Towers* unfolds a comic fate, while *Nostromo* enacts a tragic one, the defeat of the envisioned social order. In each of these exemplary novels, a society in a period of instability functions exactly as a character might, as the narrative's protagonist.

Narrative Instabilities When Society Is Protagonist

The actions of both *Nostromo* and *Barchester Towers* center on the aspirations of a social order. In *Nostromo* the supporters of the San Tomé mine hope to bring about a better society through developing the mine. The novel charts the failure of these aspirations. Originally intended to be a ray of hope for the society, the mine becomes, through its material success (bringing with it all the superficial prosperity of a developed civilization), an instrument of oppression more ruthless than any that existed formerly. This society's fate is enacted on two levels defined by the two sets of aspirations that comprise its hopes: those centered on the San Tomé mine itself, and the inchoate aspirations of the populace represented by the man Nostromo. These two hopes converge on the Gulf when Nostromo, acting to secure the safety and continuance of the mine, fails, and his failure expands into a general sense of betrayal by the whole European community.

Although the narrator depicts the ideals behind the mine as doomed from the beginning—both by including the myth of gringos in Azuera and by opening the novel with the debacle of the Blanco-sponsored Ribierist government—several aspects of the narrative insure nonetheless that these aspirations will engage us and be looked on sympathetically. Conrad includes two other commercial enterprises, the Oceanic Steam Navigation Company and the National Central Railway, whose representatives, Captain Mitchell and Sir John, see modernization as an absolute good. The former chatters about "historical events" whose importance is demonstrated by the "magnificence" and ostentation of this wealthy province, "The Treasure House of the World."[3] Blinded by sheer wealth as a measure of progress, he is a foil to the mine's principal supporters for whom material progress is a means toward a better justice. Charles Gould's statement, "I simply could not have touched [the mine] for the money alone," accords with his general emphasis on money as a "means not as an end." Emilia Gould, who need not deal in business affairs at all, lacks "even the most legitimate touch of materialism" (1, chap. 6).

The tragedy of *Nostromo* does not reside in our seeing the society at the end of the novel, a society dominated by material interests, as worse or better than the precapitalist society with its brutal and unstable governments. This tragedy consists in the fact that the development of the mine has brought about the destruction of a social potential that we have been made to endorse. The Blanco aristocrats and Nostromo, the man of the people, are the principal agents through which the tragic failure of these ideals is revealed. Nostromo's final confession to Mrs. Gould, a Blanco aristocrat ("The silver has killed me") and Mrs. Gould's reply ("Let it be lost forever") provide both a particular explanation for Nostromo's demise and a broad recognition of how their ideals have been permanently corrupted (3, chap. 12).

The action of *Barchester Towers* is similar to that of *Nostromo* in focus. It turns on abstractions, on social hopes and threats to social stability. *Barchester Towers* depicts the process by which the cathedral town of Barchester, traditionally high church, is thrown into radical instability by the appointment of a low-church bishop. He is attended by an evangelical chaplain who officially declares "war" on the high-church party by the unprecedented act of preaching in the cathedral. Grantly, leader of the high-church party, responds in kind: "War, war, internecine war was in his heart. He felt that, as regarded himself and Mr. Slope, one of the two must be annihilated as far as the city of Barchester was concerned."[4] The narrator adds, "It was not only the clergy who were affected. The laity also had listened to Mr. Slope's new doctrine." "All Barchester was in a tumult" the narrator tells us twice and reiterates: "And so all Barchester was by the ears" (chap. 7). Even the ladies find new political consciousness: "Mrs. Grantly had lived the life of a wise, discreet, peace-making woman; and the people of Barchester were surprised at the amount of military vigour she displayed as general of the feminine Grantlyite forces" (chap. 13). Mr. Slope ingratiates himself with Mrs. Bold "as he had done with other ladies, in order to strengthen his party in the city" (chap. 13).

The further action of the novel revolves around the filling of three key "political" positions: the wardenship of St. Hiram's Hospital, the deanship of Barchester Cathedral, and the husband of Eleanor Bold. Eleanor Bold, with her fortune and her position as daughter of Mr. Harding and sister-in-law of Archdeacon Grantly provides the power of money and the prestige of Barchester high-church establishment. Mr. Slope quickly divines her significance to Barchester politics and courts her because "he wanted a wife, and he wanted money, but he wanted power more than either" (chap. 24).

Instabilities increase when the low-church party, headed by Mr. Slope, wins a minor victory with the appointment of Quiverful as warden, a position for which Mr. Harding is a top contender, but the novel resolves into a comic stability when the high-church party wins the major battle over the deanship in the appointment of Mr. Arabin, who confirms his position and that of the high church by marrying Eleanor Bold. That comic stability is fully guaranteed in the expulsion of Mr. Slope.[5]

The progress of these campaigns, or wars, is dramatized when characters come together in social gatherings or in literal battles. In *Barchester Towers*, two major gatherings take place. First, Mrs. Proudie's reception brings all the characters together and draws up lines of conflict. Second, Ullathorne sports extend over one fourth of the novel. During and after these gatherings, major developments in the power struggle are clarified.

A brief comparison of these scenes with social gatherings in a novel like *Adam Bede* helps illustrate the differences in treatment and significance. In George Eliot's novel, the prominent social gatherings—Dinah's sermon on the green, Arthur Donnithorne's coming-of-age party, and the harvest supper—immerse characters in the environment, which can either nurture them with traditions and stability or confine them in limiting expectations. The chief narrative point of such episodes is to depict the tensions within individuals who must define themselves and their desires apart from social expectations. In *Adam Bede*, the social world on balance nurtures individuals and enables them to survive the destruction of Hetty Sorrel.[6] In Trollope's novel, however, the tensions are not within characters. They themselves embody only one aspect of the novel's set of opposing tensions. A character represents either high church and tradition or low church and social aspiration, and so, Trollope's social gatherings manifest this conflict in *Barchester Towers*.

In similar fashion, the action of *Nostromo*'s Separatist Revolution, a series of literal battles, dramatizes the conflict of social principles. These battles have a more poignant effect than those in *Barchester Towers* because, although the revolution succeeds and Sulaco becomes an independent republic, each step toward assuring victory of the Separatist Revolution necessitates a sacrifice of some of the ideals behind the mine and works toward the ultimate collapse of those ideals.

Treatment of setting and social order also furthers the narrative shift from an action involving individuals to one concerning a society's fate. Because the central identity of the work belongs to society and social organization, action is carefully circumscribed within a specific, relatively isolated scene. *Nostromo* opens with a sensuous evocation of the province of Sulaco with its natural barriers of broad, placid gulf, towering mountains, and vast plain. Sulaco is isolated not only geographically but temporally as well because its geographical isolation has long protected it from incursions of the modern, commercial world. This sense of self-containment is vital to the novel's effect: "Sulaco had found an inviolable sanctuary from the temptations of a trading world in the solemn hush of the deep Golfo Placido as if within an enormous semicircular and unroofed temple open to the ocean, with its walls of lofty mountains hung with the mourning draperies of cloud" (1, chap. 1). Likewise in *Barchester Towers*, the cathedral city and its immediate environs conscribe the total world of Trollope's novel. We follow characters outside this realm only insofar as they conduct the business of Barchester. In introducing the infant John Bold, for instance, the narrator cuts off his discussion with the comment: "Our present business at Barchester will not occupy us above a year or two at the furthest, and I will leave it to some other pen to produce, if necessary, the biography of John Bold the Younger" (chap. 2).

If we compare *Barchester Towers* and *Nostromo* with a novel like *Middlemarch*, we discover great differences in the representation of locality. Although Middlemarch is a specific place, it is not isolated from the outside world. Rather, it extends easily into that world because George Eliot's society is primarily a set of values, norms, and expectations that exist equally in Middlemarch, Bath, London, and even in Rome. In *Middlemarch* and such other novels as *Pride and Prejudice*, *Vanity Fair*, or *Bleak House*, there is an extension and dilution, which contrast sharply with the containment and distillation we find in a *Nostromo* or *Barchester Towers*. A centrifugal effect operates in the former; the world's values, embodied in the characters, accompany them everywhere. Society in Brussels during the crucial battle of Waterloo in Thackeray's novel differs not at all from society in London. It does not matter to the representation of society whether Napoleon or the English win. The represented social values are the same.

In *Barchester Towers* and *Nostromo*, society is defined in clear geographical and political terms; it is a particular set of social principles and political ideologies that are tied to a specific place. Where society is protagonist, we feel a centripetal effect; all that come within the boundaries of its world inevitably participate in its

immediate concerns, even if oblivious to them before. Martin Decoud in *Nostromo* and the Stanhope family and Arabin in *Barchester* testify to the power of the social world to involve individuals.
Defined by the narrator as "idle boulevardier," Martin Decoud is
nonetheless seized upon by Blanco aristocrats as "Son Decoud," a
savior to the threatened forces. Upon arrival in Costaguana, he
finds himself "moved in spite of himself" and now enlisted as
"Journalist of Sulaco"; the "right man had been found" (3, chap.
3). Arabin is that "right man" for Barchester, and "Dr. Gwynne
and Dr. Grantly together had succeeded in persuading this eminent
divine that duty required him to go to Barchester" (chap. 14).
Both Barchester "parties," high and low church, conceive Stanhope
to be their man: "The Stanhopes were all known by name in Barchester, and Barchester was prepared to receive them with open
arms. The doctor was one of her prebendaries, one of her rectors,
one of her pillars of strength; and was, moreover, counted on, as a
sure ally, both by Proudies and Grantlys" (chap. 9). Mr. Slope
expects to "enlist Dr. Stanhope on his side, before his enemies
could out-manoeuvre him"; Grantly "did not doubt but that the
newcomer would range himself under his banners" (chap. 9).

Society Manifest in Human Lives

The self-contained, well-defined societies of *Nostromo* and *Barchester Towers* are comprised of characters who are highly representative of values. No single character can embody fully the positive possibilities for a society. Thus, *Nostromo* emphasizes that
heterogeneous group of characters who inhabit the province of Sulaco in Costaguana. The Englishmen, Charles and Emilia Gould,
backed by the American financier, Holroyd, hope to bring better
justice to their adopted country through the development of its
material interests. The Goulds' efforts are furthered by Mrs.
Gould's ardent admirer and sufferer under the old regime, Dr. Monygham. Their ideals find support in Don José Avellanos, member
of the early local Spanish aristocracy, historian, and diplomat for
Costaguana; in his daughter, Antonia; and in Martin Decoud, lover
of Antonia and articulate spokesman for the cause. To broaden the
base of this idealistic venture, Giorgio Viola, an Italian and life-
long fighter for liberty and justice, shares their hopes for the devel-

opment of the San Tomé mine, the "ray of hope" for the people of a
corrupt country. Those people, in turn, are represented by Nostromo, "our man," the Mediterranean sailor. These several characters—the Goulds, Monygham, Viola, Nostromo, Avellanos, and
Decoud—are the principal agents who embody society's positive
values, and in their fates those values are seen, tragically, to fail.

Similarly, *Barchester Towers* focuses on the Barchester church
members. The church is the central social and political institution
of this cathedral town, but it comprehends a social range from
squirarchy to tenant farmers. The high-church party, dominated
by the militant arm of Archdeacon Grantly, finds support in the
cathedral clergy headed by Trefoil as dean, in the aristocracy represented by Mr. Thorne, and extends into personal relationships
through the women, Grantly's wife, Susan, and his sister-in-law,
Eleanor Bold. Mr. Harding adds spiritual warmth to the high-
church group, and Mr. Arabin brings intellectual power. Together
this group embodies a comic fate for the society by emerging collectively victorious. Their several triumphs reaffirm and reestab-
lish the social principles we have been made to endorse.

Techniques of characterization in these novels are tied clearly to
an individual's social role. After a few pages, we have no difficulty
in identifying Trollope's characters by their social positions; "the
archdeacon" is interchangeable with Grantly; "the bishop" with
Proudie; "the chaplain" with Slope; "the warden" with Harding,
then Quiverful; "the dean" with Trefoil, then Arabin. In *Nostromo*,
characters' identities often depend on nicknames: Gould is El Rey
de Sulaco; Decoud, the journalist of Sulaco; Nostromo is our man,
the "capataz"; Viola, the Garibaldino; Monygham is the mad doctor; Mrs. Gould, the good fairy.

Once established, these tags stimulate our identification with
social aspirations and principles as opposed to individual fates.
Two moments of crisis in *Nostromo* will illustrate this technique. In
one, we hear that the "incomparable Nostromo, the capataz, the
respected and feared Captain Fidanza, the unquestioned oracle of
secret societies, a republican like Old Giorgio, and a revolutionist
at heart (but in another manner), was on the point of jumping
overboard from the deck of his own schooner" rather than face the
loss of his reputation (3, chap. 12). The role-call of social tags
at the moment of Nostromo's crisis limits any internal view of

his mind. The narrator never addresses Nostromo's suffering; he stresses instead social roles, suggesting the social ideals and principles at stake in the loss of Nostromo's personal reputation. Anticipating Decoud's suicide, the narrator says, "The brilliant 'Son Decoud,' the spoiled darling of the family, the lover of Antonia and journalist of Sulaco, was not fit to grapple with himself single-handed" (3, chap. 10). Again, a personal fate is bound up in the social ideals it betrays and augurs the novel's tragic resolution.

Barchester Towers uses the same technique when social aims are compromised by individual action. In distress, Grantly contemplates Arabin's conduct with the unscrupulous Madame Neroni: "That paragon of a clergyman, whom he had bestowed upon St. Ewold's, that college friend of whom he had boasted so loudly, that ecclesiastical knight before whose lance Mr. Slope was to fall and bite the dust, that worthy bulwark of the church as it should be, that honoured representative of Oxford's best spirit, was—so at least his wife had told him half a dozen times—misconducting himself!" (chap. 47). As in *Nostromo* during moments of crisis, we are not invited to share an individual's dilemma or personal anguish. The narrator's rhetoric directs us to the social ideals embodied in individual characters.

Our identification with social ideals, of course, also depends on each novel's rhetoric of heroism. Usually a character's heroism rests in his ability to transcend society, to defy the conventional. When society is protagonist, the heroic qualities of characters reside in their ability to embody particular positive principles or hopes of the society. This different heroic in *Barchester Towers* and *Nostromo* stems from the fact that, as protagonist, society is seen as good. Heroic characters subordinate personal desire to the furtherance of social ideals, and their heroism exists principally in this capacity to identify with larger ends. In *Nostromo*, as we have seen, the mine, its supporters, and Nostromo, the representative of the common people, anchor our social hopes. In *Barchester Towers*, we identify with the high-church party, strengthened by the starch of aristocratic tradition embodied in the Thornes of Ullathorne.

Opposing or negative principles also have representatives, characters who are despicable because they use party lines and ideologies for personal, even antisocial, ends. In *Nostromo*, the Montero brothers, Sotillo, Fuentes, Gamacho—plus the memory of Guzman

Bento, who lives still in the minds of Monygham, Avellanos, and Charles Gould—represent a past and present history of unstable, greedy, corrupt, and brutal governments. *Barchester Towers* locates its negative social possibilities primarily in Mr. Slope, who therefore commands a central position in the novel, but this unscrupulous social climber finds his counterparts in the Lookalofts. Often poorly understood by critics, Trollope's Ullathorne chapters offer a fine stage for the conflict of opposing principles, a conflict that begins when the Lookalofts obtrude themselves into the Thorne's drawing-room. All of the admirable characters in *Barchester Towers* pit themselves against such incursions on the existing social order, so that the Greenacres are to be celebrated for knowing their place.

Interlopers or threats to positive principles are invariably painted in black and white terms. Although Conrad and Trollope depict other characters with subtlety and complexity, they leave no grounds for sympathy with the representatives of opposing principles. Even the potentially laughable General Barrios achieves dignity as head of the Separatist forces, but Sotillo, Fuentes, Gamacho, and the Montero brothers are foolish or, worse, despicable, and Mr. Slope is comprehended in the kind of foolish or contemptible behavior that arises from a character's constant desire for self-aggrandisement. Their motives are narrowly selfish, a narrowness and selfishness intensified by their constant juxtaposition with characters who have larger, social goals in mind.

Because agents of the novels' antagonistic social values are governed by private and selfish motives, readers easily reject them. We come to see them collectively as expressions of a contending, undesirable social idea. The narrator of *Barchester Towers* seems to exceed his role in his vituperative comments against Mr. Slope: "I never could endure to shake hands with Mr. Slope. A cold, clammy perspiration always exudes from him" (chap. 4). Likewise, the ridiculous behavior of the would-be Sulacoan dictators seems almost parodic. We recall, for example, the bravado of the provincial excellency whom Gould bribes, a distracted Sotillo dragging the Gulf for silver, or a commandante of the National Guard, Gamacho, lying "drunk and asleep" after destroying the palace and offering to declare war against France, England, Germany, and the United States. Such simple and crude depictions are essential to enlisting our sympathies with the abstract, social alternatives. Rejection of the negative possibility encourages identification with the positive possibilities for society, which must take much more complex form not only in characterization but in action.

Finally, both *Nostromo* and *Barchester Towers* create a special character, "the mercenary," to serve their ends of making society protagonist. Although this character does not embrace the social principles we have come to value, his efforts contribute to their realization. He belongs neither among the proponents of the positive principles nor among the antagonistic agents. In *Nostromo* the mercenary is Hernandez, the bandit, and in *Barchester Towers*, it is Madame Neroni. Although we feel sympathetic toward Hernandez, Charles Gould's decision to enlist his aid is a qualified moment in the novel. Gould suddenly realizes that he and this bandit "were equals before the lawlessness of the land. It was impossible to disentangle one's activity from its debasing contacts. A close-meshed net of crime and corruption lay upon the whole country. An immense and weary discouragement sealed [Gould's] lips for a time" (3, chap. 3). Although Gould finally gives the required pledge to Hernandez, he must sacrifice the ideals that the mine was to nurture, a sacrifice that underlines tragic expectations for the plot.

In *Barchester Towers*, the comic tone depends on the characters' ignoring the positive effects of Signora Neroni. To acknowledge her is to compromise their principles, but this unscrupulous lady with her machinations both guarantees Slope's demise and assures Arabin's rise. She has seduced Arabin, who hangs "enraptured and alone over the signora's sofa" (chap. 37), yet she resolves "to do a good-natured act for once in her life, and give up Mr. Arabin to [Eleanor Bold] whom he loved" (chap. 38). Her effects are all on the side we value, yet she never embraces its principles. At the end, this mercenary figure finds no place in the comic stability of Barchester's world, and she returns with her family to the banks of the Como.

The mercenaries occupy a middle ground between the positive principles and their antagonists. In so doing they reduce the tendency to see the major confrontations solely in terms of black and white. Mme. Neroni and Hernandez create complexities that engage us more deeply in the society's fate. They pose moral dilemmas for a society, which must use them to achieve its principles and thereby compromise these principles. The acknowledgement of such a compromise or the lack of such acknowledgement helps establish tragic or comic expectations.

Society in Action

The structure of action and selection of incidents work with techniques of characterization to create a protagonist out of society. Since the concerns of no single character can dominate our interest, each novel opens by introducing us to several characters, none of whom compels our attention for long. Every reader of *Nostromo* has felt some puzzlement and perhaps frustration as he has made his way through the novel's opening chapters. Captain Mitchell, Ribiera, Nostromo, Viola, the Goulds, Avellanos—names and unexplained relationships proliferate. *Barchester Towers* does not immerse us in the same initial confusion; relationships among characters are at least clear. Still, no one character commands our attention for long, and although we may develop an initial interest in a character, no single, personal instability gives focus to that interest. Grantly, the Proudies, Slope, Mr. Harding, and Eleanor Bold crowd the narrative, yet the narrator delays still longer to introduce the Stanhopes.

Novelists like Dickens, George Eliot, and Thackeray certainly pack their opening scenes with characters, too; yet one or two of those characters quickly command the center. We can soon identify them as the novel's protagonists, not because of the order in which they are introduced or their prominence in the opening scenes, but because the personal fates of these individuals are early complicated by the introduction or revelation of an instability. Thus, *Middlemarch*'s Dorothea Brooke is a marriageable girl whose tendencies toward martyrdom and rash idealism are likely to interfere with her lot's being decided according to custom and "merely canine affection." The introduction of Casaubon develops these revealed instabilities in her life, even as George Eliot connects them to larger philosophical and social questions.[7]

In *Nostromo* and *Barchester Towers*, multiple centers of interest and the narrative fragmentation reflect worlds in the process of definition. We do not perceive a single underlying social order or set of principles, which gives a sense of unity to diverse characters, situations, and relationships. Rather, we recognize alternate ordering principles, and this conflict of possibilities, expressed in the characters' vulnerability to social forces, compels our interest.

In light of this narrative strategy, the initial sustained identification in *Nostromo* with the Violas, relatively minor characters, makes artistic sense. The Violas' fates depend on the fate of the society. From the beginning, this family is particularly vulnerable to social upheaval. They are threatened by the events of the revolution—the mob violence and Sotillo's inquisition—and also by the development of material interests in Costaguana. Mrs. Gould must save their house from destruction by the National Central Railway even though it does not lie "in the way of the projected harbor branch of the line in the least" (1, chap. 8).

Barchester Towers, too, minimizes interest in individual fates by making them dependent on a larger social action. The narrator's treatment of Eleanor Bold, whose love affairs might occupy the center of our attention, signals this broader narrative intent. In what critics have seen as a clumsy gesture, Trollope's narrator removes much of the suspense about Eleanor Bold's fate barely one fourth of the way into the novel: "But let the gentle-hearted reader be under no apprehension whatsoever. It is not destined that Eleanor shall marry Mr. Slope or Bertie Stanhope" (chap. 15). The narrator then develops an aesthetic about the role of suspense in a novel, arguing that a novel's effect should not depend on a reader's uncertainty about what will happen. That aesthetic, however, applies principally to the issue of Eleanor Bold's spouse. By contrast, the narrator is not so precipitate in assuring us that Slope will not become dean. In essence, he insures that the interest of the novel will not reside in the particular fates of individuals by precluding romantic interest to focus on jockeying for political and social control of Barchester instead.

Of course, novels depend, in part, on engaging us with individual actions and motivations, but when society is protagonist, individual fates must be developed so as to keep the significance of individual actions subservient to an unfolding story of a society's change. We might recall that when Nostromo and Decoud launch out into the darkness of the Golfo Placido on a lighter full of silver, the narrator claims, "There was no bond of conviction, of common idea; they were merely two adventurers pursuing each his own adventure" (2, chap. 8). However Decoud and Nostromo conceive of their tasks, the narrator places their motives and actions within the context of larger social goals to be realized. The characters may not share a reality; nonetheless their actions shape a common end. Decoud's suicide is affecting because it has deprived the emerging country of its most articulate spokesman and its only counterweight to the obsession of Charles Gould. Nostromo's failure touches us because it embodies the crushed, inchoate aspirations of the common people.

Dr. Monygham's story further underlines the way in which individual development is subordinated to a society's fate. While it is true that Dr. Monygham undergoes a personal rehabilitation and redemption,[8] marked by his changed and meticulous attire and the "almost complete disappearance from his dreams of Father Beron" (3, chap. 11), he also participates in a larger, social action. For that participation, he is finally punished or "defeated" by Nostromo in Mrs. Gould's refusal to disclose the secret of the capataz to him.

Monygham's response to the reappearance of the capataz, who was supposedly killed on the lighter, determines Nostromo's subsequent actions. Monygham's lack of interest in Nostromo's "desperate affair" and his suggestion that Gould would approve of using the silver to buy up Sotillo—a tactic Gould has expressly rejected—destroy the seriousness with which Nostromo has accepted his mission and betray the ideals behind the mine. Its silver has always carried a tacit weight of idealism Nostromo has recognized. Dr. Monygham's subsequent refusal to let Nostromo see Gould, for fear of his being recognized, intensifies Nostromo's feelings of being betrayed by the whole European community, which Monygham now represents to him. The dual hopes for the society, embodied in the mine and Nostromo, converge in the fate of the silver. Initially an instrument to realize a better justice for the people, the silver now becomes a force to destroy Nostromo, who is their representative. On one level, then, we might talk of Monygham's personal redemption, but the predominant patterns of the novel ask us to see his actions as contributing to the failure of social aspirations we have been made to share.

In a similar way, Mr. Harding's role in *Barchester Towers* emphasizes a society's rather than an individual's fate. This long-suffering precentor is considered for positions as both warden and dean, receives neither, and yet his deprivation is not artistically disruptive of our expectations. It would be difficult to name a more deserving character, and yet the work affects us as a comedy in which good is rewarded. The narrator's comments serve to shape our attitude toward Harding's fate: "It was droll to observe how these men [Dr. Gwynne and Dr. Grantly] talked of Mr. Harding as though he were a puppet, and planned their intrigues and small ecclesiastical manoeuvres in reference to Mr. Harding's future position, without dreaming of taking him into their confidence. There was a comfortable house and income in question, and it was very desirable, and certainly very just, that Mr. Harding should have them; but that, at present, was not the main point; it was expedient to beat the bishop and if possible to smash Mr. Slope" (chap. 34). As a consequence of such comments, we perceive rewarded good in social terms, in the establishment of certain social principles, which are more guaranteed by the appointment of staunch high-church Mr. Arabin as dean than by the appointment of a deserving Mr. Harding. It is true that Harding is offered the deanship and rejects it, preferring to continue as precentor of Barchester and pastor of St. Cuthbert's even though he is urged to strive for this position by Grantly, but Harding's decision only reveals how little the instabilities of the novel revolve around individual fates. Furthermore, Harding's final determination to escort Quiverful into his duties as warden of St. Hiram's Hospital—"to walk in, arm in arm with Mr. Quiverful, and to ask from these men their respectful obedience to their new master" (chap. 52)—further guarantees the social stability and emphasizes its importance. All Barchester will no longer be "by the ears."

It is hard to think of a comparable novel, say a comedy by Jane Austen, in which a major deserving character ends the novel with his condition unchanged. It is unthinkable that Jane Bennet might not marry Bingley in *Pride and Prejudice*. Her happiness is requisite to Elizabeth's; her expectations must be equally realized in this comic resolution. But in *Barchester Towers*, Mr. Harding's fate contributes to stabilizing the social situation and to a satisfactory resolution of social instabilities. The fact that his personal situation does not and need not change measures the difference between this novel and novels with individual protagonists.

Finally, the novels' conclusions invite us to evaluate the fate of a society not of an individual or group. In *Nostromo*, this fulfillment is tragic; in *Barchester Towers*, it is comic. Indeed, when opposing principles are at stake, there seem to be no other possibilities. Idealization and abstraction preclude compromise, and the definition of protagonist is too complex, the identification too delicately balanced, to allow anything other than complete triumph or total defeat. For this form of novel, complexity and subtlety lie in using various characters as agents to realize a society's fate not in defining a complex and subtle fate for an individual hero. Even in *Nostromo*, where the tragic possibilities do not reside in a return to the old regime but in a perversion of the positive ideals and principles, the principles themselves either succeed or fail. Technically, fulfillment is expressed through a staggered resolution so that each central agent enacts one part of society's fate.

Because characters' fates are embodying a larger fate, special demands govern their final representation. Novels usually stress the growth or change of individuals; *Nostromo* and *Barchester Towers* stress the lack of change. Not only do characters not grow, but in many cases they cannot grow if the artistic end is to be realized. The reasons are evident. If novels reveal individual change by measuring the protagonist against an unchanging society, allowing both his final failure and triumph to become clear, then a changing society requires, too, its points of stability and contrast. These points are the novel's characters who must stay the same, or have their initial roles recalled, to reveal how society has been reaffirmed in *Barchester Towers* and defeated in *Nostromo*.

Charles and Emilia Gould, Monygham, Decoud, Viola, and Nostromo are the points of stability by which we measure the fall of Conrad's social order.[9] Each of the characters, whose role was initially colored with heroism, now finds himself within a changed society that ironically forces him to continue playing the old roles. The characters' understanding, or lack of understanding, of their altered circumstances contributes to our sense of what has been lost for society. Charles Gould becomes more and more fixed in his obsessions. There is no possibility that he will recognize the failure of his ideals, and his lack of recognition makes their failure more poignant. His wife understands that "he did not see it. He could not see it." She, herself, struck with the desolation of this failure, still plays the good fairy, forced to continue as sacred guardian of now betrayed ideals: "She saw herself surviving alone the degradation of her young ideal of life, of love, of work—all alone in The Treasure House of the World." Monygham is still a "dangerous enemy of the people" (3, chaps. 11, 12), despite his self-sacrificing devotion in the Separatist Revolution. Decoud—boulevardier, dilettante, victim of his own skepticism—is the Apostle of Separation, commemorated in the cathedral. Viola, the old revolutionary, prowling and protecting his grounds at night shoots his beloved, adopted son, Nostromo. Nostromo, his muscular limbs confined in a brown tweed suit, still commands the social respect of the magnificent, magnetic, incorruptible capataz de cargadores who was so compelling in the opening scenes of the novel. Only now he is a common thief, stealing silver and Giorgio Viola's daughter. Social role and social reality jar, and that discord helps measure the fall of *Nostromo*'s society.

The prominence of "our man" Nostromo in the novel's concluding scenes confirms that society is Conrad's protagonist. Of all the characters, Nostromo is the only one who changes significantly, and his changes fully accord with his representative function as "Man of the People, their very own unenvious force."[10] His sense of betrayal spells the betrayal of the people through destruction of the social ideals the mine and its silver originally promised. His death is a tragic fulfillment in which the "genius of the magnificent capataz de cargadores" is reaffirmed in Linda Viola's cathartic cry ringing around the Gulf. Nostromo's moral destruction, too, emblematizes the failure of the capitalistic revolution to realize a better justice. His death, however, offers a denouement that affirms the power of the common people to enact change through a now-threatening proletariat revolution, but that story is beyond the province of *Nostromo*'s plot.

The formal expectations in *Barchester Towers* do not demand so complex a resolution as do those in *Nostromo*. In depicting a comic fate for society, Trollope makes social role and social reality accord. Characters continue in their representative capacities and in that continuation affirm the triumph of their principles. Mr. Arabin, the very highest of the high-church party, is established in the deanery; Mr. Harding is ensconced there as well; Susan Grantly strengthens ties with her sister, Eleanor Arabin. The Proudies, who introduced Slope into Barchester, are themselves removed for large periods by the bishop's appointment to the House of Lords. Furthermore they have learned: "Mr. Slope tried his hand at subverting the old-established customs of the close, and from his failure

[Mrs. Proudie] has learnt experience." The narrator can thus assure us that "nothing can be more pleasant than the present arrangement of ecclesiastical affairs in Barchester" (chap. 53).

Society as Protagonist: The Artist's Intuition

A set of social principles would seem to make a cold protagonist, but we discover the power of art to compel our interest in its fate. That final "arrangement of ecclesiastical affairs in Barchester" gives joy; the destruction of the social hopes embodied in the Blanco aristocrats and in the man Nostromo moves us powerfully. The all-encompassing scope of the comedy or tragedy—nothing less than a whole society's fate—of course, contributes to narrative power, but essential to its force are the special techniques each novelist has discovered to engage us with an abstraction and to delineate its fate.

We might finally want to ask why Conrad and Trollope explored the possibility of society as protagonist and whether they did so accidentally or deliberately. Although Trollope never addressed the issue directly, his sophistication in novel theory suggests an experimental attitude toward his craft.[11] Furthermore, he loved political machinations, and he particularly understood the political power vested in the clergy of a cathedral city. Once he had envisioned the microcosm of Barchester, the possibility of evolving a political faction for protagonist seems an inevitable consequence, especially since Trollope often conceives of characters as political beings.

Conrad, on the other hand, wrote particularly to this question of making a social order protagonist. His "Note" to *Nostromo* discloses his dissatisfaction with the initial subject he saw: that of a rogue who stole a lighter full of silver. Once Nostromo's representative capacities as a man of the people began to emerge and Sulaco, as a place, achieved clearer definition, Conrad may well have discovered a much more interesting and broader subject. Shortly after he completed the novel, Conrad wrote an essay "Autocracy and War" in which he speaks of the state as a kind of protagonist: "States, like most individuals, having but a feeble and imperfect consciousness of the worth and force of the inner life, the need of making their existence manifest to themselves is determined in the direction of physical activity."[12] Conrad was clearly thinking in terms that would lead an artist to explore the unusual narrative possibility of society as protagonist.

We need not argue for conscious authorial intention. We need only acknowledge artistic achievement. Seeing society as protagonist in *Barchester Towers* and *Nostromo* resolves crucial critical problems in both novels and offers a cogent theory for their art.

This alternative is not immediately obvious because readers tend to take a partial and individual view of the world. The novel lends itself to exploration of individual psychologies and perspectives. We expect it to do so. Its technique, the basic fact that novels are narratives, encourages us to share the dilemmas of individuals, and the common subject matter of novels, as Dorothy Van Ghent has argued, is "human relationships in which we are shown the directions of men's souls . . . the procedure of the novel is to individualize."[13] If society is not a backdrop to the actions of individuals, we begin to move away from what we generally conceive of as the province of the novel. When society is protagonist, we move toward the subject matter of history. Van Ghent further comments, in distinguishing the novel from history, that "[history] treats people as groups; and when individuals appear they appear as catalysts of large collective actions or as representatives of groups, their significance being that of the group forces, the collection, the sum."[14]

Her description of history recalls my description of *Nostromo* and *Barchester Towers*. Although neither Trollope nor Conrad is writing explicitly *about* history (Trollope less than Conrad), each strategically uses the historian's techniques. Their novels move toward the representative rather than the particular; they move toward conflicts of principles rather than conflicts between individuals. That movement, the desire to interpret the larger processes of history in the novel, led Conrad and Trollope to discover special techniques of artistic representation that characterize *Nostromo* and *Barchester Towers*. By accommodating the techniques of the historian to fiction, these writers expanded significantly the province and vision of the novel and brought to historical process the immediacy and power of fiction.

Existence Beyond: Reality
in Brontë and O'Connor

*"I cannot express it; but surely you and everybody have a notion
that there is, or should be, an existence of yours beyond you.
What were the use of my creation, if I were entirely contained
here? My great miseries in this world have been Heathcliff's miseries, and I watched and felt each from the beginning; my great
thought in living is himself. If all else perished, and* he *remained,
I should still continue to be; and, if all else remained, and he
were annihilated, the Universe would turn to a mighty stranger. I
should not seem a part of it."*
—Catherine Earnshaw speaking to Nelly Dean in
　Emily Brontë, *Wuthering Heights*

*If the writer believes that our life is and will remain essentially
mysterious, if he looks upon us as beings existing in a created order to whose laws we freely respond, then what he sees on the
surface will be of interest to him only as he can go through it into
an experience of mystery itself.*
—Flannery O'Connor, "Some Aspects of the Grotesque in
　Southern Fiction"

Early in *Wuthering Heights*, Catherine Earnshaw cries out, "Surely
you and everybody have a notion that there is, or should be, an
existence of yours beyond you."[1] Although such a notion is "non-

sense" to an uncomprehending Nelly Dean, the reality of "an existence of yours beyond you" in fact determines the characters' fates and shapes the role of society in Emily Brontë's novel. While social norms—in the persons of the narrators, Nelly Dean and Lockwood —and social institutions, especially inheritance laws, figure prominently in the novel, fictional society does not serve as the medium in which the protagonists define themselves. Human beings live in societies, and meaning on earth is determined by social expectations and institutions, but there exists a larger, transcendent sphere in which to interpret and evaluate these characters' lives. That sphere is not created by man; his participation in it is not willed or chosen. If Conrad and Trollope approach the subject matter of history, Brontë addresses a subject matter of philosophy and religion: the possibility of a supranatural existence, a dimension of existence beyond that apprehensible by our senses.

I have pointed out earlier that the twentieth-century novel has increasingly looked elsewhere than society for a medium in which to interpret meaning and value. Brontë's novel does not participate in the movement that, under pressure of man's increasing social alienation and subjectivity, seeks meaning in alternative mediums such as art, language, sensibility, and myth. These mediums, like societies, are man-made systems of value. Brontë, on the contrary, glimpses a life beyond man-created forms, and her novel explores its meaning through her protagonists' lives. She precludes society as a significant context for individual meaning but includes it as the context that necessarily governs human behavior on earth and that becomes our means through which to apprehend the possibility of suprahuman existence.

The novel's reality depends on this grounding in the usual. As a result, the fictional society appears to play a role similar to its role in other novels. In fact, some critics have interpreted *Wuthering Heights* as a novel of class conflict.[2] A homeless, Liverpool orphan boy is rescued by a kindly gentleman, loved by this man's daughter, but degraded and abused by his son. This is the sense that the 1942 Lawrence Olivier movie made of Brontë's novel. But the novel itself continually precludes social mores and morality as a medium in which to understand the protagonists and their dilemma.[3]

Flannery O'Connor, although separated from Emily Brontë by a century and an ocean, shares Brontë's preoccupation with the uselessness of our creation if we are "entirely contained here." Like Brontë, O'Connor creates a transcendent realm in which to see her characters' fates. Although her realm is pointedly religious, it is not one of dogmas and dictates. Hence O'Connor avoids the didacticism that poses a danger to the religious novelist. O'Connor recognized organized religion, with its commandments and ethics, as part of society, man's interpretation of the divine, not divinity itself. She does not, therefore, preach the merits of one dogma over another, even though many of her characters are such prophets or preachers. Instead, she pursues the inexplicability, the mystery of divinity, of a life beyond the one we know. She recognizes that people need society, with its categories and values, to live together on earth, but she explores the possibility of another realm in which other kinds of relationships exist. To do so, she, like Brontë, focuses closely on society as a necessary step to precluding it as the significant realm for individual meaning. O'Connor has a firm grasp of social class and racial conflict; she captures the exigencies of daily social life with its inevitable concussions, but society becomes for her a vehicle to explore the larger, more elusive reality of the divine and mysterious action of grace.

Although both O'Connor and Brontë were influenced by the gothic, and Brontë also by the romance, their own formal achievement is distinctive and unique. Both create a convincing realistic world in which to place their characters; their depictions of society do not exceed probability. In fact, both writers locate their fictions in the worlds they knew personally. So faithful are both to social customs, dialects, and conditions that, even in the absence of extratextual information, we would have little difficulty determining period and locale. Any exaggeration resides in individual characters not in the representation of society. Brontë and O'Connor use an ordinary, realistic social medium as access to their mystery.

Indeed, in contrast to the gothic novelist, who focuses on the decadent or violent, O'Connor stipulates that the violence in her art stems from the conflicting realities: the social and the transcendent. "It's not necessary to point out that the look of this fiction is going to be wild, that it is almost of necessity going to be violent and comic, because of the discrepancies that it seeks to combine."[4] She illuminates that combination of two points in terms Emily Brontë would understand: "One is a point in the concrete, and the other is a point not visible to the naked eye, but believed in by him [the writer] firmly, just as real to him, really, as the one that every-body sees."[5] Only by going through "a point in the concrete" do we approach that "point not visible to the naked eye."

The Extraordinary in *Wuthering Heights*

Emily Brontë's novel opens with Mr. Lockwood gloating over hav-ing found in Thrushcross Grange and Wuthering Heights a "per-fect misanthropist's heaven" (chap. 1). Misanthropist implies, of course, a relationship of man to society, in this case a desire to be "completely removed from the stir of society." Lockwood's fancied empathy with Heathcliff—"how my heart warmed towards him"—suggests that he expects to find his landlord a man like himself, diffident in high society, averse to "showy displays of feeling" (chap. 1). While Mr. Lockwood eulogizes the supposed virtues of his new neighbor and situation, he quickly reveals his own person-ality. Conceited, stuffy, self-satisfied, and obtuse, he knows himself so little that he calls himself a misanthropist yet spends each day pursuing company rather than solitude. Of course, Lockwood is not an unattractive character; he is even likeable, but because his self-satisfaction is partially responsible for his later discomfiture in the society of Wuthering Heights, we find him ludicrous even as we sympathize with him for the difficulty of his situation.

His difficulty stems from the almost complete absence of social decorum at Wuthering Heights. Even minimal social etiquette is ignored, and nothing short of his dogs attacking his guest can rouse Heathcliff to perform any duties of host. We recognize two things: one, that Lockwood's perspectives provide an inadequate framework for judging the situation; and two, his perspectives are, however, socially normative. They acquaint us with Mr. Lock-wood's ordinariness, and, more important, with the extraordinari-ness of Wuthering Heights and its inhabitants.

Mr. Lockwood's presence in the scene makes clear that Heath-cliff is not a social recluse even though it gives us no further insight into Heathcliff or his behavior. Although we recognize that Heath-cliff rarely fulfills a social form, this recognition does not accom-plish what it does in most novels in which it facilitates our judg-ment of the characters. Authors usually make major judgments of character through social norms. For example, we might decide that

Heathcliff is a boor for what Lockwood calls "churlish hospitality" or, alternatively, interpret his actions as transcending social considerations. Henry Fielding provides an example of the first type of judgment in *Joseph Andrews* when Parson Adams visits Parson Trulliber: "Whilst they were at table, her husband gave her a fresh example of his greatness; for, as she had just delivered a cup of ale to Adams, he snatched it out of his hand, and, crying out, 'I *caal'd vurst*,' swallowed down the ale."[6] By social lights, we understand the irony in "a fresh example of his greatness" and conclude that the implied author has judged the man a boor.

D. H. Lawrence's *Women in Love* includes the type of judgment in which we interpret a character's actions as transcending social considerations. Birkin arrives to propose marriage to Ursula and is confronted by her father, Will Brangwen:

> "What I mean is that my children have been brought up to think and do according to the religion I was brought up in myself, and I don't want to see them going away from *that*."
>
> There was a dangerous pause.
>
> "And beyond that—?" asked Birkin.
>
> The father hesitated, he was in a nasty position.
>
> "Eh? What do you mean? All I want to say is that my daughter"—he tailed off into silence, overcome by futility. He knew that in some way he was off the track. . . .
>
> There was a complete silence, because of the utter failure in mutual understanding. Birkin felt bored. Her father was not a coherent human being, he was a roomful of old echoes. The eyes of the younger man rested on the face of the elder. Brangwen looked up, and saw Birkin looking at him. His face was covered with inarticulate anger and humiliation and sense of inferiority in strength.[7]

Birkin himself realizes his superiority, a fact substantiated by the implied author's judgments, which reflect negatively on Brangwen and reveal Birkin to be a man admirable in his transcendence of worn-out and empty conventions.[8]

Fielding and Lawrence demonstrate ways in which included social norms reveal character. Those social norms imported by Lockwood in *Wuthering Heights*, however, offer little such insight into Heathcliff's character. Heathcliff's inattention, his "habitual moroseness," and his indifference suggest that he neither ignores nor transcends social decorum. He seems, rather, simply oblivious to it. The demands of ordinary social intercourse distract him. In other words, Brontë's novel does not endorse or discredit social norms as a measure of character, rather it includes them to reveal their lack of explanatory power.

Brontë's achievement in *Wuthering Heights* has two dimensions: first, she suggests two realms for existence by making the ordinary or social contexts inadequate to explain Catherine and Heathcliff. The second dimension of her achievement relates to the first but has not been remarked by critics for its significance to the novel's formal ends; that is, although Catherine and Heathcliff share an immediate and intuitive knowledge of each other, they fail to share even the most basic social values, and therefore they rarely understand each other's actions. Communication between them, within social forms, is frustrating and destructive, because social forms fail to express what they are about.

In this framework, we easily see that fictional society is both important and unimportant in *Wuthering Heights*. It is the means through which we understand Catherine and Heathcliff, but it is not the medium in which their lives and fates have their meaning. In this sense, Brontë precludes ordinary social reality. Society and its expectations are present as a window to another reality. Like the window, society allows us to see beyond, but to see through the window, one must finally ignore it. If one concentrates on it or, by analogy, on society, he will never see outside, see the mystery beyond.

By rendering the usual social categories inadequate in explaining Catherine and Heathcliff, Brontë suggests two contexts for existence. First Lockwood and then Nelly Dean—with her complacent, solid, unimaginative, socially normative morality—attempts to explain Heathcliff and Catherine to us, and their failures should stimulate in us a search for alternative categories for judgment. By evoking all the norms and expectations of society, the novel's narrators render those perspectives useless as ultimate explanations.[9] We may return to Lockwood's description of Heathcliff as misanthropist, for instance. This opinion initially suggests that he might be a disappointed lover, another tragic Don Lockwood, but that phrase cannot explain Heathcliff's enmity toward his daughter-in-law, his degradation of Hareton Earnshaw, or his frantic response to his visitor's dream about Catherine Earnshaw. Likewise, Nelly

Dean's characterization of Catherine as a "wicked girl" for wanting to marry Linton while maintaining her relationship with Heathcliff makes Catherine into an amorous Becky Sharp. It ignores entirely the strange bond that exists between Catherine and Heathcliff. That bond expresses a reality of elemental union beyond social custom and convention, beyond all the trappings of ordinary human intercourse.

Two conflicting realities exist in *Wuthering Heights*. Nelly Dean and Lockwood articulate the first, a social reality, which is focused in Thrushcross Grange. The second resides in the implied author and is shared by the protagonists. This set of values stems from a belief in an "existence of yours beyond you." Wuthering Heights and, more particularly, the moors provide a local context for this reality. Catherine tries to articulate the elemental, nonhuman existence in her famous conversation with Nelly Dean. This conversation is striking for its depiction of failure to communicate and deserves our close attention.

Although the two characters appear to be speaking and responding to each other, each fails to convey her meaning because each proceeds from entirely dissimilar premises about human existence. The conversation has great importance because it demonstrates the incommensurability of the human and suprahuman perspectives. Catherine and Heathcliff are doomed because they seek a solution to their impulses, desires, and dilemmas in a world that can offer no accommodation to those who respond to a suprahuman dimension of existence.

The conversation begins with Catherine's admission that she has agreed to marry Edgar Linton and her request to know "whether [she] was wrong." Nelly refuses to answer this question, perhaps partly to provoke her charge, but also because there is, in her mind, no question: "You have pledged your word, and cannot retract." Catherine and Nelly do not mean the same thing by "wrong"; for Nelly, it involves a social ethic, a promise made cannot be broken. Catherine is speaking of her soul's and heart's resistance to her decision. The succeeding irrelevant catechism to which Nelly subjects Catherine—"Do you love Mr. Edgar?" "Why?" etc. —provokes impatient responses from Catherine, who finally orders Nelly to "speak rationally." If we accept that Catherine is not being perverse but that she recognizes a deep logic of her nature, which Nelly has not addressed, then her renewed appeal, "You have not told me whether I'm right," makes sense. Nelly's sarcastic response once again invokes the social ethic and expectation: "Perfectly right; if people be right to marry only for the present . . . you will escape from a disorderly, comfortless home into a wealthy, respectable one . . . where is the obstacle?" Nelly's responses are never adequate to Catherine's questions; she never proceeds from the same assumptions. She uses the same vocabulary, which persuades them they are speaking the same language, but their words, like "right" and "wrong," never mean the same thing.

To Nelly, the logical consequence of Catherine's marriage to Linton, the one dictated by social morality, is that Catherine will give up Heathcliff, and he will "be quite deserted in the world." Catherine vehemently refuses this logic—it is, after all, not the logic of her premises and their development—and suggests that she will destroy anyone who comes between her and Heathcliff. "I shouldn't be Mrs. Linton were such a price demanded!" It is Catherine, not Nelly, who suddenly glimpses the other perspective, "I see now, you think me a selfish wretch," but she immediately resumes her own logic, "If I marry Linton, I can aid Heathcliff to rise." To Nelly the most discreditable motive, it is to Catherine the best and leads to her attempt to make Nelly see her perspective: "But surely you and everybody have a notion that there is, or should be, an existence of yours beyond you. . . . Nelly, I *am* Heathcliff." Nelly's only response can and must be from that social world she represents: "You are ignorant of the duties you undertake in marrying; or else . . . you are a wicked, unprincipled girl." The failure of communication between the characters is complete (chap. 9).

The reader, however, enjoys the advantage of distance. It is tempting to follow Nelly's logic; she, after all, has the last word, and hers are the lights by which most of us live. That temptation must exist because only by rejecting the obvious limitations of Nelly's perspectives can the reader approach any understanding of Catherine and Heathcliff. To facilitate that approach, Brontë is careful to make Catherine logical and coherent once her premises are understood. Catherine assumes that inarticulate, noncorporeal bonds such as she shares with Heathcliff are common. If one's existence extends beyond self—in Catherine's case, she *is* Heathcliff—then it is wrong to violate oneself in acting against oneself. In Catherine's implicit logic, such behavior is contra-nature and therefore unnatural. Social ethics can explain nothing that Catherine needs to know, but social ethics govern behavior on earth, and in the confusion of two ethical systems Catherine anticipates her own destruction, because the bond she shares with Heathcliff can find no social correlative.

In its formal juxtaposition of two value systems, this scene between Catherine and Nelly anticipates the later descriptions of Heathcliff's violence against Hindley. This violence has often been seen by critics as evidence of a desire to avenge social wrongs, but a look at these two accounts of Heathcliff's brutality toward Hindley shows us once again that we are dealing with a situation that must be interpreted in different lights. As Isabella relates the episode to Nelly, Heathcliff is a madman motivated by revenge against Hindley: "[Heathcliff's] adversary had fallen senseless with excessive pain and the flow of blood that gushed from an artery, or a large vein. The ruffian kicked and trampled on him, and dashed his head repeatedly against the flags, holding me with one hand, meantime, to prevent me summoning Joseph" (chap. 17). Isabella's whole account accords with her understanding, which is dictated by norms of social class and power. To the extent that Heathcliff exceeds those, he becomes a demon or a devil. She cannot see other explanations for his behavior. As a result, when Heathcliff later describes this episode we might easily fail to recognize it as the one reported by Isabella. In his version, he is oblivious to Hindley, to revenge, to degradation, to all except the spirit of Catherine whom he pursues in anguish and loss:

> "I felt that Cathy was there, not under me, but on the earth.
> "A sudden sense of relief flowed from my heart through every limb. I relinquished my labour of agony, and turned consoled at once, unspeakably consoled. Her presence was with me; it remained while I re-filled the grave, and led me home. You may laugh, if you will, but I was sure I should see her there. I was sure she was with me, and I could not help talking to her.
> "Having reached the Heights, I rushed eagerly to the door. It was fastened; and, I remember, that accursed Earnshaw and my wife opposed my entrance. I remember stopping to kick the breath out of him, and then hurrying upstairs, to my room and hers. I looked around impatiently—I felt her

by me—I could *almost* see her, and yet I *could not!* I ought
to have sweat blood then, from the anguish of my yearning,
from the fervour of my supplications to have but one
glimpse!" [chap. 29].

The details that compose pages of Isabella's narrative comprise a
fleetingly remembered interruption in Heathcliff's. The inclusion
of a second narrative of the same events establishes a sequence of
motive and behavior other than that explained by the social norms
that usually shape interrelationships.

Brontë also succeeds in precluding society as an obstacle to
Catherine and Heathcliff by limiting the ways in which the protagonists know and understand each other. Although Catherine
and Heathcliff know each other in an instinctual way, they understand each other's actions no better than they are understood by
others. Their failures at social communication are appalling. On
earth, they are often ciphers to each other. We have seen earlier
that society is the medium for character action, which partially or
wholly determines individual fates. It is a medium that implies
shared communal values. Because Catherine and Heathcliff must
act in society and because they themselves share no values, goals,
and aims except the inarticulate one of elemental oneness, every
attempt to communicate within that system fails. Every act is at
variance. Society does not and cannot destroy them unless by "society" we mean any conceivable human—that is, social—arrangement. But nineteenth-century English social class and customs do
not destroy them.

Catherine and Heathcliff are truly amoral. Dorothy Van Ghent
has astutely noted that the "difficulty of defining, with any precision, the quality of the daemonic that is realized most vividly in the
conception of Heathcliff . . . [is] a difficulty that is mainly due to
our tendency always to give the 'daemonic' some ethical status—
that is, to relate it to an ethical hierarchy."[10] Van Ghent sketches
the ethical history of the outsider/devil figure with his various sea
changes and shifting ethical valence, and she concludes that
Heathcliff is an exception because he is related to no ethical hierarchy.[11] Van Ghent's point is the essential one to make about Heathcliff. To it, must be added that precisely because Heathcliff and
Catherine share no social values, even between themselves, and
can be placed in no ethical hierarchy, they appear animal, ele-

mental, outside the human. Humanity depends on shared values. Catherine and Heathcliff share two things basically: earthly existence and an intense consciousness of each other. The suprahuman intercourse that they crave, and that was most closely approximated as children in their wild, sexless, and therefore unembodied, freedom on the moors, is an impossibility, but the inescapability of their mutual consciousness and drive for union on earth will determine their destruction of themselves and all about them.

Catherine and Heathcliff are destroyed by the impossibilities of a human union and their acting on earth in a way that is comprehensible to the other. For example, Catherine's decision to marry Linton provokes Heathcliff's departure, which initiates her fever, more an emotional than physical response. Catherine intends to benefit Heathcliff; instead he feels degraded. To her, he is in error; to him, she errs. Upon Heathcliff's return, Catherine chides him for his absence: "Cruel Heathcliff! you don't deserve this welcome. To be absent and silent for three years, and never to think of me!" He, expecting to find her changed, has planned to "settle my score with Hindley; and then prevent the law by doing execution on myself." This initial plan of Heathcliff's to destroy himself is so unexpected by the reader that it can stem only from a complete failure to understand Catherine's actions: "Her [unexpected] welcome has put these ideas out of [his] mind" (chap. 10). Once Catherine and Heathcliff have matured and left the moors where understanding was automatic and intuitive, understanding can never again exist between them. Their final words to each other are words of both reproach and blame: Catherine charges Heathcliff, "You and Edgar have broken my heart . . . I shall not pity you, not I. You have killed me—and thriven on it, I think. How strong you are!" Heathcliff, impassioned, replies, "You teach me now how cruel you've been—cruel and false. *Why* did you despise me? *Why* did you betray your own heart. . . . You loved me—then what *right* had you to leave me? . . . Because misery, and degradation, and death, and nothing that God or Satan could inflict would have parted us, *you*, of your own will, did it" (chap. 15). Both characters remain oblivious of wrong-doing, to themselves and to others.

Acting against each other and ultimately thus against themselves, they destroy themselves and each other. Catherine cries, "They may bury me twelve feet deep, and throw the church down over me, but I won't rest till you are with me. I never will" (chap.

12). And Heathcliff anticipates his anguish, "Oh God! Would *you* like to live with your soul in the grave?" and at her death howls "Oh God! it is unutterable! I *cannot* live without my life! I *cannot* live without my soul!" (chap. 16).

The nature of corporeal existence, not society, destroys Catherine and Heathcliff. Society provides a window to that alternative possibility. Heathcliff's subsequent revenge, the destruction of all those about him, is a manifestation of his passion to destroy the physical and human bonds that keep him from Catherine. At the end he confesses to Nelly, "I have to remind myself to breathe— almost to remind my heart to beat! And it is like bending back a stiff spring; it is by compulsion that I do the slightest act not prompted by one thought, and by compulsion, that I notice anything alive, or dead, which is not associated with one universal idea. I have a single wish, and my whole being and faculties are yearning to attain it. They have yearned toward it so long, and so unwaveringly, that I'm convinced it *will* be reached—and *soon*— because it has devoured my existence. I am swallowed in the anticipation of its fulfillment" (chap. 33).

As this transcendent consummation with Catherine approaches, Heathcliff becomes indifferent to revenge: "My old enemies have not beaten me; now would be the precise time to revenge myself on their representatives: I could do it; and none could hinder me. But where is the use? I don't care for striking, I can't take the trouble to raise my hand!" (chap. 33). Heathcliff's fulfillment must be expressed in something other than the destruction of the society around him. It must be expressed in his achievement of transcendent union with Catherine, a union expressed in death by his "frightful, life-like gaze of exultation" (chap. 34). With that consummation the social order reasserts itself, but not by any victory over Heathcliff. Heathcliff has won his battle, a battle to be united with Catherine in a oneness beyond embodiment.

Society in *Wuthering Heights* is not the medium that determines what happens to Catherine and Heathcliff. It is true that society contributes to their destruction, but it does so simply because it is there, and, like other forms of human existence, is thus an obstacle to suprahuman existence. But society does not have the same importance in shaping the quality of individual lives and fates as it has in other novels. Rather, the characters are driven by their belief in an existence beyond themselves.

The ordinary social order depicted in *Wuthering Heights* serves as our vehicle for understanding Catherine and Heathcliff. One is a background for defining the other, as a shape with no color (black) is defined by placing it against a color. The novel uses society as a vehicle to the beyond and so challenges us to transcend the limits of what we can humanly know and to contemplate the elemental, the material, the suprahuman in which we might also participate.

"Rumbling Toward Heaven": Dual Contexts for Being in O'Connor's Fiction

Flannery O'Connor's fiction poses the same challenge as Brontë's. Of her own work O'Connor said, "If the writer believes that our life is and will remain essentially mysterious, if he looks upon us as beings existing in a created order to whose laws we freely respond, then what he sees on the surface will be of interest to him only as he can go through it into an experience of mystery itself."[12] Although the writer's words do not necessarily offer insight into her work, O'Connor's comments suggest her own impulse to be similar to Brontë's. O'Connor argues that the region, the local environment, is something that the writer has to use in order to suggest what is beyond it: "Fiction begins where human knowledge begins—with the senses—and every fiction writer is bound by this fundamental aspect of his medium," but the writer must make "his gaze extend beyond the surface, beyond mere problems, until it touches that realm which is the concern of prophets and poets."[13] A writer must use the region to suggest what is beyond it. A similar concept informed Brontë's novel. Through Nelly Dean and her normative perspectives we were able to glimpse beyond, because the characters were "incoherent" or inexplicable by Nelly's standards. For Flannery O'Connor, too, "the characters have an inner coherence, if not always a coherence to their social framework. Their fictional qualities lean away from typical social patterns, toward mystery and the unexpected."[14]

O'Connor, for all her theological differences from Brontë, speaks of action in the same way that Brontë's *Wuthering Heights* reveals her to have understood it, that is, as illuminating an existence of ours beyond us. This is what the offering of grace means to an O'Connor protagonist, not a validation of doctrine and dogma, but an entry into the mystery of existence beyond human forms and institutions.

Society in O'Connor's fiction concentrates largely on the middle and lower classes in the American South, a world of sharp divisions between black and white, old and new, bankrupt aristocracy and white trash. It is a world highly conscious of itself and its divisions. Julian's mother in "Everything That Rises Must Converge" says of blacks, "They should rise, yes, but on their own side of the fence."[15] Or she proudly asserts of the other women in her reducing class, "Most of them in it are not our kind of people . . . but I can be gracious to anybody. I know who I am."[16] Knowing who one is and where one fits in the social structure is a surety and clarity typical of an O'Connor protagonist. Both Julian and his mother are sure they know who they are.

Yet this firm grasp of social reality marks a major limitation of character in O'Connor's world. In *The Violent Bear It Away*, the old man, Tarwater, says of his nephew, Rayber, "He don't know it's anything he can't know. . . . That's his trouble."[17] That failure defines a great sin, the refusal to recognize the limits of one's ability to know. It is the great, self-professed sin of intellectuals. Rayber shares it with Julian of "Everything That Rises," Asbery Fox of "The Enduring Chill," and Shepherd of "The Lame Shall Enter First." These characters seek to control reality by making everything into a stateable formula or concept. Old Tarwater rails at Rayber because "he felt he was tied hand and foot inside the schoolteacher's head" (chap. 2). The metaphorical straightjacket of Rayber's mind recalls the literal one in which Rayber's parents confined the old man. Those who do not accept earth-bound reality are branded by society as crazy. "Reality" for these would-be intellectuals consists of knowable, limited social facts. Rayber argues with Old Tarwater over the boy: "This one is going to be brought up to live in the real world. He's going to be brought up to expect exactly what he can do for himself." No mysteries of salvation here. Rayber resents having been pushed "out of the real world and I stayed out of it until I didn't know which was which" (chap. 2). He has straightened his own confusion "by pure will power," blocking the "irrational and abnormal," which focus in his unreasoning love for his idiot child, Bishop: "a love . . . so outrageous that he would be left shocked and depressed for days, and trembling for his sanity" (chap. 4).

Through characters who insist on concrete "reality," Flannery O'Connor empowers us to glimpse the mystery beyond. Their impoverished reality points unswervingly to an alternative. The more they insist on seeing the "truth," the less they seem to see. Blind and deaf, they construct their worlds to keep out light and sound. Rayber maintains a precarious balance by not looking at anything too long; anything he looked at too long could overwhelm him with horrifying love. So he starves himself; "he denied his senses unnecessary satisfactions" (chap. 4). He is literally deaf—in need of a hearing aid, which appears to wire his head with electric current. His son, Bishop, represents both the love he has repressed and his access to a larger reality. Young Tarwater sees the boy and his father as inseparably joined: "The child might have been a deformed part of himself that had been accidentally revealed" (chap. 3). When young Tarwater drowns the child, Bishop's bellow echoes in Rayber's hearing aid: "The machine made the sounds seem to come from inside him as if something in him were tearing itself free" (chap. 9). But the schoolteacher, who has denied any larger reality and who has starved his senses, cannot feel even "the intolerable hurt that was his due" (chap. 9). He confronts simply emptiness.

O'Connor grounds her intimation of another life in the details of this one. Her images and language operate on two levels, one literal and one metaphoric. She speaks articulately of this process of "looking for one image that will connect or combine or embody two points; one is a point in the concrete, and the other is a point not visible to the naked eye, but believed in by him firmly, just as real to him, really, as the one that everybody sees."[18] These images are not metaphors in the usual sense, that of one thing standing for another, as in *Bleak House*, where Chancery stands for the confusion, obfuscation, and enmiring of all society, or in *Middlemarch*, where the web describes the nature of human relationships. In O'Connor's and Brontë's fiction, images are rather translucencies through which alternative meanings are glimpsed simultaneously. Images are a route to prophecy, which, in O'Connor's words, is "a matter of seeing near things with their extensions of meaning and thus of seeing far things close up."[19] In Brontë's novel, the elemental images—weather, rock, landscape—bring the far close up. For example, Lockwood's floundering through snow drifts, which erase the route markers between Wuthering Heights and Thrushcross

Grange, provides an image for the experience of his entering the Heights where social markers are erased. It is a treacherous world for Lockwood, but one in which Heathcliff and Catherine are at home.

Hunger is the dominant transparency in *The Violent Bear It Away*. This image expresses the concerns of quotidian existence while suggesting the realm of the extraordinary, and the ordinariness of this image becomes a vehicle for that mystery. The characters feel hunger, seemingly a physical desire for food, but the physical act of eating never satisfies Old or young Tarwater. Old Tarwater eagerly anticipates his death so that he can sit by the Sea of Galilee and feast on Christ's multiplied loaves and fishes. The old man's literal-minded, fundamentalist application of the biblical story to his life has its laughable aspects. To the boy, his great-uncle's preoccupation stimulates in him "a hideous vision of himself sitting forever with his great-uncle on a green bank, full and sick, staring at a broken fish and a multiplied loaf" (chap. 2).

The narrator's perspective is always outside young Tarwater's literalmindedness. In fact the narrator uses this literal interpretation of religious metaphor to resuggest the mystery of hunger and satiety. The characters are not satisfied; they remain empty. The schoolteacher deliberately starves his senses to stave off "madness": "He kept himself upright on a very narrow line between madness and emptiness, and when the time came for him to lose his balance, he intended to lurch toward emptiness and fall on the side of his choice." When confronted by the boy, the little that Rayber has in reserve is consumed, because the boy's look, "something starved in it, seemed to feed on him" (chap. 4).

In comic and poignant scenes, Rayber tries to tempt Tarwater's appetite with foreign dishes, but the child rejects the food and stares rapt at a single loaf of bread in a bakery window with "the face of someone starving who sees a meal he can't reach laid out before him" (chap. 5). Young Tarwater eats, but the emptiness inside him cannot be filled. "You can't eat," scoffs the schoolteacher, "because something is eating you" (chap. 9). Rayber, who thinks he has the answer—understanding and facing reality—is himself a vessel of emptiness. The boy's stomach gnaws at him, but he insists he " 'ain't hungry for the bread of life' " (chap. 10). Jesus, the bread of life, is, according to Old Tarwater, the only one who can appease hunger. O'Connor often uses this double entendre as an echo in "reality" of the other spiritual plane. This hunger is at the heart of Old Tarwater's madness, and emptiness is the price that Rayber pays for refusing to accept the madness of his hunger.

The boy, too, wants to reject his great-uncle's vision, and his plight is poignant and real. Offered ravioli, hot dogs smeared with mustard, chile, sandwiches, and liquor, the boy eats and drinks in a real effort to be sated. His vomiting becomes an image of a soul-searing hunger unsatisfied by ordinary food and by ordinary existence. In this way, hot dogs and chile are vehicles employed to approach the mystery of Christ's body, his sacrifice and man's salvation, the offering of grace as man's reality. The boy's final recognition is homely and concrete: "When I come to eat, I ain't hungry. . . . It's like being empty is a thing in my stomach and it don't allow nothing else to come down in there. If I ate it, I would throw it up" (chap. 10). He finally accepts that "nothing on earth would fill him. His hunger was so great that he could have eaten all the loaves and fishes after they were multiplied" (chap. 12). His destiny, "GO WARN THE CHILDREN OF GOD OF THE TERRIBLE SPEED OF MERCY," is revealed as his eyes are opened to a new reality.

This transcendent reality arrests the characters in O'Connor's world. They seek to control their existence, to know who they are, to anatomize the social structure and their place in it; they seek, in other words, to lock reality into their heads. For example, Mrs. Turpin, in "Revelation," has her world well figured out: "Sometimes Mrs. Turpin occupied herself at night naming the classes of people. On the bottom of the heap were most colored people, not the kind she would have been if she had been one, but most of them; then next to them—not above, just away from—were the white-trash; then above them were the home-owners, and above them the home-and-land owners, to which she and Claud belonged. Above she and Claud were people with a lot of money and much bigger houses and much more land."[20] But a larger reality waits to confront her. It may, as it does in "Revelation," look out unexpectedly from strange and hostile eyes, and the challenge may be delivered in pungent and colloquial diction: "Go back to hell where you came from, you old wart hog."[21] Mrs. Turpin may seek to deny the truth of that statement, but the revelation of a larger reality cannot finally be denied:

A visionary light settled in her eyes. She saw the streak [of light] as a vast swinging bridge extending upward from the earth through a field of living fire. Upon it a vast horde of souls were rumbling toward heaven. There were whole companies of white-trash, clean for the first time in their lives, and bands of black niggers in white robes, and battalions of freaks and lunatics shouting and clapping and leaping like frogs. And bringing up the end of the procession was a tribe of people whom she recognized at once as those who, like herself and Claud, had always had a little of everything and the God-given wit to use it right. She leaned forward to observe them closer. They were marching behind the others with great dignity, accountable as they had always been for good order and common sense and respectable behavior. They alone were on key. Yet she could see by their shocked and altered faces that even their virtues were being burned away.[22]

In this vision the fiction's meaning lies.

Society has thus become a vehicle to explore a larger reality beyond itself. Characters' responses to society's expectations do not invest their lives with meaning. That meaning waits for an elemental or transcendent reality, "an existence of yours beyond you." Only in that sphere are burning hungers appeased—Heathcliff's for unity with Catherine, Tarwater's for satiety.

That larger meaning can be approached only through spheres of the ordinary. Thus society has assumed a special and important function. It is our means for apprehending the mysterious. Images, too, become windows from one world to another, translucencies through which alternative meanings are glimpsed; to paraphrase O'Connor, the near with its extensions of meaning makes the far close up.

Social norms, attitudes, values, and expectations help us chart the characters' progress within their societies, but they cannot explain the forces that drive the characters. We discover an unusual divorce between what is happening socially to a character and the locus of his or her meaning. As Tarwater simultaneously baptizes and drowns the idiot child, Bishop, he is becoming increasingly alienated from his society, but he is approaching his self-realization. The fact that he is guilty of murder is relatively unimportant.

Likewise, Heathcliff's frustration and vengeance lead to social alienation, but the havoc he wreaks in his world pales in importance beside his approaching unearthly consummation with Catherine.

Ethical questions arrest us in our reading of these novelists. Society is the context in which we usually explore morality. When society is precluded as a significant context for meaning, ordinary ethics become strikingly irrelevant. O'Connor and Brontë are no longer concerned primarily with how individuals can peacefully coexist, with what kind of relationships they can evolve to fulfill both themselves and their roles in society. Although man lives in society, he is not conceived primarily as a social being. Catherine Earnshaw voices the challenge that these novelists pose: "What is the use of our existence if we are entirely contained here?" Most writers assume that the meaning of our existence must be predicated on the fact that we are largely contained here; we make our world even as it makes us. This position has obvious consequences for ethics.

It is strange to call a religious novelist like Flannery O'Connor nonethical, but that is precisely the issue here. Brontë and O'Connor come to the novel at that point before philosophy becomes ethics, the point at which one is still querying the nature of existence. Ordinary ethics, social ethics, are predicated on a conclusion that these novelists are not willing to draw. They pose, instead, the question of reality itself and argue the simultaneity of human and suprahuman existence.

8

Society and the Problematics of Knowledge in Faulkner, Kafka, and Pynchon

"Jesus, if I was going to spend nine months in this climate, I would sure hate to have come from the South. Maybe I wouldn't come from the South anyway, even if I could stay there. Wait. Listen. I'm not trying to be funny, smart. I just want to understand it if I can and I don't know how to say it better. Because it's something my people haven't got."
—Shreve speaking to Quentin in William Faulkner,
  Absalom, Absalom!

Instead they let K. go anywhere he liked—of course only within the village—and thus pampered and enervated him, ruled out all possibility of conflict, and transposed him to an unofficial, totally unrecognized, troubled, and alien existence. In this life it might easily happen, if he was not always on his guard, that some day or other, in spite of the amiability of the authorities and the scrupulous fulfillment of all his exaggeratedly light duties, he might—deceived by the apparent favor shown him—conduct himself so imprudently as to get a fall. . . .
—Franz Kafka, *The Castle*

Brontë and O'Connor use society to capture a mysterious reality beyond human, social reality; they look for a source of mystery outside society, but other novelists recognized that society itself might become the mystery that the characters seek to penetrate. In the modern novel, where knowledge is problematic, society gives focus to a novelist's epistemological questions. Twentieth-century novels employ society in a new way, a way that might be called the "excluded middle" as Pynchon's Oedipa Maas terms her experience in *The Crying of Lot 49*. What is excluded? These novelists exclude a knowable reality, that which in the nineteenth-century novel defines a character. In the nineteenth-century novel, a character's conflict with and accommodation to a world outside himself, potentially knowable and autonomous, defines him and shapes his fate. Characters in these novels can be defined and their destiny charted by the degree to which they are capable of transcending self, of imagining community, of understanding the nature of their worlds and their possibilities in them. Society was not easily known nor its influence easily grasped, so the degree to which characters mastered their mediums became a subtle indication of personality and worth. Most novels function in this middle ground of a difficult, knowable reality, not easily knowable but potentially knowable. Its influence is real and tangible. When it is possible to know, one's perceptions are tentative, the progress slow, often painful. Life expresses the effects of one's medium.

When knowledge of truth, of society, is impossible, then one's perceptions become absolute and definitive for oneself. An individual has no choice but to act on what he or she believes, to shape a personal destiny by the perception of one's medium. In an individual's pursuit of meaning, society often assumes bizarre forms, forms that suggest the projection of individual mind and ego on the object in quest. Often the vision dims; the doubt sets in. Has one discovered an autonomous and self-sustaining reality, or has one only projected one's deepest wishes and fears into fantastic visions and chimeras?

The formal role of society in these quest novels is interwoven with themes that are defined as the novels develop. Society is both the medium in which individual actions and fates unfold and the object or end that the characters seek. As a result of this dual role, society is not a fixed or constant set of values. It becomes instead a more crude set of impressions and glimpsed truths, which the questor attempts to order and to understand. Thus, in *Absalom, Absalom!*, Quentin Compson struggles to find a social truth about Sutpen and the South in order to locate and come to terms with his own place in contemporary society, while in *The Castle*, K. seeks underlying connections between the Castle and the village to discover both meaning and affirmation for his existence. Finally, in *The Crying of Lot 49*, Oedipa Maas seeks an alternative to her southern California "tower" by exploring the limits to that culture. In each case, society is both the medium for the characters' actions and fates, and the key to unlocking the meaning of their quests.

Despite great doubts about the ability to know reality and even about objective reality itself, Faulkner, Kafka, and Pynchon share an important conclusion with earlier novelists we have looked at, and that is that society, whether real or imagined, exerts an enormous influence on individual life. This combination of doubt about the nature of reality and of certainty about the need for individuals to confront, or if necessary to create, a world outside themselves has generated new forms of tragedy and pathos. However destructive these imagined systems, they are a hedge against an individual's self-absorption; they express commitment and relationship to something beyond self, whether hated or desired.

Mystery at the Heart of Society in *Absalom, Absalom!*

When Quentin Compson breathes into the cold dark of New England, "*I dont hate it* [the South]! *I dont hate it*," he is rebelling against something so tenuous and intangible that his Canadian friend, Shreve, cannot even begin to understand. Yet tenuous and intangible as that world is, it is the central shaping force in Quentin's life.

Absalom, Absalom! details several quests for meaning that offer varied interpretations of the novel's events. Sutpen and his life provide the object for that larger search. He serves, thus, as one center of the novel, but the quest focuses upon young Quentin Compson, ready to leave for the North and Harvard College, yet bound by a world from which he cannot escape: "The Quentin Compson who was still too young to deserve yet to be a ghost, but nevertheless having to be one for all that, since he was born and bred in the deep South."[1] Sutpen's life is explained variously but the terms of explanation all revolve around social norms, expectations, and conventions and are born of social definitions of responsibility and success. Quentin now seeks to liberate himself from this entangling medium, a medium that has sown the seeds of destruction for Sutpen, Judith, Henry, and Charles Bon. Whether real or imagined, however, that shaping medium is woven into his existence. In *Absalom, Absalom!*, then, Faulkner shows us that while society may not be an autonomous thing, subject as it is to individual interpretation and perception, society is nonetheless the medium that forms human experience. Although Quentin cannot "know" his world, it is ineluctably shaping his destiny. This merging of society as medium for definition and object of quest gives rise to the tragic poignancy of *Absalom, Absalom!*

Olga Vickery has postulated a tension in Faulkner's novels, a tension between mystery and reality. This tension expresses Faulkner's contrary aims. On the one hand, he seeks to capture truth: concrete, tangible truths based in the land, people, and customs. On the other hand, he acknowledges the primacy of mystery, a final unknowingness. In Vickery's words, Faulkner "ventures into the unknown and interrogates the known."[2] This procedure sounds reminiscent of Brontë and O'Connor, but no separate planes exist in Faulkner. For him, the unknown lies at the heart of the known, and the more the characters probe the known, the more elusive becomes the truth they seek.[3]

Elements of Faulkner's novel make it paradigmatically southern. Embroidered as the story is with chivalrous distinctions among ladies, women, and females, with class distinctions between plantation owners and "white trash," and with racial distinctions, it is both a story of Sutpen's destruction and of the forces that destroy the culture.[4] In their interpretations of Sutpen, four minds—Rosa Coldfield's, Quentin's father's, his grandfather's, and Quentin's—reflect not only his significance but the significance of a whole culture embodied in individual lives.[5] Thus, as Sutpen's story unfolds, Quentin, though two generations later, feels increasingly trapped by the same forces that defeated Sutpen. But the social categories that defined Sutpen, and that now define Quentin, become increasingly elusive and insidious. The relatively simple categories from the first generation are inadequate for later generations, but the imperative to know increases with the oppressive, cumulative weight of culture.

Elementally opposed in their interpretations, Rosa Coldfield and Quentin's grandfather, both from Sutpen's generation, present an interesting contrast. To the former, Sutpen's story embodies his diabolicism; to the latter, Sutpen's history reflects a basic innocence. These terms, diabolical/demonic and innocent, derive their meaning from the cultural perspectives of the speakers. We saw earlier that the uniqueness of Brontë's Heathcliff among demonic figures stems from Brontë's refusal to place him within any ethical hierarchy. This, too, was Dorotohy Van Ghent's point: "Heathcliff is no more ethically relevant than is flood or earthquake or whirlwind. It is as impossible to speak of him in terms of 'sin' or 'guilt' as it is to speak in this way of the natural elements or the creatures of the animal world."[6]

Clearly established in an ethical hierarchy, Sutpen is no Heathcliff. On Rosa Coldfield's scale of values, Sutpen is a demon. In her discursive opening narrative, she tenaciously returns to issues of respectability and establishment. The fact that Sutpen has usurped civilized appearances outrages her sensibilities and merits the epithets "fiend blackguard and devil" for him:

> He wasn't a gentleman. He wasn't even a gentleman. He came here with a horse and two pistols and a name which nobody ever heard before, knew for certain was his own any more than the horse was his own or even the pistols, seeking some place to hide himself . . . and Jefferson gave him that. Then he needed respectability, the shield of a virtuous woman, to make his position impregnable . . . and it was mine and Ellen's father who gave him that . . . and he, fiend blackguard and devil, in Virginia fighting, where the chances of the earth's being rid of him were the best anywhere under the sun, yet Ellen and I both knowing that he would return, that every man in our armies would have to fall before bullet or ball found him . . . a man who so far as anyone . . . knew either had no past at all or did not dare reveal it . . . a man who fled here and hid, concealed himself behind respectability. . . .
>
> No: not even a gentleman. Marrying Ellen or marrying ten thousand Ellens could not have made him one. Not that he wanted to be one, or even be taken for one. . . . And the very fact that he had had to choose respectability to hide behind

was proof enough (if anyone needed further proof) that what he fled from must have been some opposite of respectability too dark to talk about [chap. 1].

To Rosa, demonism means a major breach of decorum, of convention. "He wasn't even a gentleman," and he does not care. Sutpen ruthlessly purchases or otherwise acquires the appurtenances of respectability, and in his person reveals the impotence of a decaying world. Rosa's gothicism—her talk of "fatality and curses on the South and on our family," "dark forces of fate" (chaps. 1, 5)—is grounded in a sense of "right" and right violated. For Sutpen's travesty of that which is sacred, this sacred vessel of southern gentility rains imprecations on his head. Rosa furiously affirms her interpretation of cultural imperatives and insists on the value of tradition. Shreve later picks up her vocabulary, calling Sutpen "this Faust, this demon, this Beelzebub" to capture her "mortal affront" at Sutpen's suggestion that he and Miss Rosa "breed together for test" before marriage (chap. 6).

Quentin's grandfather proceeds from the opposite assumption, that "Sutpen's trouble was innocence." Innocence stems from an ignorance of social reality and social convention. In his view, Sutpen suffered an insult at age fourteen that transformed his life. He was told by a "monkey-nigger . . . never to come to that front door again but to go around to the back" (chap. 7). In this episode, Sutpen discovered what he had not even known "existed to be wanted," that "there was a country all divided and fixed and neat with a people living on it all divided and fixed and neat because of what color their skins happened to be and what they happened to own" (chap. 7). He discovers, in short, civilized society, an order not governed simply by strength or endurance: "He had learned the difference not only between white men and black ones, but he was learning that here was a difference between white men and white men, not to be measured by lifting anvils or gouging eyes or how much whiskey you could drink then get up and walk out of the room" (chap. 7). He cannot resolve *this* insult by shooting the "nigger monkey"; he needs a bigger rifle. He needs, in short, "land and niggers and a fine house"; "to combat them you have got to have what they have that made them do what the man did" (chap. 7). So, to Quentin's grandfather, Sutpen sets out to found his dynasty, to drag civilization out of the hostile land so that his son and his son's son may inherit after him.[7]

Sutpen's description of this action as creating a "bigger rifle" is an apt one, since he pursues one set of social goals but lives by the more primitive ones by which he was raised. Hence he is "innocent," as Quentin's grandfather explains; he believes that "the ingredients of morality were like the ingredients of pie or cake and once you had measured them and balanced them and mixed them and put them into the oven it was all finished and nothing but pie or cake could come out" (chap. 7). It is an "innocence" that leads to Sutpen's particular insensitivity and ruthlessness. It is, then, innocence or demonry—whichever way one looks at Sutpen's responsibility to the social ethic—that enables him both to insult Miss Rosa by suggesting they breed before marrying, or, more serious, to refuse to acknowledge Charles Bon as "my son."

From Miss Rosa and Quentin's grandfather, we have two versions of Sutpen, each interpretation dictated by the teller's understanding of social convention and expectation and by what each concludes Sutpen either did not know or ignored.

All of the characters must construct a reality that forms and informs their lives, but that reality becomes increasingly elusive, subtle, and complex. So Mr. Compson, Quentin's father, provides an elegant interpretation of Henry's outrage at Charles Bon. He refuses the simpler categories, innocent or demonic, but his are also firmly grounded in his ideas about society. He takes his distinctions from prerogatives of blood and kinship set against those of inheritance, class, and race.

Lacking knowledge of Sutpen's relationship to Charles Bon and of Charles Bon's Negroid blood, he fabricates a story that proves remote from the literal "truth". His narrative dwells on the ceremony between Bon and an octoroon woman, the ceremony at which Henry must have rebelled and for which he must finally have killed Bon. This elaborate tale distinguishes among ladies, women, and females: "the virgins whom gentlemen someday married, the courtesans to whom they went while on sabbaticals to the cities, the slave girls and women upon whom that first caste rested" (chap. 4). Since riding and hunting "make importunate the blood of a young man," Henry himself must have yielded to Negroid flesh, so it cannot be the mere fact of Charles Bon's relationship with a Negro that is in question. No, it is the ceremony, a "ceremony entered into, to be sure, with a negro, yet still a ceremony" (chap. 4). Mr. Compson calls Henry's reaction a "fetish-ridden moral blundering which did not deserve to be called thinking" (chap. 4), but in so doing he affirms the authority of social conditioning.

Mr. Compson's whole explanation is finally shown to have little basis in fact, but, ironically, the spirit of his account, with its discriminations and distinctions, is relevant. As we untangle layers of rationales for Henry's shooting Bon—first the ceremony, then the incest, then the fact of Bon's Negroid blood—we move back to the basic assumptions of Mr. Compson's narrative, that the Negroid blood made Bon's relationship with the octoroon essentially unserious, that it invalidated the ceremony. Only now Bon is the Negro, and a black man may not impregnate the "ladies," "the virgins whom gentlemen someday married." For Judith to marry Charles Bon would defeat Sutpen's dynasty, which is built on distinctions between "white men and black ones," between "white men and white men," which are not distinctions of strength. For the same reason that Judith cannot marry Bon, Sutpen cannot acknowledge Bon;[8] it would interfere with a design predicated on a country "all divided and fixed and neat." Sutpen is heroic in his way if we see heroism as describing man's relationship to his society, his affirmation of order, his commitment to ideals, but Sutpen is tragically heroic since he denies the human heart, treating his son, Charles Bon, with the same contempt that greeted him as a fourteen-year-old child: "He just told you [Bon tells Henry], sent me a message like you send a command by a nigger servant to a beggar or a tramp to clear out" (chap. 8). Of course, too, the ideals that Sutpen upholds have decayed. Quentin, reporting his father's words, explains Mr. Coldfield's decision to help Sutpen as born of a hope that "the South would realize that it was now paying the price for having erected its economic edifice not on the rock of stern morality but on the shifting sands of opportunism and moral brigandage" (chap. 7).

In the center of all of these explanations for Sutpen's life and destruction stands the questing figure of Quentin. The whole culture culminates in Quentin, and the only way to escape this hall of mirrors is to disentangle its meaning. Even at the novel's beginning Quentin feels himself trapped by his southern heritage; "his very body was an empty hall echoing with sonorous defeated names; he was not a being, an entity, he was a commonwealth" (chap. 1). Quentin's fate is tragic because he cannot finally master and quiet these echoes.

What society is actually must remain a personal interpretation, unknowable by others. At Harvard Quentin is set apart because of his social heritage: *"Tell us about the South. What's it like there. What do they do there. Why do they live there. Why do they live at all"* (chap. 6). Shreve scoffs, "Jesus, the South is fine, isn't it. It's better than the theatre, isn't it. It's better than Ben Hur, isn't it. No wonder you have to come away now and then, isn't it" (chap. 7). Shreve will try to argue against the authority of that experience, distinguishing it from his own: "We dont live among defeated grandfathers and freed slaves . . . and bullets in the dining room table and such, to be always reminding us to never forget. What is it? Something you live and breathe in like air? . . . a kind of en-tailed birthright father and son . . . so that forevermore as long as your childrens' children produce children you wont be anything but a descendant of a long line of colonels killed in Pickett's charge at Manassas?" (chap. 9). Quentin's reply is, of course, "You cant understand it. You would have to be born there."[9]

Quentin's fate expresses the effects of having been "born there." He sees his destiny as a rippling of endless effects from the past: "Maybe nothing ever happens once and is finished. Maybe happen is never once but like ripples maybe on water after the pebble sinks, the ripples moving on spreading" (chap. 7)[10] and desper-ately speculates, "Am I going to have to hear it all again . . . I am going to have to hear it all over again. I am already hearing it all over again" (chap. 7).[11] Later he broods, "Nevermore of peace. Nevermore, Nevermore, Nevermore" (chap. 9).

Because the story of Sutpen is finally an hypothesis, a piecing together of facts, an interpretation, which takes as its premise the authority of that particular experience that is southern experience, what should impress us is the "reality" of that authority and not its objective "truth." It is precisely the speculation that takes place throughout the novel that takes us to the heart of the mystery. The reality of that experience cannot be known, but the reality of the authority is everywhere present. Hence, when Shreve expresses his incomprehension and asks his unanswerable question, "Why do you hate the South?" Quentin vehemently refuses, *"I dont hate it! I dont hate it!"* (chap. 9). Quentin expresses the desperate attempt to live with something he can neither escape nor fully understand.

Quentin is finally furiously in conflict with his own experience of a society, an experience grounded in his interpretation of a past. Both personal experience and interpretation haunt him. He needs them even as he needs to reject them. So society is presented, paradoxically, as unknowable, yet inescapable. It functions as Quentin's own inner imperative that is given objective force in his life.

Through a Glass Darkly: Society in *The Castle*

The Castle is reminiscent of Brontë's and O'Connor's fiction because of its interest in separate realities. K.'s search can be seen as one for the "unaccessible transcendent world," the novel's central theme as "the grotesque unconnection between the human being and the transcendental; the incommensurability of the divine."[12] Although similar in this way, Kafka differs from the others in the formal arrangements between character and the society he creates. O'Connor and Brontë stress the duality of human and suprahuman existence; society, as represented, is ordinary and recognizable. It comprises a familiar locale, familiar expectations and conventions; it exploits familiar distinctions among classes: rich/poor, master/servant, white/black. We approach the mystery of a reality beyond by discovering the irrelevance of social norms, conventions, and expectations to explain the characters' fates.

In Kafka's novel, by contrast, society assumes fantastic dimensions. Rather than emphasizing the duality of human and suprahuman existence, Kafka has fused the two. Quotidian reality blends into a bizarre, surrealistic landscape. Thrust into this fantastical milieu, the hero becomes a questor. K. seeks to penetrate the Castle, but his meaning and significance finally come through his experiences in the village. There, characters attempt to mirror what they believe exists in the Castle but cannot know with any certainty. Reminiscent of Brontë's and O'Connor's transcendent realms of existence, Kafka's *Castle* differs substantially in form. Here, the protagonist's only meaning comes through the village, that commonplace reality that, however convoluted and distorted, may be, after all, the only source of man's meaning.

K.'s quest for the Castle ends in neither success nor failure, not simply because Kafka did not finish the novel, but also because K. can never be perfectly objective in his search for the social reality of the scene. As perceiver, he inevitably becomes part of the village and obstructs his own "objective" line of sight. Messages, as from Klamm, themselves prove ambiguous and unreliable. We are left finally with the village as the source of K.'s achievement; it encompasses what he knows, and, because the implied author does not reveal the Castle, suggests to us the limits of what any one can ever know. Society cannot be precluded in favor of an alternate realm for knowledge and existence as it is in Brontë and O'Connor. Rather society can only be made a mirror of the characters' desires for such a realm. The village itself remains the source of quests and the shaper of fates.

The Castle encompasses three sets of values: those belonging to K., those of the village, and those of the Castle. K. looks to the village as an image of the Castle and attempts to approach the Castle by conforming to the village. The village is represented as a society, but to speak of society in this novel is problematic because fictional societies are usually mimetically convincing even if they are not determined solely by mimetic considerations. We recognize a real place, logical and coherent relationships.

Kafka's world belongs to the realm of nightmare. For example, K. is appointed—or imagines he is or only wishes he were—land-surveyor. He has "new assistants" who are his "old assistants," the ones whose arrival he has been awaiting. Days end suddenly, seemingly just begun: "Just a short time ago it had been uniform daylight, and now the darkness of night was upon them."[13] These are not just irrational projections of one character's mind. Others share them. For example, Pepi points out that winter is protracted eternally: "spring and summer seem as short as though they didn't last much longer than two days, and even on those days, even during the most beautiful day, even then sometimes snow falls" (chap. 20). In the face of this bizarre order of existence, a "normal" suggestion, such as Frieda's request that she and K. go to the South of France or Spain, sounds absurd and improbable. The seeming absurdity of the normal is perhaps the point. Kafka's village has all the properties of societies: norms, taboos, restrictions, ostracisms, hierarchies, class distinctions, and an economic structure of some kind. We recognize, for example, that K. had more status as land-surveyor than he does as school janitor; he sinks still further when he accepts a bed with the chambermaids. The village establishes its own probabilities, even if the probable is bizarre and exaggerated, and we respond to them as does K.: they are potentially knowable. In this respect, Kafka's novel illustrates a basic point: that, when we look for society in a novel, we search for patterned values not for mimetic accuracy.

The village has built its structures on what it believes is happening at the Castle, but its beliefs are mere hypotheses. The structures, however, are not. They have real consequences for the characters. As in Faulkner, belief in a structure gives it the power to affect lives. When Olga Barnabas tells the story of her family's ruin, she insists that "it's all engineered from the Castle" (Amalia's Secret). Her recital of the community's ostracism provokes K.'s question, "And where do you see in all this the influence of the Castle? . . . So far it doesn't seem to have come in. What you've told me about is simply the ordinary senseless fear of the people, malicious pleasure in hurting a neighbor, specious friendship, things that can be found anywhere" (Amalia's Punishment). In short, to K., the Barnabas family's assumption of guilt has provoked society's punishment of them. Their belief in the Castle's censure has changed the structure of their lives. As if in confirmation, Olga admits: "It wasn't our family that was taboo, it was the affair. . . . So if we had quietly come forward again and let bygones be bygones . . . and reassured public opinion that it was never likely to be mentioned again . . . everything would have been made all right in that way too" (Amalia's Punishment). Still, even in the face of Olga's recognition, it is not clear that this ruin was not engineered by the Castle. What is clear is the characters' inability finally to know the source of their condemnation. Whether it stems from the Castle itself or only from their belief in that authority remains in doubt. At all times the characters seek to model their social existence in the village in accordance with what they perceive to be the Castle's policy. Of course, they can never know that policy; they can only confront its inexplicability.

Kafka's *The Castle*, like Faulkner's *Absalom, Absalom!*, raises major epistemological questions. K. is pursuing the meaning of the transcendent, "a clearer meaning than the muddle of everyday life" (chap. 1), but he must pursue it through the muddle of everyday life. He originates interpretations, and his own understanding of village society and its relation to the Castle becomes the authority on which he acts and by which he relates to the world around him. Society, for Kafka's K., must be the medium for his search, but frustrating that search is the recognition that the medium is not the goal of his quest. K.'s ordeal is further complicated by his unfamiliarity with the village and its customs. He is an outsider, the alien, the stranger. A local landlady tells him, "You are not from the Castle, you are not from the village, you aren't anything" (chap. 4). Later she chastises him, "Your ignorance of the local situation is so appalling that it makes my head go round to listen to you and compare your ideas and opinions with the real state of things," and so she cautions, "never forget that you're the most ignorant person in the village" (chap. 4). The village mayor confirms K.'s naivete: "All those contacts of yours have been illusory, but because of your ignorance of the circumstances you take them to be real" (chap. 5). But K. feels that only by establishing certain kinds of social relationships can he proceed to acquire necessary knowledge. Later, of course, he is assured that his procedure has been ridiculous: "According to the reports I've received he takes everything too seriously. He has just got to the village and starts off thinking that a great experience, whereas in reality it's nothing at all" (chap. 16). Nonetheless, even in the face of these negations, K. has no choice but to value and to act on his experience in the village as he interprets it. There exists no other measure by which he, or in fact anyone else, can live. Whether he has understood any part of his experience rightly, he must proceed on the basis of his interpretation.

Then, again, these negations are not definitive because surviving in the village may guarantee access to the Castle. The schoolteacher early corrects K.—who, looking for his peers, complains, "I don't fit in with the peasants, nor, I imagine, with the Castle"—with the caution, "There is no difference between the peasantry and the Castle" (chap. 1). Propaganda or truth? It may be that Godhead expresses itself in human community.[14] In the reported end of the novel, K. is finally granted permission to live in the village. He has succeeded not through his efforts but only through "certain auxiliary circumstances."[15] His quest, then, for the Castle is concluded by his official establishment in the community.

In short, uncertain meanings of K.'s experience do not affect his fate. Paul Goodman's formal analysis of *The Castle* concludes that "the particular allegories . . . are important not in content but in form, just as man substitutes one ideology for another and still is unchanged in character and destiny."[16] *The Castle* is not allegorical in the sense that the *Faerie Queen* is. By comparison, *The Castle* becomes a kind of existential *Faerie Queen* with the Red Cross Knight narrating, the meaning of his experience and fate uncertain, but that experience and fate remain unchanged despite the uncertainty of meaning.

Of special interest to our study of society in the novel, then, are the ways in which K. is limited by his humanness. Having no way to apprehend the Castle, he must rely on social structures, on structuring meaning in terms of social experience, seeking truth through the village. For example, K. responds to Klamm's first letter only after examining it closely, an examination predicated on ideas about social organization: "These were inconsistencies, no doubt about it. They were so obvious that they had to be faced. It hardly occurred to K. that they might be due to indecision; that seemed a mad idea in connection with such an organization. He was much more inclined to read into them a frankly offered choice." We are invited to consider an alternative interpretation to K.'s, but we have no way of deciding other than he does: "Only as a worker in the village, removed as far as possible from the sphere of the Castle, could he hope to achieve anything in the Castle itself" (chap. 2).

Later he reaffirms his perception, "He had been persuaded that in this village everybody meant something to him, and indeed he was not mistaken" (chap. 2). He seizes on Frieda, Klamm's mistress, as an avenue to Klamm; he pursues the Barnabas family for the same reason; he questions Hans Lasemann in a scene that provokes Frieda's conclusion that "before you knew me you were without any hope, but . . . now you imagine that in me you have a reliable means of reaching Klamm certainly and quickly and even with advantage to yourself" (chap. 13). Finally, he feels drawn to Pepi because, as Frieda's successor, "she too, apparently, had connections with the Castle" (chap. 8).

K. looks to these socially well-established or socially disenfranchised creatures as a means of rescue, but just as he, as outsider, wants to use them to advance himself, so these same individuals see him as a possible avenue of escape from their social dilemmas. K.'s pursuit of these figures and their pursuit of him parodies basic fairy-tale patterns, that of the beast redeemed to humanity by the beautiful woman and that of the maiden in distress rescued by the arrival of a strange prince.[17] Unlike the fairy tale, however, a miraculous clarity and rescue are not likely here. K. expects rescue by Frieda, by Olga, by Hans's mother, by Pepi. As he appropriates them, they take on a new significance that is shaped by their relationship to him. Frieda is no longer Klamm's mistress, only K.'s fiancée. He is a man who "has ruined our dear little Frieda and whom we must unfortunately accept as her husband" (chap. 4). In seeking to approach the Castle, K. has only entangled himself in social relationships that culminate in his "alleged unfaithfulness" to Frieda (chap. 18).

Yet this "truth" is not definitive either. Did K. ruin Frieda? Pepi depicts him as Frieda's rescuer and as her own. The precariousness of Frieda's position in the tap room was such, claims Pepi, that she needed a man with whom she could run off, but "though it had to be a common man, if possible even lower than a servant, much lower than a servant, yet it must be one on whose account one would not be laughed to scorn by every girl" (chap. 20). The land-surveyor fit the role. For Pepi, the removal of Frieda became her avenue of promotion: "K. had appeared, a hero, a rescuer of maidens in distress, and had opened the way upstairs for her" (chap. 20). The final irony is that K., even as knight-errant, has no power to resolve the dilemmas confronting each girl. He temporarily assuages a social problem of prestige and image, but each girl is ultimately returned to her original position, apparently still struggling with the same dilemma.

What are they struggling for? For position and power. They evolve elaborate strategies for gaining and keeping positions in the village, positions that seem to reflect some official sanction by the Castle. Whether they do or not is never known, cannot be known.

Perhaps characters cannot alter their destinies, but they have to care about their destinies. That incessant caring is what links us with K. That caring is what makes *The Castle* more novelistic than allegorical. We share K.'s struggles, his perceptions, his failures. The characters have no choice but to establish some recognizable structures by which to evaluate their progress and their fates. These structures are the structures of a society. Like Faulkner's Quentin, K. finds an essential mystery at the end of his quest, a meaning of existence that cannot be summarized. He has charted a path toward that end by the familiar landmarks of social hierarchies, norms, values, and expectations, all of which have authority for him because they are the source of whatever meaning he actually attains or only imagines. The society is, perhaps, only a source for negation, for concluding what is not truth, but negation, what is not, may be the only avenue to affirmation, to what is. Even here we cannot rest. Burgel suggests the teasing alternative, "I don't want to inquire into what all this really amounts to, perhaps the appearance does really correspond to the reality" (chap. 18).

What distinguishes K.'s quest from that of other questors in the novel is that he seeks his meaning in a social organization. Society, in Kafka's novel, is bizarre and fantastic because it depicts the attempts of a community to make its reality reflect the unknowable. So K. focuses on the village to understand his destiny. The medium for his quest is the bizarre world of the village although the goal of his quest is the Castle itself. Other quest-novels—such as Conrad's *Heart of Darkness*, Proust's *À la recherche du temps perdu*, or Joyce's *A Portrait of the Artist as a Young Man*—rely on social norms and expectations to shape the protagonist's search, but the questor is not seeking to penetrate a social order. It is Kafka's fusion of two orders of existence that enables him to portray the quotidian as an approach, if a futile one, to the transcendent. Since the transcendent is unknowable, society remains the medium in which individual fates are shaped and defined, the object of whatever knowledge is gained.

Pynchon's *Everyman*: Searching for an Alternative Society in *The Crying of Lot 49*

Thomas Pynchon not only makes society the medium for the quest, but he makes discovery of an alternative social order the end of the search. Oedipa Maas, the heroine of Pynchon's *The Crying of Lot 49*, enacts a secular version of *Everyman*, finding at the end of her quest not the heavenly sphere but a "secular Tristero. Power, omniscience, implacable malice, attributes of what they'd thought to be a historical principle, a Zeitgeist, are carried over to the now human enemy."[18]

That alternative order may be real or only imagined, but for Oedipa Maas, it does not finally matter. Either an alternative exists or she will imagine one in an "orbiting ecstasy of true paranoia."

Pynchon would probably argue that any fiction cannot explain the world at all, because fiction is self-referential. Reality is phenomenal, therefore partial and subjective. His resolution to *The Crying of Lot 49* can maintain that philosophy by allowing its protagonist to affirm a society that may or may not exist, but the fact that she needs to believe in it stresses the need all of us feel for a perspective outside ourselves, a meaningful human community in which to understand personal experience and to shape individual destiny.

The novel begins with Oedipa Maas returning from a Tupperware party, a quintessential American social experience, to the news that she has been named executrix of Pierce Inverarity's estate. Her quest begins with her attempts to untangle the extent and legal intricacies of this estate. The world from which she launches herself is an empty one. Her husband, Mucho Maas, her psychiatrist, Dr. Hilarius, and her lawyer, Mr. Roseman, abandon her even at the outset of her quest, but this abandonment anticipates the fairy-tale motif of Pynchon's novel—that of Rapunzel in her tower. Pynchon's use of a fairy-tale motif is reminiscent of Kafka's. In Pynchon, too, the questor must reject the idea of rescue from the outside. Here, more clearly than in Kafka, Oedipa must rely on herself, on her own capacity to penetrate and understand her society in order to free herself, but at the beginning she postulates her tower and her presence there as "visited on her from outside and for no reason at all":

> Such a captive maiden, having plenty of time to think, soon realizes that her tower, its height and architecture, are like her ego only incidental: that what really keeps her where she is is magic, anonymous and malignant, visited on her from outside and for no reason at all. Having no apparatus except gut fear and female cunning to examine this formless magic, to understand how it works, how to measure its field strength, count its lines of force, she may fall back on superstition, or take up a useful hobby like embroidery, or go mad, or marry a disk jockey. If the tower is everywhere and the knight of deliverance no proof against its magic, what else? [chap. 1].

Oedipa seeks to discover the "what else," to find out "if the tower is everywhere." The paradigmatic society she encounters at San Narciso (Inverarity's domicile and headquarters) presents a landscape as bizarre as Kafka's. Scale, dimension, and color are heightened to almost hallucinatory proportions. Society is represented as "less an identifiable city than a group of concepts—census tracts, special purpose bond-issue districts, shopping nuclei, all overlaid with access roads to its own freeway" (chap. 2). The images that strike Oedipa include the "vast sprawl of houses" resembling a radio's printed circuit, Yoyodyne Inc., represented by "two sixty-foot missiles," barbed wire, and a thirty-foot, sheet-metal nymph with "enormous vermillion-tipped breasts and long pink thighs" (chap. 2). The images suggest an impersonal, electronic, nuclear-powered, defensive materialism.

Oedipa initially responds to this world by confirming her imprisonment in the tower, seducing and being seduced by her new lawyer, Metzger. That infidelity, however, brings her to the possibility of "an end [to] her encapsulation in her tower . . . as if there were revelation in progress all around her." She discovers "what she was to label the Tristero System or often only The Tristero" (chap. 3). Whether the connections really exist or whether Oedipa only imagines them stands at the heart of this novel. Clearly dissatisfied and feeling imprisoned, Oedipa is ripe for an alternative.

Oedipa must live out her destiny in this increasingly inimical world even as she is searching for a key to an alternative destiny. To alter that destiny she must envision a new world. Oedipa writes in her memo book, *"Shall I project a world?"* (chap. 4). She deeply desires to penetrate her ignorance, to attain the illumination that seems to hover about her. She examines Pierce Inverarity's will and concludes, "If it was really Pierce's attempt to leave an organized something behind after his own annihilation, then it was part of her duty, wasn't it, to bestow life on what had persisted" (chap. 4). She reflects, "I am meant to remember. Each clue that comes is *supposed* to have its own clarity, its fine chances for permanence" (chap. 5). And all of her clues lead her to project a Tristero.

Tristero focuses on the mail system: "Delivering the mail is a government monopoly," what Mike Fallopian sees as "a parable of power, its feeding, growth and systematic abuse" (chap. 3). Through pursuing subtle hints and connections, obscure editions of the *Courier's Tragedy,* elusive references and allusions, sounds, symbols, seemingly chance circumstances, and children's games, Oedipa pieces together a story of an alternative private channel of communication. She discovers a "separate, silent, unsuspected world," an alternative in America to the public U.S. mail, an alternative to the "life of the Republic": "For here were God knew how many citizens, deliberately choosing not to communicate by U.S. Mail. It was not an act of treason, nor possibly even of defiance. But it was a calculated withdrawal, from the life of the Republic, from its machinery. Whatever else was being denied them out of hate, indifference to the power of their vote, loopholes, simple ignorance, this withdrawal was their own, unpublicized, private. Since they could not have withdrawn in a vacuum (could they?), there had to exist the separate, silent, unsuspected world" (chap. 5). The elaborate history of Tristero which Oedipa unfolds begins in 1577 in the northern provinces of the Low Countries. It is a history that includes not only America but Europe, a history of continuous rebellion against social subjugation.

This discovery of an alternative "society," and thus of an alternative destiny, leads Oedipa to the novel's single moment of tenderness, warmth, and compassion when she cradles a dying, drunken sailor in her arms and offers to deliver a letter to his wife through the underground W.A.S.T.E. As she succors a fellow creature in distress, she prepares for her violent and precipitous weaning from all the men in her life, from her dependencies on familiar social roles. First she loses her psychiatrist, Dr. Hilarius, to madness, then her husband, Mucho, to LSD, and finally her lover, Metzger, to a fifteen-year-old chick: "They are stripping from me . . . they are stripping away, one by one, my men" (chap. 6). Oedipa increasingly relies on herself, increasingly lets go of the supports to her life and, in this process, frees herself for the discovery of alternatives. She must free herself from social assumptions about herself—assumptions based, for example, on the Rapunzel myth that she shares—and she must free herself of her need for these men in order to begin to glimpse alternatives. In pursuing the meaning of Pierce Inverarity's will she discovers that alternative, the "true continuity": "San Narciso had no boundaries. . . . She had dedicated herself, weeks ago, to making sense of what Inverarity had left behind, never suspecting that the legacy was America" (chap. 6). Oedipa finally confronts America; she is now no longer automatically assimilated into that culture but rather is given distance from it by the possibility of Tristero.

At this point, essentially at the end of her quest, Oedipa has to face what is, ultimately, its central question. It is an epistemological question, the problem of how she knows what she knows: whether she is hallucinating and is the victim of an elaborate practical joke by Pierce Inverarity, whether she is hallucinating such a joke, or whether she has actually stumbled, "without the aid of LSD or other indole alkaloids, onto a secret richness and concealed destiny of dream; onto a network by which X number of Americans are truly communicating whilst reserving their lies, recitations of routines, arid betrayals of spiritual poverty, for the official government delivery system; maybe even onto a real alternative to the exitlessness, to the absence of surprise to life, that harrows the head of everybody American you know" (chap. 6).

Oedipa's quest recognizes the need for some alternative destiny to the "exitlessness . . . that harrows the head of everybody American you know." It predicates that new destiny on the discovery of an alternative social order. The sustained lyricism of the conclusion supports the legitimacy of what Oedipa has discovered and gives authority to her perceptions, whether real or imagined:

> Suppose, God, there really was a Tristero then and that she *had* come on it by accident. If San Narciso and the estate were really no different from any other town, any other estate, then by that continuity she might have found The Tristero anywhere in her Republic, through any of a hundred lightly-concealed entranceways, a hundred alienations, if only she'd looked. She stopped a minute between the steel rails, raising her head as if to sniff the air. Becoming conscious of the hard, strung presence she stood on—knowing as if maps had been flashed for her on the sky how these tracks ran on into others, others, knowing they laced, deepened, authenticated the great night around her. If only she'd looked. . . . What was left to inherit? That America coded in Inverarity's testament, whose was that? She thought of other, immobilized freight cars, where the kids sat on the floor planking and sang back, happy as fat, whatever came over the mother's pocket radio; of other squatters who stretched canvas for lean-tos behind smiling billboards along all the highways, or slept in junkyards in the stripped shells of wrecked Plymouths, or even, daring, spent the night up some pole in a lineman's tent like caterpillars, swung among a web of telephone wires, living in the very copper rigging and

secular miracle of communication, untroubled by the dumb voltages flickering their miles, the night long, in the thousands of unheard messages. She remembered drifters she had listened to, Americans speaking their language carefully, scholarly, as if they were in exile from somewhere else invisible yet congruent with the cheered land she lived in; and walkers along the roads at night, zooming in and out of your headlights without looking up, too far from any town to have a real destination. And the voices before and after the dead man's that had phoned at random during the darkest, slowest hours, searching ceaseless among the dial's ten million possibilities for the magical Other who would reveal herself out of the roar of relays, monotone litanies of insult, filth, fantasy, love whose brute repetition must someday call into being the trigger for the unnamable act, the recognition, the Word [chap. 6].

This wisdom affirms the value of Oedipa's discovery: this world may be hers to create if it does not already exist. The fact that she perceives it, that she believes it might exist, has the authority to make it real. She concludes she is "either Oedipa in the orbiting ecstasy of a true paranoia, or [there is] a real Tristero. For there either was some Tristero beyond the appearance of the legacy America, or there was just America and if there was just America then it seemed the only way she could continue, and manage to be at all relevant to it, was as an alien, unfurrowed, assumed full circle into some paranoia" (chap. 6).

Whether Tristero is real or imagined does not finally matter. Oedipa has changed her destiny by belief in an alternative social order. She exists now as an alien to the legacy of America, a would-be member of Tristero should it exist.

One's beliefs remain hypotheses, questioned by other hypotheses. For characters, this unknowable society can be enabling or destructive. Certainly, Quentin Compson is finally unable to cope with the cumulative force of his interpretation of social experience. Oedipa Maas, in contrast, finds the cumulative weight of a potential society the major source of her affirmation. K., too, needs his conception of social structures to continue his quest, but his success seems even more precarious than Oedipa's, as any achievement of a fate must be precarious when society is presented as both unknowable and desirable. Society functions finally as simply the characters' own inner wishes given objective force in shaping their fates. This final formal role underlines the authority society assumes in narrative structures even when it remains an hypothesis.

We, like Oedipa, K., and Quentin, must define ourselves against something, and many characters and their authors want something like a society or human community, a merging with something larger than oneself. Society, a system of order outside onself, may be only a projection of mind, but it gives meaning to individual experience, and it determines individuals' destinies. Finally, it ceases to matter whether it is real or not; in seeking to know the source of their destinies, characters draw conclusions that hasten them toward ends, whether hated or desired, constructive or destructive. Their belief has a reality sufficient for their fates.

Society in the Novel

A writer is worthy of interest insofar as he is not totally bound by his milieu.
—Eugene Ionesco, "Interview," *Critical Inquiry*, 1, no. 3

Before raising some final questions about society in the novel, it is useful to survey briefly the ground covered. This book defines a range of formal roles for society that seems comprehensive. The four outer boundaries located in preceding chapters suggest comprehensiveness. We found in Austen that society, responsive to merit, functions as a context for individual fulfillment, whereas Dreiser and Zola instanced the opposite formal possibility, a society that functions to determine individual merit and to destroy individual potential. Along a second scale, we saw that society could act as protagonist of a novel—as in Conrad's *Nostromo* and Trollope's *Barchester Towers*—or, at the opposite end, that social considerations could be largely precluded as significant contexts for individual fates, as in Emily Brontë's and Flannery O'Connor's fictions.

We also examined some of the varied and subtle possibilities within these broad boundaries in the works of writers as diverse as Fielding, Thackeray, Dickens, Eliot, Hardy, Lawrence, Faulkner, Kafka, and Pynchon. For Fielding, Thackeray, and Dickens, the idea of society in the fiction insists that human life should and can be better; social probability is therefore secondary to moral imperatives. Eliot, Hardy, and Lawrence believe in the idea of community, but its realization is increasingly precarious and remote. Finally, for Faulkner, Kafka, and Pynchon, the idea of society exists as only that: an idea in the minds of the characters. Nonetheless, as idea, it has an authority sufficient for their fates.

It is possible that we might ultimately wish to make finer distinctions or, indeed, identify yet other basic formal roles for society in the novel. That desire would support the broad premise from which I have proceeded, that society plays a variety of roles in the formal construction of the novel, and that we need to give closer attention to that variety and the framework for interpretation it suggests.

Basic Assumptions about Society

This brief recapitulation leads inevitably into larger, more speculative questions about society in the novel. To what extent is our idea of society an understanding of Western society? To what extent has our limited understanding of the formal roles of society restricted our appreciation of the art of the novel?

We might ask our first question in another way: is it not possible that the values of a fictional society might be so remote from our experience that they are no longer intelligible? Perhaps, like those linguists who postulate a deep structure to language, we need to postulate a deep structure to society. What a novelist "argues" or articulates in the novel, all careful readers can interpret. We have been talking, by and large, of society as that which is created and structured toward certain formal ends, but there are a number of behavioral taboos that form the deep structure of Western society and need no justification or explanation at all. The prohibition against incest, for example. As we have seen, Tolstoy uses this broad social taboo to convey the turpitude of Anatole and Hélène Kuragin. He need do nothing more than hint at a sexual relationship between brother and sister to arouse our disgust. We might number other social taboos or prerogatives among this group. For example, we accept that special bonds, obligations, and responsibilities exist between parent and child, that parents will protect and nurture their children, that children will honor their fathers and mothers that their days may be long. Tolstoy plays with these attitudes, too, suddenly redeeming the cold, self-interested Dolohov by reporting his unparalleled devotion to his aging mother and hunchbacked sister. In contrast, a character will inevitably appear vicious if he attacks his parents or abuses his children, and particularly strong effects are available by representing these things directly. Such a social dictate partially determines the fact that Hetty Sorrel's child-murder in *Adam Bede* is represented only indirectly and retrospectively through Hetty's tortured consciousness. Even that reprobate Moll Flanders, who is only too eager to shift unwanted children off her hands, offers a brief narrative of their fates, because, for Defoe's fiction to engage us, we must feel that she cares for them and would tend to them personally were it within her means to do so. In his last novel, Defoe will make one of Roxana's abandoned children pursue and threaten to reveal her. Such behavior makes sense to a reader only if he accepts an inalienable bond between parent and child. That "social" bond, however, is not particular to English society; it is general at least to Western society and stems from Judeo-Christian religions. It may be held part of a deep structure of our society.

Certain twentieth-century writers have enjoyed playing with these broad taboos. Vladimir Nabokov's *Lolita* depicts a sexual relationship between a forty-year-old man and a prepubescent girl, his charge and stepdaughter; his later novel *Ada* portrays a life-long love affair between half brother and sister. Our immediate response to such relationships is negative. It is significant that great energy in both of these novels is directed to making us see and experience these affairs in a new light. Both novels, but especially *Lolita*, can start from the assumption that our distaste will be there; Nabokov need not labor to create those responses. If we examine *Lolita*, we see that the emotional power of the novel finally depends on that response, depends on our rejecting Humbert Humbert's lively self-justifications, recognizing his real and poignant love for Lolita beneath the humbug, and yet perceiving the destruction he has wrought in the child's life. It is a complex and unusual power possible only by exploiting this social taboo and our basic feeling that, despite everything, Humbert's behavior cannot be condoned.

If we turn to a novel from the Eastern tradition, Tsao Hsueh-chin's *Dream of the Red Chamber*, we discover that part of our difficulty in interpreting it stems from a different fundamental social structure. Mark Van Doren, in his preface, admits that "much here will strike a Western reader as strange, and naturally so, since a Chinese household of the eighteenth century is about as far away as the imagination can travel."[1] Van Doren adds, however, that the reader will also find "its essential features . . . recognizable because they are features of the human mind and heart."[2] This distinction corresponds roughly to a distinction I would like to make between the representation of society and the representation of character. This Chinese "novel of manners" leaves us baffled and puzzled at key points because we understand the characters' feelings and actions but not the social context in which we are to interpret those feelings and actions. In other words, we lack the means to intuit the novel's formal principles. For example, the novel's hero, Pao-yu, has an explicit dream in which the Goddess of Disillusionment helps initiate him into the mysteries of sex. We all understand the youthful eagerness of the boy, appetite whetted, which leads him to propose to Pervading Fragrance, one of his handmaidens, that he demonstrate what the Goddess has taught him. The narrator reports, "At first Pervading Fragrance refused but in the end she acquiesced, since she knew that she would eventually be Pao-yu's concubine. Thenceforward, Pao-yu treated her with more tenderness than ever, and the maid on her part ministered to the comforts of her young master even more faithfully than before."[3]

We can understand the human heart—the boy's tenderness, the maid's devotion—but it is impossible to tell whether what has happened is good or bad in social terms and thus to determine whether the couple faces likely separation and punishment or continued joy in each other's arms. Pervading Fragrance is certainly no shrieking, fainting Pamela Andrews, and we know with certainty that relationships between masters and maids carry different expectations in Chinese society. Pervading Fragrance clearly anticipates a time when she will be Pao-yu's concubine, but have she and her master acted prematurely? Are there explicit social forms to be observed? That kind of knowledge is generally taken for granted. We may recall that Faulkner's *Absalom, Absalom!* made distinctions among females, women, and ladies and that black females were simply to be had for the asking by their white masters, but we also knew that those relationships were temporary and carried no obligations and no expectations. This same casualness does not exist in *Dream of the Red Chamber*, but the Western reader is uncertain of the social responsibilities and prerogatives that do exist.

Familial relationships in *Dream of the Red Chamber* are even more problematic. A father, Shih-yin, is comforting his "pretty and lovable" daughter, Lotus, when he is approached by a Buddhist monk who bursts out, "What are you carrying that ill-fated creature for? She will only bring misfortune upon her parents. . . . Give her to me as a sacrifice to Buddha" (chap. 1). Shih-yin's human annoyance at these comments does not fully acquaint us with the proper response to what seem, to this reader, to be outrageous suggestions. Their prophecy, we recognize, will no doubt be fulfilled, but what is a parent's responsibility to his child? What is the status of the family in the presence of divine prophecy? Western tradition's Abraham and Isaac cannot help us here, since the parents are simply supposed to get rid of an ill-fated child not offer a supreme sacrifice to God.

After Shih-yin loses his daughter, he meets a Taoist and suddenly leaves his wife. The narrator says, "Shih-yin's wife spared no effort in trying to locate her husband, but how can one find a man who wants to be lost?" (chap. 1). Of course, we all understand the feeling that would prompt Feng-shih's effort to find her husband, but, once again, we cannot interpret the significance of this event. Do husbands regularly desert their wives? Shih-yin, we are told, "had always been a man of great intuitive understanding" (chap. 1). Has he glimpsed a valuable secret of life that he must follow, the conjugal ties being slight by comparison? It is hard to determine without a thorough knowledge of that culture.

On a simpler level, the narrator tells us that the matriarch loved Black Jade best although she was not her "real granddaughter." Having pursued complicated genealogies, the Western reader is amazed at this information since Black Jade is the matriarch's daughter's daughter, but the translator informs us that "a daughter's child, having a different surname, is only an 'outside' or pseudo grandchild" (chap. 4). All well and good; the grandmother's partiality is only human, but within this society will it have negative or positive consequences since Black Jade is not her "real grandchild"? Will that partiality make life easier or more difficult for Black Jade? More frustrating still, does it even matter? It is difficult to anticipate since we lack explicit knowledge of the deep structure of family relationships and social expectations that underlie such comments. This is the first point I would like to emphasize.

A second issue that *Dream of the Red Chamber* helps clarify is the assumed relationship between individuals and societies. Critics such as Ian Watt have documented at length that the English novel arose simultaneously with certain social changes: increasing economic individualism and Protestantism, both of which emphasize the individual apart from society. The Western novel is predicated on conflict, potential or actual, between an individual and his social milieu. Novels have interpreted that conflict and its resolution differently, but it exists even in such precursors of the novel as the picaresque *Lazarillo de Tormes*. Cervantes' *Don Quixote* becomes increasingly less picaresque, but both its picaresque and novelistic parts pit the idealistic Don against an inimical world. Don Quixote, tilting at windmills, is tilting against inimical aspects of his society, real and imagined.

Dream of the Red Chamber early offers an explanation of character that contradicts the assumption that individual and social expectations will conflict:

> "I am afraid that you misjudge Pao-yu. . . . I think he probably represents one of those exceptional beings who are born under a special set of circumstances and who are not generally appreciated and therefore often misunderstood. Generally speaking, Heaven and Earth endow the generality of men with the same mediocre qualities, so that one is hardly distinguishable from another. Not so, however, in the rare instances of the Exceptionally Good and the Exceptionally Evil that flash through the pages of history. The first embodies the Perfect Norm of Heaven and Earth; the second, its Horrid Deviations. . . .
>
> "Today, under our divine Sovereign, peace and prosperity reign, and the Perfect Norm is exemplified everywhere. . . . there is no place under the clear sky and bright sun for the Deviations from the Norm. . . . But occasionally, pressed upon by the clouds or wafted by the winds, traces of these evil elements find their way into the upper air and clash with traces of the Norm, causing violent storms and thunder and lightning.

"It is under these special circumstances that the unusual
type that I spoke of before comes into being. This represents
the embodiment of a new force, the result of a union of
traces of the Norm and of its Deviations" [chap. 2].

In an attempt to explain the hero's personality, Yu-tsun invokes a
theory of the Perfect Norm of Heaven and Earth in contrast to its
Horrid Deviations. Because at the time the novel is set "the Perfect
Norm is exemplified everywhere," Pao-yu, the novel's hero, is "one
of these admirable deviates from the Norm"; he represents the
embodiment of a new force, the result of a "union of traces of the
Norm and of its Deviations" (chap. 2). The implications of this
theory, borne out in the novel, are that one is innately deviant or
conformist. Individual struggles against a society dominated by the
Perfect Norm would be ridiculous or meaningless. The characters
in conflict are born that way; this society does not generate conflict
within individuals or give rise to individual alienation. Characters
who are born out of Harmony with the Perfect Norm experience
difficulties reminiscent of those of characters in the Western tradition, but their problems can never call into question the value of
the society and its norms. That value is assumed, even when it
leads to the degradation of impoverished relatives, to suicides, or
to brutal and "arbitrary" beatings.

Even as I describe these events, I am interpreting them in lights
that distort their cultural significance. After one poor woman has
begged some silver from the wealthy Phoenix, Phoenix says to her,
"Come often when you have nothing to do, as relatives should"
(chap. 5). Such begging is accepted; even its seeming humiliation
is deemed appropriate because it validates class differences. As
another example, a father's brutal beating of his son is curbed by
the mother's reminding the father of his duty to himself and to the
matriarch: "Though Pao-yu deserves punishment, Lao-yeh must
also consider his own health and not overexert himself. . . . It
would matter little if Pao-yu perished under your punishment, but
what if Lao Tai-tai should suffer?" (chap. 20). Such a set of social
relationships, and therefore such a scene, could not exist in a Western realistic novel without some indictment of the society these
characters inhabit. In the Western novel, such brutalization would
force us to examine not only the characters but the social milieu
that has created them. The value of custom, convention, and law

would be deeply questioned; indeed, censure would seem to be demanded. Such basic assumptions about individuals' relationships to their worlds lie at the heart of our novel.

Milieu and the Artistic Act

Problems for Western readers raised by a novel like *Dream of the Red Chamber* also help focus on our second larger question about society in the novel: the question of evaluation, particularly the evaluation of society. To begin to shape an answer, we might examine the assumption, underlying much of Marxist criticism, that artists consciously or unconsciously reflect their social milieus in their fictions. The result, a Marxist might say, are novels full of unexamined assumptions about the ways individuals relate to society.

Dream of the Red Chamber helps us see, to some extent, that novelists are culture-bound, accepting social taboos and values as normative. But, the position implicit in much Marxist criticism that most novelists do not or cannot consider with some critical objectivity the societies they depict is undercut by the many formal roles for society we have here discovered. The variety of these roles and their clear relationships to the expressive ends of novels can only argue for authorial selectivity and autonomy in creating and shaping fictional presentations of society.

Further, Marxism is itself a Western philosophy and proceeds from the same basic assumptions about the individual's relationship to society and history that shape Western novels. The Western novel and the philosophies of capitalism and Marxism are all products of industrialization and the corollary concept of the individual as an economic unit whose labor has value and whose products are his belongings. It is hard to imagine a Marxist analysis of *Dream of the Red Chamber* that would do justice to that Far Eastern vision. Thus Marxism is not nearly so useful an interpretive tool for Far Eastern society as it is for Western society.

The work of Terry Eagleton provides a fine insight into the strengths and limitations of a Marxist interpretation of literature. As we saw earlier, Eagleton recognizes that literature cannot provide a mirror image of some real, outside world. The text's "pseudo-real" or imaginary situations are signifiers of social or historical ideology, which is itself a signification of history. Thus what the text represents is, like itself, only a system of signs. So, Eagleton recognizes the gap between text and real world, but he does so by denying the knowability of a "real world." He then collapses the gap between text and world in another way, by acknowledging the phenomenal nature of both text and world. Yet, beyond our experience of text and world, there clearly exists for Eagleton an absolute: history itself, which has produced the general ideology that has produced the text. Despite layers of ideologies, history or historical fact always exists for Eagleton. It is from this basis of fact (Britain's volume of world trade rose rapidly and money-wages probably rose by at least a third between 1850 and 1870) that he constructs the prevailing ideology, "class patriotism" and "richer growth of our national politics," and then articulates the formal character of, for example, George Eliot's fiction: "Eliot's work attempts to resolve a structural conflict between two forms of mid-Victorian ideology: between a progressively muted Romantic individualism . . . and certain 'higher', corporate ideological modes."[4]

These are perceptive comments on the ideology of a text, but George Eliot's great novel, *Middlemarch*, becomes only one more example of an ideology entering into "grievous conflicts which its aesthetic forms betray in the very act of attempted resolution." Such destruction of ideology "in the aesthetic region" is, however, essential "not only for a scientific knowledge of a literary past, but for laying the foundation on which the materialist ethic and artistic practices of the future can be built."[5] A critical perspective concentrating on the artistic production of ideology cannot at the same time do justice to the question of art's broad capacity to express values.

Eugene Ionesco, in an interview with Gabriel Jacobs, pinpointed these limitations to Marxist criticism which have not changed, despite its new phenomenological base:

> Taine, who believed that a work of art was the product of an age, a race, a milieu, said precisely what the Marxists now say: man is the expression of his milieu and his society. That is both true and untrue, or rather it's true but it's more complex than that. First of all, a man may be not the product of his society, but someone who rejects it; or he may be the product of that society, and yet be against it. He can also be

against a State. When Russian leaders say: "Man is the product of Society," it may be true, but exactly which society do
we mean? . . . Another point: a man may be the product of
his milieu but that in no way explains a work of art. . . . You
might put it like this: A writer is worthy of interest insofar as
he is not totally bound by his milieu.[6]

In the several discussions of literature and society undertaken in
this study, we have seen that society is something different for
different novelists and novels, and the social inclusions depend as
much on artistic needs as on unconscious influences. Furthermore,
there exists a higher artistic purpose to which a novel's society is
subordinated. The Marxists would, of course, argue that their central position remains unchallenged; novelists who fail to articulate
the dialectic of history are blind to the social influences in their
work. But if novelists fail to measure up to this Marxist yardstick,
it cannot be concluded that they therefore present in their fiction a
mere social or historical ideology.

In *Pride and Prejudice* the implicit criticism of society is no-
where more cogently expressed than in the socially approved marriage of Jane and Bingley. The marriage of these two amiable, if
vapid, characters defines the limits of the society's ability to discriminate. Indeed, for that society, Elizabeth's marriage to Darcy
ranks on a par with Jane's to Bingley. Austen has made us feel the
vast superiority of the former union over the latter, but that superiority is not generally acknowledged in the world that Elizabeth and
Jane inhabit. Society, then, becomes a leveler of experience. Although a novelist can sharpen our perceptions by including a society, that society remains dull in its own discriminations of value.

We discover a similar truth in other novels. Dorothea Brooke
from *Middlemarch* demeans herself in society's eyes by marrying
Will Ladislaw; Celia Brooke is the much more socially successful
sister with her marriage to the bland Sir James Chettam. Rosamond Vincy, having helped to destroy Lydgate, is rewarded by
society at his death with a rich doctor. Indeed, no character has the
same value in his society as he bears in our more privileged eyes.
Tess Durbeyfield and Clyde Griffiths are convicted murderers; Ursula Brangwen appears isolated and self-absorbed. The fine discriminations we make of individual achievement and failure do not
belong to members of the society: those discriminations remain

privately revealed rather than socially acknowledged. Although Marxist critics would locate man's meaning in his relationship to his society, no novelist in fact lets his vision stop there. He is neither himself so bound by his society, nor are his characters so bound, that an individual's achievement will be measured solely by his status in the world he inhabits.

The novelists who make society's evaluation most closely accord with ours are those who manipulate the expectations and probabilities of their represented worlds: Fielding, Thackeray, and Dickens. Dickens's Esther Summerson finds wide acclaim for her goodness and generosity. Thackeray's Becky Sharp finds "a strong party of excellent people [who] consider her to be a most injured woman" (chap. 67). Although Amelia Sedley gets her Dobbin, she is not allowed the complacency of *Middlemarch*'s Rosamond Vincy, who sees her rich doctor as a "reward" for putting up with Lydgate. Finally, Fielding's Tom Jones is universally vindicated and welcomed as Allworthy's nephew and heir, but, then, we readers know that things do not happen this way in the "real world." The narrators of these novels let society reflect our evaluations to encourage our participation and responsibility in creating more adequate social structures. We are, for a time, especially in Fielding's novels, architects of worlds constructed on better, more equitable principles, and if, as in Thackeray, a society cannot better itself, it shall, at least, not unduly reward its beneficiaries nor unduly condemn its victims.

Nostromo, in which I have defined society as the formal protagonist, presents another phenomenon. Perhaps the most telling implicit criticism of represented society resides in our recognition that none of the characters who embody society's hopes are contemptible or mere aggrandizers, yet all participate in realizing a society that ultimately has the production of wealth as its end. Here, society becomes larger than its component parts in its destructive powers. It assumes a life and purpose of its own, subverting an idealistic character like Charles Gould to its own ends.

In the twentieth-century novel, where subjectivity and alienation from social forms are the norm, a Marxist might wish to argue the novelists' total incapacity to surmount their own social alienation and subjectivity that give rise to their novels. These novelists express as ultimate and true that which is a process: transitory and temporal, and this has always been the failure of writers in Marxist

eyes. It is interesting that none of the writers considered here—
Faulkner, Kafka, and Pynchon—is content with concluding that
absolute subjectivity prevails when they look at society. They chart
their characters' quests. All of them validate the search for larger
truth even if that search will not be attended with certainty. In so
doing, they question the value of particular social organizations
and assert the validity of some social organization.

Works such as *Wuthering Heights* and *The Violent Bear It Away*
present a final challenge to the Marxist position. As we have seen,
"society" exists in Brontë's and O'Connor's novels, but it does not
explain or determine the protagonists' fates. In novels like these,
we are meant to feel that any meaningful engagement with a fate
exists outside the social order—in some religious, supranatural, or
spiritual state. By locating human meaning outside social conditions, these novelists render social determinism impotent. These
writers acknowledge society by including it but accord it minimal
formal significance in defining their characters' fates. In these novels, most obviously, to focus, as the Marxist critics do, on the included society would seem to miss the artistic point.

Although the problems for Marxist critics are perhaps more
radical in *Wuthering Heights* or *The Violent Bear It Away*, they do
not differ in kind from those in any of the other novels I have
discussed. This formal approach, however, is not necessarily at
odds with Marxism. Such close attention to the artistic demands
made by the work itself can only enrich and further validate a
Marxist approach. To limit one's vision to the way history and the
ideologies produced by history shape novelists and their novels, to
fail to acknowledge the high degree of social examination and criticism present, to fail to recognize the way in which superior individuals transcend the norms and conventions of their milieu, to fail
to recognize the diverse relationships among individuals, society,
and the implied author that are at the heart of society's many
formal roles in the novel is ultimately to commit an injustice to the
novel's full artistic achievement. Novelists, by their understanding,
free themselves in part from the assumptions and limitations of
their societies and align themselves with the universal.

This book began with a formal rather than a mimetic purpose; it
has focused not on the power of the novel to mimic a real milieu
and period but rather on its power to generate its own terms for
evaluation. That power is a power to create and shape reality, to

acquaint us with possibility, to question our assumptions about individual relationships to society. Of course, we are finally dealing with imitation in its Aristotelean sense. We do not look to the novel primarily for social documents; social historians and sociologists can tell us about particular societies. Novelists teach us the varied meanings that society has for individuals and for human life; they instruct us in the mutual responsibilities of individuals and societies; they use depictions of society to speak truths about what men and women are, singly and communally, and what they might be. We look to the novel for what we ultimately find there, imitations and intimations of human life in society.

Notes

Chapter 1

1. Knoepflmacher, *Laughter and Despair*, p. 3. It is interesting, also, to note that Knoepflmacher's caution is written several decades after a similar *caveat* from Mikhail Bakhtin whose work has been rediscovered for its relevance today: "As we have already said, there is a sharp and categorical boundary line between the actual world as source of representation and the world represented in the work. We must never forget this, we must never confuse—as has been done up to now and is still often done—the *represented* world with the world outside the text . . ." (*Dialogic Imagination*, p. 253).

2. Mikhail Bakhtin develops a similar point about the importance of discussing the relationship of art to life: "However forcefully the real and the represented world resist fusion . . . they are nonetheless indissolubly tied up with each other and find themselves in continual mutual interaction. . . . We might even speak of a special *creative* chronotope inside which this exchange between work and life occurs" (*Dialogic Imagination*, p. 254). At the heart of Bakhtin's theory is the chronotope, an abstraction of historical time-space. Bakhtin explains the relationship of chronotope to meaning in this way: "whatever these meanings turn out to be, in order to enter our experience . . . they must take on the *form of a sign* . . . [a] temporal-spacial expression. Consequently, every entry into the sphere of meanings is accomplished only through the gates of the chronotope" (p. 258). This conception of chronotope is a theory of form upon which, as we see, all meaning depends. Thus, Bakhtin says, as do I, that we cannot confuse art and life. But there is a vital interaction between them, and Bakhtin has recourse, as do I, to *form* not content in explaining the relationship of life and art. This emphasis we share; the relationship of art to life depends on some theory of forms since content or meaning is always expressed through forms.

3. Levine, *Realistic Imagination*, p. 3. See also Said, *The World, The Text, and The Critic*, who has moved away from his strong endorsement of deconstruction in his *Beginnings: Intention and Method* and argues in his new book that "texts are worldly, to some degree they are events, and, even when they appear to deny it, they are nevertheless a part of the social world, human life, and of course the historical moment in which they are located and interpreted."

4. Levine, *Realistic Imagination*, p. 4.

5. Ibid., p. 6.

6. Eliot, *Adam Bede*, chap. 17.

7. Tolstoy, *War and Peace*, Book 1, pt. 1, chaps. 1, 2.

8. Harvey, *Character and the Novel*, p. 56.

9. Trilling, *Liberal Imagination*, p. 206.

10. Shroder, "Novel as a Genre," p. 16.

11. Friedman, *Turn of the Novel*, p. 10.

12. Society as protagonist has been used in this sense by such critics as Williams, *English Novel*; Lucas, *Melancholy Man*; Van Ghent, *English Novel*. See especially, Van Ghent's essay on *Adam Bede* in this volume.

13. This is not a new idea. It has been developed most forcibly by Booth, *Rhetoric of Fiction*, and Grossvogel, *Limits of the Novel*, pp. 6–43. Both Booth and Grossvogel point out that it is impossible to avoid beliefs in fiction and that the very form a fiction takes implies beliefs or values of one kind or another. Booth makes helpful distinctions among what he terms qualitative, intellectual, and practical beliefs. See his chapter "Beliefs and the Reader."

14. That the proper subject of the novel is man in society has been a conclusion of critics working within very different frameworks. For example, Allen's *English Novel*, pp. xv–xvi, vigorously defends the novel's newness as a genre—decrying attempts to find its tradition and history in earlier fictions. Allen identifies the novel's interest in individuals' relationships to society with the special conditions that dictated its rise in the eighteenth century. Frye, *Anatomy of Criticism*, pp. 303–12, locates the novel's "chief interest . . . in human character as it manifests itself in society," and he creates other categories of prose fictions—romance, anatomy, confession—to account for the genre's later preoccupation with metaphysical or psychological questions. Finally Lukács, *Historical Novel*, p. 139, has distinguished the novel from drama through the novel's greater commitment to evoking the "totality of the process of social development. . . . Society is the principal subject of the novel, that is, man's social life in its ceaseless interaction with surrounding nature, which forms the basis of social activity, and with the different social institutions or customs which mediate the relations between individuals in social life."

15. Harvey, *Character and the Novel*, p. 57, made this point early: "Indeed, one can think of remarkably few novels in which the protagonists achieve reality while remaining isolated from some social context." Graff, *Literature Against Itself*, pp. 211, 213, has recently reiterated this point in locating the failure of modern fiction in a failure to embody society.

16. My own theory of the novel bears essential similarities with that defined by other critics, especially critics of the nineteenth-century novel upon which my study focuses. Of special note is Miller, *Form of Victorian Fiction*, whose thesis is that a "novel is a structure of interpenetrating minds, the mind of the narrator as he beholds or enters into the characters, the minds of the characters as they behold or know one another. Not isolated consciousness, not consciousness at grips with natural objects, not consciousness face to face with God in meditation but consciousness of the consciousness of others—this is the primary focus of fiction. The novelist's assumptions, often unstated ones, about the ways one mind can interact with other minds determine the form his novel takes" (p. 2). I emphasize three points of values; Miller emphasizes two: narrator and characters. But we note that his category "character" implies two spheres of value: individual and communal. He concludes that society depends upon rules established by the individual human heart interacting with other hearts, and it is this dialectic that fiction portrays (pp. 139–40). Miller has defined his theory in a fruitful way to address the problem he sees—the intensified subjectivism of Victorian fiction—but it is a theory that cannot account for varieties in the formal role of society since, by definition, it implies one formal role. My study makes a clear theoretical separation of society and character in order to explore diverse formal roles, although individual formal roles for society may close that distance between social order and character in varying ways.

17. Berlin, *Hedgehog and the Fox*, pp. 67–68, 71.

18. See Watt, *Rise of the Novel*; Berger, *Real and Imagined Worlds*; and Ariès, *Centuries of Childhood*, for concurrent views of a literary critic, a sociologist, and an historian on this subject.

19. See, for example, Cazamian, *Social Novel in England*.

20. Eliot, "Three Months in Weimar," p. 89.

21. Harvey, *Character and the Novel*, p. 45.

22. Swinden reaches this conclusion in *Unofficial Selves*, p. 4.

23. Stevenson, *Victorian Fiction*, p. 13.

24. Kermode, "Novel and Narrative," p. 156.

25. See Williams, *English Novel*, pp. 30–31, 57.

26. Brontë, *Jane Eyre*, chap. 12.

27. Ibid., chap. 12.

28. Woolf, *Room of One's Own*, p. 73.

29. Brontë, *Jane Eyre*, chap. 12.

30. My conclusions here are founded on principles of artistic coherence articulated by critics working within the tradition of Chicago neo-Aristotelian theory. For example, Rader, "Concept of Genre," p. 86, points out that in reading we search for coherent form, "for a comprehensive infer-

ential grasp of an author's overall creative intention in a work, which allows us to eliminate in the act of reading any potential incoherencies and ambiguities which cannot be resolved within our appreciation of the coherence of the whole." See also Rader, "Fact, Theory, and Literary Explanation," pp. 245–72.

Rader's theories are by no means generally accepted. Garrett, *Victorian Multiplot Novel*, has summarized the controversy between proponents of monological readings (as he characterizes the neo-Aristotelians) and those of deconstructive readings. He finds himself to have charted a "middle ground," advancing a theory of "dialogical form" that recognizes the "importance of basic conventional organizing patterns yet challenge[s] traditional assumptions about unity by attempting to demonstrate the presence of multiple and irreconcilable patterns" (p. 16). Garrett's own goal is to show how narrative elements "produce effects of remarkable and irreducible complexity" (p. 17).

Garrett is somewhat harsh with neo-Aristotelians, like Rader, who, he is persuaded, consistently ignore and repress incoherencies and ambiguities in a quest for "monological" readings. It is interesting that Garrett has essentially faulted the neo-Aristotelian critics for assuming an artist's constructive intention, yet he himself presumes such intention in his conception of "dialogic form."

My own understanding and practice of neo-Aristotelian theory allows for ambiguity and irreducible complexity in narratives; and it also acknowledges the possible presence of *unintentional* self-contradictory aspects of a text like those I have defined in *Jane Eyre.*

31. See, for example, Berger, *Real and Imagined Worlds*, who, as a sociologist, offers the broad distinction that the novel deals with moral implications of social issues while social sciences deal with variables involving social change and are not primarily concerned with moral issues although they touch on them; or Marcus, *Representations*, who focuses on questions similar to Berger's but from a literary critic's point of view.

32. Watt, *Rise of the Novel*, still stands as the definitive account of social and historical conditions in the eighteenth century which gave rise to the novel as an art form. See also Spearman, *Novel and Society* (New York: Barnes and Noble, 1966).

33. A significant number of critics have looked at the ways in which novels both reflect and shape the societies that give rise to them. Major studies of the sociology of the novel include the pioneer study, originally published in 1904, of Cazamian, *Social Novel in England*, which states as its purpose the illumination of the relationship between literary and social evolution. More recent treatments of the selected aspects of this subject include Sussman, *Victorians and the Machine*; Basch, *Relative Creatures*;

and Brantlinger, *Spirit of Reform*. For good general theoretical discussions of the relationship of art to life see Harvey, *Character and the Novel*; Hardy, *Appropriate Form*; Frye, *Stubborn Structure*; and Daiches, *Literature and Society*.

34. Major studies include Williams, *English Novel* and his *Country and the City*; Kettle, *Introduction to the English Novel*; Lucas, *Literature of Change*; and Craig, *Real Foundations*. All of these critics share the broad aim of combining an examination of what people have made of their situation (literature) and the situation itself (history).

35. Georg Lukács, the Marxist critic, is the most famous of a group of critics who articulate a historical dialectic in the novel. See, for example, his *Theory of the Novel*; *Historical Novel*; and *Studies in European Realism*. For those who explore the theoretical implications of a sociology of the novel, see Demetz, *Marx, Engels, and the Poets*; Sammons, *Literary Sociology and Practical Criticism*; and Orr, *Tragic Realism and Modern Society*.

36. See, for example, Jameson, *Marxism and Form*; Jameson, *Political Unconscious*; Eagleton, *Criticism and Ideology*; and Eagleton, *Marxism and Literary Theory*.

37. Eagleton, *Criticism and Ideology*, p. 80.

38. Berger, *Real and Imagined Worlds*, p. 26.

39. I have found very fruitful, in a general way, Bachelard, *Poetics of Space*. The bases for Bachelard's theoretical reflections on space are very close to mine on society. Both insist on art as autonomous (the image is not "a simple substitute for a perceptible reality"), and both recognize the ways in which form and image interrelate. Bachelard speaks of adopting a "phenomenological attitude" toward reading: "It asks us to produce within ourselves a reading pride that will give us the illusion of participating in the work of the author of the book. Such an attitude could hardly be achieved on first reading, which remains too passive. . . . After the sketchiness of the first reading comes the creative work of reading. We must then know *the problem* that confronted the author" (p. 21). My own analyses always probe this question of *the problem*: not *what* meaning is created, but *how* meaning is created.

40. Duckworth, *Improvement of the Estate*.

41. Whereas I move from form to theme, other critics have moved from theme to form to approach some of the same issues and problems I confront. The most notable is Williams, *English Novel*, pp. 13, 16, who defines society as an agency or process, replacing God as "active creator, the destroyer of the values of human relationships." Williams's thesis makes a thematic statement about society as protagonist, but that statement has immediate implications for the form of the novel, some of which Williams

explores. But he does not fully pursue formal implications and stays within his general thematic claim, which enables him to emphasize similarities among Dickens, Eliot, and Hardy, whereas I define strong formal differences.

Chapter 2

1. Two recent critics have also reached this conclusion that Jane Austen's novels present a fluid, balanced interchange between private and social lives, an interchange new to the novel. Hardy, *Reading of Jane Austen*, p. 21, the first to speak out for Austen's "flexible medium," applauds the perfect ease with which "We move from the innermost recesses of heart and mind to the most extrovert social occasions. . . . It is this formal balance, ease and harmony which is scarcely found before Jane Austen, though frequently afterwards." Brown, *Jane Austen's Novels*, p. 5, echoes this perception in distinguishing Austen's novels from those of the eighteenth century: "The eighteenth-century novel, derived from allegory and romance, still sought to define social experience in relation to an absolute."

2. Critics of Jane Austen have invariably focused on her attitudes toward society and on the relationship between society and individuals. While sociological and thematic critics have acknowledged the hardnosed truth of Austen's novels—particularly in her understanding of the economic base of personal relationships—these same critics are troubled by the implied author's attitude toward these values. Fleishman, *Reading of "Mansfield Park,"* pp. 9–13, has done an excellent job of surveying that criticism, which has taken many forms, from criticizing Austen's social conservatism (Mudrick, *Jane Austen*), to praising her understanding of the weaknesses of an open society (Trilling, "Mansfield Park," in *The Opposing Self*, and Litz, *Jane Austen*) to finding her novels to be social documents of the rise of the bourgeoisie (Greene, "Jane Austen and the Peerage," pp. 1017–31). Fleishman acknowledges that, of these critics, Kettle, *Introduction to the English Novel*, 1:99–100, attempts the greatest sociological sophistication in treating Austen's works to rescue them from the Marxists. But his analysis, too, lacks the "historical specificity and terminological precision" needed to validate its conclusions. For a fuller discussion of these perspectives, the reader should see Fleishman.

Avrom Fleishman's own approach is to provide that "historical specificity and terminological precision" and, in so doing, to document that "a major writer can no more offer blanket affirmations of a society's or a class's way of life than she can wholly reject it" (*Reading of "Mansfield Park,"* pp. 17–18). His specificity allows him to discover in *Mansfield*

Park that "the novel does not take sides with the gentry, but instead takes that class's historical situation as its *donnée*—and then seeks out a way to survive within it" (p. 18). Fleishman concludes, "Society is, for Jane Austen, both the horizon of our possibilities and the arena where we destroy each other" (p. 81).

Fleishman's work set a tone for later critics of society in Austen's novels. Subsequent critics have acknowledged the scathing critique of that world, yet recognized, too, that Austen's superior individuals not only survive in society but achieve a complete fulfillment therein. Duckworth, *Improvement of the Estate*, shares this general conclusion but focuses on the estate, which, as "an ordered physical structure," is a "metonym for . . . society as a whole" (p. ix). Duckworth concludes, "In her close attention to physical fact, Jane Austen declares her belief, not in man as the creator of order but in man's freedom to create within a prior order" (p. 34).

Finally, feminist critics, like Gilbert and Gubar, *Madwoman in the Attic*, have raised within this same framework other important thematic issues for Austen's canon. Gilbert and Gubar recognize social weaknesses specifically in options for women—weaknesses that encourage women to become "diseased shrews" or "dying fainters"—but they also recognize that "a few of her heroines do evade the culturally induced idiocy and impotence that domestic confinement and female socialization seem to breed" (p. 183).

All of these thematic studies—diverse as they are—basically recognize flaws within the society Austen presents but acknowledge the possibility of individual fulfillment within that world. My study essentially provides a formal foundation for these several thematic studies. I am concerned with the narrative techniques Austen found to create her unique vision of the fulfilled individual in a potentially constricting society.

3. Austen, *Pride and Prejudice*, in *Novels*, vol. 1, chap. 1. Subsequent references to volume and chapter will appear parenthetically in the text.

4. Butler, *Jane Austen and the War of Ideas*, p. 299, defines as Austen's central question in her fiction "what was the moral nature of the individual, and what his true role in society?" (p. 298). To Butler, Austen answers that question as only a *novelist* can: "Because the marriages which end her novels can be made to symbolize so much for the heroine as an individual, and for her role in society, Jane Austen's fable carries her partisan meaning further than it could be carried in reasoned argument, even by Burke." Butler acknowledges what I want to document, that the form and techniques of art can accomplish what great feats of reasoned argument cannot.

5. Austen, *Emma*, in *Novels*, vol. 3, chap. 19, and Austen, *Northanger Abbey* and *Persuasion* in *Novels*, vol. 4, chap. 12.

6. Williams, *English Novel*, pp. 18–27, has reached a similar conclusion and also distinguishes Austen's depiction of society from that of novelists to follow.

7. Tave, *Some Words of Jane Austen*, pp. 1–35, has pointed to this metaphor of dance as an apt one for understanding the relationship of Austen's characters to their social milieus.

8. Lewes, "Novels of Jane Austen," p. 326.

9. Ibid., p. 327.

10. Ibid., pp. 328–29.

11. Hardy, *A Reading*, p. 165.

12. See Tave for a full discussion of Jane Austen's language and the ways in which certain words achieve special meaning and weight. Tave's study deals most closely with the language that interests me here. Other significant studies have documented that Austen's "stylistic base derived from commerce and property, the counting house and the inherited estate." See Schorer, "Fiction and the 'Matrix of Analogy,'" pp. 539–60, who concentrates on *Persuasion*. See also Van Ghent, *English Novel*, pp. 107–11, who does a similar analysis of *Pride and Prejudice*.

13. Bachelard, *Poetics of Space*, was useful in developing my own discussion of houses. Bachelard notes, "On whatever theoretical horizon we examine it, the house image would appear to have become the topography of our intimate being" (p. xxxii). Of course, we discover that houses can define very different kinds of intimate spaces; indeed, the ways in which houses define that intimate space have, as I show, major implications for the characters' relationships to their society.

14. See, for example, Mudrick, *Jane Austen*, p. 102.

15. Brown, *Jane Austen's Novels*, pp. 46–49, has also addressed this question of the narrator's function in Jane Austen's novels, and she also links narrative commentary with the formal end of Austen's novels, but she does not explore the relationship of that commentary to the representation and role of society.

16. Forster, *Howards End*, chap. 41.

17. Wharton, *Age of Innocence*, chap. 12.

18. Auerbach, *Communities of Women*, pp. 60–61, 62, 73. Auerbach shapes her discussion of family to a different end than I do mine; she is ultimately interested in exploring the viability of communities of women. But we share similar preoccupations with how family functions in society. Barbara Hardy has also explored the "strength of family life" in Austen's novels, and she concludes that "family ties are very strong" (*A Reading*, pp. 129–31). My conclusions dispute hers unless she is implicitly defining family as I have and not as a biological unit.

19. Several critics have commented on the marked differences between *Persuasion* and the earlier novels. Woolf, *Common Reader*, pp. 148–49,

was one of the first to point out these differences. More recently, in look-ing at the estate as a measure of social vitality, Duckworth, *Improvement of the Estate*, p. 208, has noted in *Persuasion* "an incipient doubt as to the continuance of a socially based morality."

Chapter 3

1. Forster, *Aspects of the Novel*, p. 67, made this now famous distinc-tion between flat and round characters. Flat characters are those who "in their purest form . . . are constructed round a single idea or quality."

2. Fielding, *Tom Jones*, book 3, chap. 2.

3. See, for example, Crane, "Concept of Plot"; and Sacks, *Fiction and the Shape of Belief*.

4. Price, "Fielding," p. 415, makes a related point about reward: "Fielding can reward his heroes because they do not seek a reward. . . . The comic resolutions are not devices for saving these heroes from facing moral consequences but rewards for their having done so."

5. Crane, "Concept of Plot," has explored the comic power of the novel and has distinguished it from that of a "merely amiable comedy." He concludes, "We are not disposed to feel, when we are done laughing at Tom, that all is right with the world or that we can count on Fortune always intervening, in the same gratifying way, on behalf of the good" (p. 84).

6. Alter, *Fielding and the Nature of the Novel*, pp. 61–71, has explored the various techniques Fielding uses to give his characters a sense of depth.

7. James, preface to *Princess Casamassima*, p. 68.

8. Alter, "Fielding and the Uses of Style," 53–63, has looked at style to explain our sense of fullness in Fielding's depiction of society: "Since Fielding's plots obviously represent a relatively limited selection of social possibilities and moral situations, it is chiefly through his integrating style that he achieves the artistic illusion of an all-encompassing vision of con-temporary life."

9. Sacks, *Fiction and the Shape of Belief*, p. 198, here echoes R. S. Crane's observation that *Tom Jones* is not merely an amiable comedy.

10. Ibid., 163–92.

11. See Iser, *Implied Reader*, pp. 29–56, for one discussion of the con-cept of implied reader and of the implied reader in Fielding's novel. Iser concludes, "The role of the reader as incorporated in the novel must be seen as something potential and not actual. His reactions are not set out for him, but he is simply offered a frame of possible decisions, and when he has made his choice, then he will fill in the picture accordingly"

(p. 55). Preston in *Created Self*, speaking of judgment and the role of the reader, concludes, *"Tom Jones* shows, though, that we cannot choose not to judge. Nor can we avoid being judged, however 'prudent' our lives. But we can and should learn to judge with knowledge, that is with full experience and full sympathy; above all we have to learn how to forgive" (p. 132). Booth's early discussion of the concept of reader in *Rhetoric of Fiction*, pp. 215–18, is also helpful.

12. Battestin, "Fielding's Definition of Wisdom," 188–217, has discussed the "deliberately complex" concept of prudence that Fielding employs in the novel.

13. Critics have explored at length the structure of the novel, the ways in which Thackeray parallels the lives of the two women, stressing both thematic oppositions and similarities. See Taube, "Contrast as a Principle of Structure in *Vanity Fair*," pp. 119–35; and Harden, "Discipline and Significance of Form in *Vanity Fair*," pp. 530–41.

Loofbourow, *Thackeray and the Form of Fiction*, finds the novel's generic heritage in neoclassical forms like the pastoral and mock epic, which *Vanity Fair* parodies, and his focus leads him to define numerous salient contrasts between the women: "Amelia acts out archaic obsession . . . Rebecca reveals tribal mores" (p. 90). Loofbourow, in general, discusses Thackeray's characters as he sees Thackeray to have conceived them "primarily as types" (p. 91).

Ray, *Thackeray*, p. 422, gives one typical response to the deliberate paralleling of Becky's and Amelia's stories. He claims that "Becky's career is admirably suited to illustrate the destructive operation of the standards of Vanity Fair, but Thackeray desired through Amelia's history to show what he would put in their place, the life of personal relations, the loyalty and selflessness inspired by home affections." Other critics have found explicit and consistent criticism of Amelia and what she represents and have discovered in Thackeray's depiction of Amelia evidence of his desire to criticize the values she represents. But even if critics like Tillotson, "*Vanity Fair*," p. 239, acknowledge that all of Thackeray's characters "are so mixed, so often on a moral borderland," the tendency is still to see Becky as the embodiment of social morality and Amelia as the embodiment of moral goodness, even if ineffectual at times.

This tendency to define thematic oppositions and similarities has obscured Thackeray's formal innovations in *Vanity Fair*. My analysis concentrates on the similar formal roles Becky and Amelia play in the narrative, each fulfilling one important dimension of Thackeray's depiction and criticism of society. Our awareness of their formal similarity allows us to perceive, too, the special relationship among individuals, society, and narrator which characterizes Thackeray's novel.

14. Thackeray, *Vanity Fair*, chap. 53.

15. In this light, it is not surprising that both Charlotte Brontë and George Eliot admired Thackeray greatly, the latter praising him as "on the whole the most powerful of living novelists" in a letter to John Blackwood, 11 June 1857.

16. Mathison, "German Sections of *Vanity Fair*," p. 11.

17. This general complaint has been voiced pointedly by Van Ghent, *English Novel*, pp. 139–41. See also Kettle, *Introduction to the English Novel*, pp. 156–58, 169–70. Other critics, like Geoffrey and Kathleen Tillotson, introduction, *Vanity Fair*, have defended the "authorial speech and preaching as part of the structure of *Vanity Fair*"; the commentary "grows out of the action, and the telling of it, as it grows out of its final title" (pp. xiv, xv). Taking a position closer to mine, McMaster, *Thackeray*, p. 5, has argued that the "authorial presence is not the artist himself, but a humanely fallible narrator, whose failures in assessment and personal idiosyncracies are . . . open to our judgment." The novel ultimately constitutes a "confrontation . . . between author and reader."

18. Iser, *Implied Reader*, p. 120, develops a similar point: "The predominant aim [of *Vanity Fair*] is no longer to create the illusion of an objective outside reality . . . [but] to diversify his vision, in order to compel the reader to view things for himself and discover his own reality."

19. Kettle, *Introduction to the English Novel*, p. 158.

20. Booth, *Rhetoric of Fiction*, pp. 67–77, makes these helpful distinctions among narrator, implied author, and author.

21. Van Ghent, *English Novel*, p. 139.

22. Ibid., p. 139.

23. Eliot, *Middlemarch*, chap. 15.

24. Lubbock, *Craft of Fiction*, p. 95, damns Thackeray with faint praise for this achievement.

25. House, *Dickens World*, p. 220, is one of the first to note that, although Dickens recognizes the ways in which environment shapes individual action and fate, his main characters escape that shaping process. Holloway, "Dickens' Vision of Society," pp. 287–89, echoes this observation: "Dickens is not alone in seeing that you could believe in the complex integration of the social framework—the 'working of the system'—without losing this sense of mystery in humanity." Sussman, *Victorians and the Machine*, p. 73, for whom the machine becomes Dickens's image for society, reaches a similar conclusion and looks for the thematic key to this dilemma. He asserts that Dickens's "hope for reform lay not so much in transforming mechanized industry as in keeping feeling alive in a mechanized world through liberal education and through art. This belief, that the affective life could survive the advance of the machine, becomes the central theme of his writings."

Some critics, like Hardy, *Moral Art of Dickens*, pp. 3, 13–14, simply use these difficulties to argue against the formal and thematic coherence of Dickens's novels. Others attempt to deal with the difficulties in new terms. Recently, Garrett, *Victorian Multiplot Novel*, p. 29, has identified Dickens's novels as examples of dialogical form; that is, contradictory narrative possibilities simply exist simultaneously in the "element of artifice and delightfully absurd unreality" and in the "mimetic terms . . . [that assert] a correspondence to 'real life.'" For Garrett, the contradiction exists, and he finds in the irreconcilability of the two logics a key to the novels' richness.

My thesis asks us to inquire into the formal terms of Dickens's novels to discover the narrative machinery that makes us perceive these contradictions as a narrative whole rather than as disruptive fragments. Williams, *Country and the City*, pp. 153–64, has suggested an analysis similar to mine in his discussion of the city in Dickens's novels. He explores the ways in which a thematic tension—the city at once "an alien and indifferent system" and the "unknown, perhaps unknowable, sum of so many lives"—is realized in a formal whole that takes Dickens to the "dynamic center of this transforming social experience."

26. Eliot, "Natural History of German Life," pp. 271–72.

27. Lucas, *Melancholy Man*, p. 344.

28. Trilling, introduction, *Little Dorrit*, p. 375.

29. Miller, *Charles Dickens*, p. 333.

30. Lewes, "Dickens in Relation to Criticism," p. 195.

31. Miller, *Charles Dickens*, develops a similar idea, but he does not pursue the formal implications of that presentation of society.

32. Miller, "Optic and Semiotic in *Middlemarch*," p. 126.

33. Ibid., p. 126.

34. Dickens, *Bleak House*, chap. 58.

35. Miller, "Optic and Semiotic," p. 126.

36. Dickens, *Our Mutual Friend*, chap. 3.

37. I borrow the phrase from Forster, *Aspects of the Novel*, p. 82. Forster decries this aspect of Fielding's and Thackeray's work because it detracts from the "illusion and nobility" of the novel. From my study's perspective, the art of Fielding and Thackeray depends on this "chattiness."

Chapter 4

1. Bedient, *Architects of Self*, has also explored the relationship between self and society in the novels of George Eliot and D. H. Lawrence. He concludes that George Eliot's "characteristic subject is the necessary submission of individuals to their own society. . . . For her, any society is

preferable to the explosive egoism of the individual" (p. 34). Bedient then compares George Eliot to Lawrence and notes that, if for George Eliot the "social self" was all, for Lawrence, "conversely, it was the social and conscious life, the life of principle and self-giving, that he was to equate with nothingness" (p. 268). Bedient's argument seems an oversimplification of the subtle relationship between individuals and society to which I point and of the function of society in both George Eliot's and D. H. Lawrence's novels.

2. Eliot, "Amos Barton," chap. 2.

3. Ibid., chap. 2.

4. Miller, "Optic and Semiotic," p. 126.

5. Ibid., p. 127.

6. Anderson, "George Eliot in *Middlemarch*," p. 277, has focused on this aspect of George Eliot's fiction.

7. Miller, "Optic and Semiotic," p. 128. See also Stump, *Movement and Vision in George Eliot's Novels*, who examines the function of web imagery in *Middlemarch*.

8. Eliot, *Adam Bede*, chap. 3.

9. Ibid., chap. 16.

10. Marcus, *Representations*, pp. 197–98.

11. Knoepflmacher, *Laughter and Despair*, provides a full discussion of the narrator, opinion, and truth, focusing on Casaubon and culminating with the observation that "truth is multisided" (p. 188).

12. See, especially, the recent feminist critics whose most serious objections are to the heroines' self-destructive tendencies: Showalter, *Literature of Their Own*; Edwards, "Women, Energy and *Middlemarch*," pp. 223–38; Beer, *Reader, I Married Him*; and Moers, *Literary Women*. But this tension in George Eliot's resolutions had been defined even before the feminist criticisms. See, for example, Hardy, *Novels of George Eliot*; Leavis, *Great Tradition*; and Harvey, *Art of George Eliot*, critics early to raise the problem.

13. Eliot, *Middlemarch*, p. 612n.

14. Harvey, "Criticism of the Novel," pp. 133–34, looks at the contemporary reception of this deleted passage and concludes that it is "very probable that its subsequent deletion is George Eliot's response to the verdict of her reviewers" who found the emphasis on social determinism unconvincing in light of the narrative, which emphasized individual responsibility as well. The reviewers argued that Dorothea "does not yield to social pressure in marrying Casaubon, but is simply deluded about him."

Society, it is true, does not force Dorothea to marry Casaubon, but it gives an intelligent woman desiring education no option but marriage to a sickly scholar. The reviewers are right, however, in pointing out that the novel's balance between social determinants and individual possibility is upset in the deleted passage. My analysis focuses on a related balance, which is also upset, that between society as restrictive and society as constructive. My conclusions suggest a supporting reason for the deletion of the passage.

15. Eliot, *Daniel Deronda*, chap. 69.

16. Ibid., chap. 70.

17. In discussing George Eliot's movement from *Middlemarch* to *Daniel Deronda*, Garrett, *Victorian Multiplot Novel*, picks up on Calvin Bedient's observation that "the only certain injury resulting from Gwendolen's marriage is to herself" (*Architects of the Self*, p. 64). Garrett observes, "In the tightly woven fabric of Middlemarch society, morality is much more a question of obligation to others, but in *Daniel Deronda* the community has disappeared. Making Gwendolen's guilt a question of her effects on others seems an attempt to disguise the extremity of her isolation, a condition in which actions and consequences have been completely internalized" (pp. 172–73). George Levine has advanced a similar idea in *The Realistic Imagination*, p. 46: "By the time of *Daniel Deronda*, George Eliot had in effect renounced the limits of realism by renouncing the possibility of satisfactory life within society. . . . Daniel is sent off, in fact, to create a community, outside the reaches of the society. . . . The language of realism becomes fit only for that experience of loss and absence that is Gwendolen Harleth's at the end."

As I point out in my discussion of *Middlemarch*, that development is already underway, and this pattern in *Daniel Deronda* makes Hardy and Lawrence logical inheritors to George Eliot in exploring the individual in society.

18. Hardy, *Jude the Obscure*, part 4, chap. 1.

19. This conclusion contradicts some major criticism of the novel. For example, Van Ghent, *English Novel*, pp. 201–9, has argued that nature is a primary agent of Tess's destruction.

20. Social criticism of Hardy's novels stresses two kinds of conflicts, that between nature and society and that between two aspects of society: urban/rural or industrial/agricultural. Brown, *Thomas Hardy*, p. 90, defines *Tess* as "the tragedy of a proud community baffled and defeated by processes beyond its understanding or control." Brown emphasizes agricultural decline as the source of tragedy. In a similar vein, but looking at *Tess* in the context of the English historical novel, Fleishman, *English Historical Novel*, argues, "It is by now well known that *Tess*'s social theme is the destruction of the old yeoman class of small-holders and peasants (p. 190). Tess sacrifices herself to "the course of history itself . . . the tragic sense of life becomes a historical attitude" (p. 197).

Howe, *Thomas Hardy*, p. 110, has argued the first kind of conflict, that the tragedy stems from disjunctions between nature and society. He claims, "Tess derives from Hardy's involvement with and reaction against the Victorian cult of chastity. . . . Tess reaches a purity of spirit even as she fails to satisfy the standards of the world." Howe, in defining this conflict, intends to move beyond both Brown and Kettle, *Introduction to the English Novel*, 2:49, who focuses on "the peasant Tess" as representative of the "destruction of the English peasantry" and terms the novel a "moral fable." Howe wants to acknowledge Tess's "reality" and convincingness as woman and as a source of the novel's power: "What matters . . . is the figure of Tess herself. Tess as she is, a woman made real through the craft of art and not Tess as she represents an idea" (p. 130).

Other critics have moved away from dichotomies between nature and society, between agricultural and industrial, and from simple endorsements of one over the other, to argue that Hardy tempers his agricultural values with an appreciation for improvements in the social system. See Williams, *English Novel*, pp. 97–102, and Williams, *Country and the City*, which insists on a greater complexity to this issue and elucidates that complexity: "Tess is not a peasant girl seduced by the squire; she is the daughter of a lifeholder and small dealer who is seduced by the son of a retired manufacturer" (p. 210).

In all of these studies of Tess in society, we find an emphasis on Tess as representative—of purity or of class. Yet some critics look for greater subtlety. Howe's response indicates a desire to acknowledge the social themes without reducing Tess to a symbol. Williams, *Country and the City*, p. 210, urges our recognition that "the social alienation enters the personality."

My analysis looks closely at Hardy's depiction of society and its relationship to his creation of character. It studies the ways in which the character Tess retains her autonomy even as the novel develops social dimensions to her personality and social themes. It stresses the social conflicts within her as an individual: the destructive social forces are not simply outside her.

21. Williams, *Country and the City*, p. 213, has arrived at a similar position. Williams concludes of Tess, as well as of Marty South and Jude Fawley, that "people choose wrongly but under terrible pressures; under the confusions of class, under its misunderstandings, under the calculated rejections of a divided separating world."

22. Squires, *Pastoral Novel*, has done an analysis of rural society represented in what he terms the pastoral novels of George Eliot, Hardy, and Lawrence. He concludes that "illustrating the significance of an agricultural society, they bear insight into the meaning of a rural environment

and of a traditionally ordered society for those who make up the community" (p. 218). My own analysis of the rural world—albeit primarily in later novels by Hardy and Lawrence—suggests that the use of the agricultural context is more complex than Squires documents. The representation of society in fact recognizes criticism and limitation of the agricultural world. It is not simply a vantage point from which to view an increasingly urban and industrial world.

23. See my article on this subject, "A Perspective of One's Own," pp. 12–28.

24. Hardy, *Tess of the D'Urbervilles*, chap. 2.

25. Hardy, *Jude*, part 5, chap. 7.

26. Lawrence, "Morality and the Novel," p. 528.

27. "To Edward Garnett," 5 June 1914, Lawrence, *Collected Letters*, 1:281–82.

28. Moynahan, *Deed of Life*, p. 71.

29. Reported by Stephen Pile, in "A Pilgrimage to D. H. Lawrence—Warts and All," *The Sunday Times*, London, 20 July 1980, sec. 1, p. 32.

30. Lawrence, *Rainbow*, chap. 1.

31. Hough, *Dark Sun*, p. 72.

32. Mudrick, "Originality of *The Rainbow*," p. 17, makes a similar point: "The community in *The Rainbow*, like every other, is an abstraction from its individuals, who are its only embodiment; and it lives as more than a mere term of discourse only so long as it provides forms and sanctions for the abiding impulses of their separate natures. These impulses are, besides, not all of them communal and sympathetic."

33. Leavis, *D. H. Lawrence*, p. 106.

34. "To Edward Garnett," 5 June 1914, Lawrence, *Collected Letters*, p. 282.

35. Daleski, *Forked Flame*, p. 77, observes that "it takes . . . three generations to produce a genuine individual." Daleski's point is a corollary to mine, which finds Ursula's the superior achievement not only because of her inheritance but because of the superior quality of her struggles.

36. Sagar, *Art of D. H. Lawrence*, p. 66, speaks to the quality of society as included in *The Rainbow* and sees this novel as "Lawrence's Isaiah, a reaffirmation of Noah's covenant": "The structure shows how the Brangwens, beginning with the patriarch Tom, strive to keep this covenant while the society around them is devoting more and more of its energy to breaking it." Sagar points to the increasing conflict between individuals and society, although he has recognized that the *beyond* to be incorporated by successful individuals can include "unknown areas of experience within society" (p. 66). Sagar does not explore, as I do, how Lawrence's fictional society helps generate the particular effects of *The Rainbow* and *Women in Love*—where the conflict between individual and society must

somehow be resolved, because society is still a source of the essential self for Lawrence's characters.

37. See, for example, Moynahan, *Deed of Life*, p. 71, and Stoll, *Novels of D. H. Lawrence*, p. 106, who finds *The Rainbow*'s conclusion "forced and merely defiant" because Lawrence partly abandons "the struggle of the vital self to realize its potentialities" and turns attention to "an attack upon the social order." My analysis interprets this attack on an engagement with society as the means for Ursula's final vision, the realization of her vital self.

38. Sanders, *D. H. Lawrence*, p. 93, notes, at this stage in Lawrence's canon (*The Rainbow* and *Women in Love*) an insistence on "the destructive consequences of isolating oneself from the world of man. Yet from the latter chapters of *The Rainbow* onwards, his characters are in constant flight from society, they observe the 'ordered world of man,' if they observe it at all, from ever greater distances." My own analysis reaches a similar conclusion: that Lawrence in *The Rainbow* and *Women in Love* has taken his perspective as far as he can. It is a fragile accomplishment. His later career—*The Plumed Serpent, Lady Chatterley's Lover*—falls outside the bounds of this book, outside the bounds of the formal understanding of society and the individual articulated in this chapter.

39. Cited in Marcus, *Representations*, p. 199.

40. James, *Ambassadors*, book 10, chap. 2.

41. James, *Daisy Miller*, chap. 4.

42. I am indebted to Harvey, *Character and the Novel*, p. 46, for this reference and for an analysis of James significant to the development of my own thinking.

43. Ibid., p. 50.

44. James, *Ambassadors*, book 12, chap. 5.

45. Ibid., book 2, chap. 2.

46. Lukács, *Studies in European Realism*, p. 71, defines as "typical" heroes only "figures of exceptional qualities, who mirror all the essential aspects of some definite stage of development, evolutionary tendency, or social group."

47. Ibid., p. 53.

48. Tolstoy, *War and Peace*, book 2, part 2, chap. 1.

49. Ibid., part 5, chap. 1.

50. Ibid., part 1, chap. 9.

51. Anderson, "George Eliot in *Middlemarch*, p. 293.

52. Tolstoy, *War and Peace*, book 2, part 5, chap. 1.

53. Eagleton, *Criticism and Ideology*, p. 121.

Chapter 5

1. Zola, "Experimental Novel," p. 9.
2. Ibid., p. 3.
3. Tolstoy, *War and Peace*, book 3, part 3, chap. 31.
4. Zola, *Germinal*, part 1, chap. 3.
5. Sherman, "Barbaric Naturalism of Mr. Dreiser," p. 80.
6. Zola, "Experimental Novel," pp. 53–54.
7. Matthiessen, *Theodore Dreiser*, p. 192, has articulated the critical consensus on *An American Tragedy*, the story of a boy "always worked upon by his environment and circumstances."

While this perspective is not new, we need to look at what underlies it. Hakutani, *Young Dreiser*, p. 9, begins with a critical truism about Dreiser, "that the greatness of Theodore Dreiser's writing comes not so much from his technique but from his particular knowledge of American life." Hakutani's study explores the influence of French naturalism—especially the work of Balzac and Zola—upon Dreiser and concludes that that influence is superficial. Hakutani's is an historical/social study; my formal study essentially reaches the same conclusions by focusing on Dreiser's techniques, which differ markedly from Zola's.

Warren, *Homage to Theodore Dreiser*, p. 104, suggests one obvious source for Dreiser's literary naturalism—his own life: "He was not, in fact, trying to put himself imaginatively in the place of Chester or Clyde. He was not, in the end, trying to tell their story. He was trying to tell his own." See also, Moers, *The Two Dreisers*. But, as Dreiser commented in his letter of 20 April 1927 to Jack Wilgus, his *own* story is a "story so common to every boy reared in the smaller towns of America."

Dreiser achieves his naturalism, because he tends to see the general social truth in the individual life. Dreiser's greatness may finally depend on his techniques, and it is time we examined them closely, because only through those techniques is Dreiser's vision and judgment of American life and the individual realized.

8. Dreiser, *American Tragedy*, book 1, chap. 1, and souvenir.
9. Matthiessen, *Theodore Dreiser*, pp. 197–98, analyzes in detail Dreiser's weakness in the presentation of Sondra and her set, but he, too, feels that "this may have been what Dreiser intended."
10. Howe, afterword, *American Tragedy*, p. 817.
11. Eliot, *Adam Bede*, chap. 37.
12. Ibid.
13. Ibid., chap. 45.
14. Matthiessen, *Theodore Dreiser*, pp. 206–7, comments that Dreiser "sees man so exclusively as the overwhelmed victim that we hardly feel any of the crisis of moral guilt that is also at the heart of the tragic

experience." Although Matthiessen concludes that Clyde, the character, is below tragedy, he notes that Dreiser "has written out of a profoundly tragic sense of man's fate."

Chapter 6

1. Fleishman is a distinguished proponent of this position, which he articulated first in *Conrad's Politics*, pp. 161–84. In his *English Historical Novel*, p. 231, Fleishman claims that, in *Nostromo*, Conrad discovered "an aesthetic equivalent for the complex process of historical change." See also, Kettle, *Introduction to the English Novel*, 2:11, 75.

This claim is less common from critics of *Barchester Towers*, who usually do not locate social process as the center of the novel. A notable exception is Polhemus, *Changing World of Anthony Trollope*, who argues that Trollope is "chronicling imaginatively . . . forms of historical and psychological change." *Barchester Towers* offers a comic interpretation of a whole middle-class Victorian world.

2. See, for example, Hay, *Political Novels of Joseph Conrad*, especially p. 176; Guerard, *Conrad the Novelist*, especially pp. 204–7; Karl, *Reader's Guide to Joseph Conrad*, especially p. 178; and Bains, *Joseph Conrad*, especially p. 299.

Friedman, *The Turn of the Novel*, pp. 89–90, acknowledges the problems in characterization, as does Leavis, *Great Tradition*, especially p. 200.

For those who find *Barchester Towers* flawed see Booth, *Anthony Trollope*, who sees *Barchester Towers* as artistically flawed social commentary; Davies, *Trollope*, who argues that morality is a goal that excuses formal flaws; and Edwards, *Anthony Trollope*, who claims reality is a goal that excuses formal flaws.

It had been too long a critical truism that Trollope's novels lacked artistic coherence when Ruth ApRoberts, *Moral Trollope*, argued for new principles on which to judge Trollope's achievement. She points to Trollope's "moral casuistry": Trollope's novels often appear to be flawed because the shaping principle behind his work acknowledges the ambiguity of ethical problems. Kincaid, in *"Barchester Towers,"* pp. 595–612, and *Novels of Anthony Trollope*, adopts a similar strategy and formulates the principles or unity informing Trollope's work. He denies that plot consists of causal actions in a connected series and focuses on the way point of view creates a moral tension resolved by running the reforming rascals (e.g., Slope) out of town. Garrett, *Victorian Multiplot Novel*, originates the term "dialogical form" to understand the principles behind Trollope's novels. Trollope's works have irreconcilable logics that cannot be subsumed into any single theme or logic. In the tension between these logics lies the novels' richness.

Fruitful as these approaches are to Trollope's canon in general, they leave unexplored the theory of the novel and society I am advancing to explain one of Trollope's most popular novels, *Barchester Towers*. This explanation will not serve for all of Trollope's canon nor for all of Conrad's. It does explain the complexity and narrative decisions of these two rich novels.

3. Conrad, *Nostromo*, part 3, chap. 10.

4. Trollope, *The Warden* and *Barchester Towers*, chap. 6.

5. Knoepflmacher, *Laughter and Despair*, p. 39, articulates this same conflict between the low-church elements, which he identifies with London—"innovative and mechanical"—and high-church elements, which he identifies with Barchester, "conservative, organic." For Knoepflmacher, Ullathorne, so resistant to change that time seems to stand still, provides a contrast to the more flexible and healthy conservatism of Barchester. Knoepflmacher points to the same encroachment of one world upon another that I discuss, but he pursues the thematic implications of that encroachment and locates Trollope's achievement in creating a world that serves as an "impregnable bastion against the same confusion that his contemporaries could not manage to screen as easily or as completely" (p. 26). In contrast, I have restricted myself rigorously to the formal techniques a writer must employ when he is demonstrating the challenge of one society to another—that is, when society functions as protagonist. Although novelists often depict one world encroaching upon another, they do not usually focus on society as protagonist, rather on particular characters experiencing the conflicts of social change. It is Trollope's focus, not on character, but on that abstraction called society, that provided him with the narrative means to be so *thematically* affirming. In a *conflict of societies*, one society must win. From my point of view, the "homogeneity" that reigns at the end of *Barchester Towers* cannot readily be duplicated by other novelists, because Trollope's *techniques* are not duplicated. Form and meaning go hand in hand.

6. Van Ghent, *English Novel*, p. 179, talks about *Adam Bede* as a novel in which we might think of society as protagonist. But she means by protagonist that society is essential to a character's identity and that someone like Hetty "lost from the only values that can support her mediocrity . . . sinks into the chaos of animal fear." Van Ghent is not speaking, as I am, of society's acting as a human hero. Her definition of society's role in this novel accords with mine. She simply uses a term I reserve for a special function of society. Gregor and Nicholas, *Moral and the Story*, adopt a point of view similar to Van Ghent's and observe that, in *Adam*

Bede, "The communal gathering is used here partly to endorse the personal values and partly because it is the most explicit way of emphasizing the values and traditions of the community itself" (p. 18). They conclude that Hetty cannot return to Hayslope, not from shame, but from "the feeling that she has broken a social bond which cannot be retied" (p. 27). Society as protagonist here would mean what Van Ghent means: characters live by the "coercive morality of the community" (p. 26). This, of course, is the common meaning of society as protagonist: a thematic one. It is not my meaning.

7. *Vanity Fair* raises another distinction between novels with a joint protagonist and novels in which society is protagonist. Here, as we have seen, Becky Sharp and Amelia Sedley command central significance, and each seems to represent different values. Those values constitute two sides of one social vision comprising the real and the ideal. Amelia embodies society's cherished ideals of self-sacrifice and submission, Becky its pragmatic realities of self-interest and aggression. Of course, the distinction between real and ideal is not absolute, only relative, and *Vanity Fair* derives power from the moral valence of the opposing visions. While *Vanity Fair* images different aspects of one social order through Becky and Amelia, *Nostromo* and *Barchester Towers* envision different social orders, each of which has its own conflict between ideals and realities. We realize this intentional conflict perhaps most vividly in Charles Gould's continual sacrifice of the ideals behind the San Tomé mine in his pragmatic efforts to safeguard its existence.

Bleak House affords yet another distinction. Although the story actually constitutes a single action, the deliberate fragmentation (one plot divided into two seemingly separate actions) images, as Rader ("The Comparative Anatomy of Three 'Baggy Monsters,'" p. 9) has argued, "the collective guilt of a neglectful and unfeeling society," a world whose moral center has decayed. A novel like *Bleak House* may have several protagonists and the focus of interest may shift from one character to another, but each of the characters expresses some aspect of that corrupted world.

8. For many critics, Dr. Monygham's personal redemption marks his unequivocal success in the novel. See, for example, Warren, introduction, *Nostromo*, p. 11; and Leavis, *The Great Tradition*, p. 194.

9. I have been silent about Antonia Avellanos because, although she loses her fiancé, she seems to belong to the future proletarian revolution rather than the capitalist revolution enacted in the novel. She is even less fully realized as a character than the others. The psychology, so rudimentary in the other major characters, is missing entirely in her, an absence that would support my general contention that what internal psychologi-

cal development we get is provided to define the limitations of the individuals to realize society's potential. Antonia, on the contrary, becomes a promise for the future. Nostromo's final victory—expressing the resiliency of the people—and the presence of Antonia Avellanos assure us that the society has only reached one point of definition in an ongoing process. Conrad's statement, "Antonia the Aristocrat and Nostromo the Man of the People are the artisans of the New Era, the true creators of the New State" (*Nostromo*, p. 8), has an essential rightness in this context.

10. Conrad, *Nostromo*, p. 7.

11. Kendrick, *Novel-Machine*, provides a much-needed revision of our understanding of Trollope as a theorist of the novel. Kendrick defines Trollope's achievement as encompassing the very art of realism itself "in forcing writing to efface itself between the equal realities of the reader's real and the writer's represented world" (p. 4). My own point here, of course, is that Trollope had the artistic sophistication necessary to lead him to experimental forms.

12. Conrad, "Autocracy and War," p. 97.

13. Van Ghent, *English Novel*, pp. 3, 4.

14. Ibid., p. 4.

Chapter 7

1. Brontë, *Wuthering Heights*, chap. 9.

2. See, for example, Kettle, *Introduction to the English Novel*, pp. 139–55; and Collins, "Theme and Conventions in *Wuthering Heights*," pp. 43–50.

3. Garrett, *Victorian Multiplot Novel*, has argued for the "dual logic of *Wuthering Heights*." His is an interesting advance on the by-now-common discussions of thematic oppositions in Brontë's novel. Garrett notes the thematic oppositions "between the energy of natural or supernatural forces and the restraints of civilized order and reason" (p. 19), but he is interested in what he calls the novel's double plots. Traditionally, criticism has defined "a tragic metaphysical love story followed, complemented, and reversed by a comic counterplot in which less extreme versions of the original tormented lovers converge to restore civility" (p. 19).

In Garrett's view, however, we can set another pattern or plot against this first "closed, linear" one, a pattern in which "they (Catherine and Heathcliff) and their violent visionary world remain as a perpetual alternative, coexisting with the more normal, conventional world of the second generation" (p. 19). For Garrett, the two plots coexist. My own reading of the role of society in this novel essentially supports the latter reading over the former: society is represented in such a way that the visionary world remains a present, perpetual alternative throughout. The former plot presents the conventional, safe view of people like Nelly and Lockwood and seems to me to be subverted throughout. I wonder, too, how fully Garrett endorses his own dialogical reading since, when he quotes Lockwood's final lines in *Wuthering Heights*, "I . . . wondered how any one could ever imagine unquiet slumbers for the sleepers in that quiet earth," he claims that even as Lockwood's words end the narrative's movement, they also "ironically invite us to remedy his *deficient imagination*" (emphasis added, p. 20). If Lockwood's imagination is deficient, then that is a judgment of the validity of the first "plot."

4. O'Connor, "Some Aspects of the Grotesque in Southern Fiction," p. 43.

5. Ibid., p. 42.

6. Fielding, *Joseph Andrews*, chap. 14.

7. Lawrence, *Women in Love*, chap. 19.

8. Collins, "Theme and Conventions," compares Lawrence and Brontë and finds them similar in their use of society. But the similarities are only superficial; my own analysis finds a basic difference in the formal role of society in Lawrence and Brontë.

9. Van Ghent, *English Novel*, pp. 154–59, makes a related point. My broad recognition that a precise social reality provides a vehicle to the mystery is also anticipated in specific analyses of the narrative technique of *Wuthering Heights*. See Mathison, "Nelly Dean and the Power of *Wuthering Heights*," pp. 106–29.

For other critics, the technique is important not to validate Heathcliff and Catherine but to undercut the untenable theme of the "moral magnificence of unmoral passion . . . in the end the triumph is all on the side of the cloddish world, which survives." See Schorer, "Technique as Discovery," p. 70, as well as his "Fiction and the 'Matrix of Analogy,'" p. 550, in which Schorer argues that the style performs the same artistic function as the technique: the "rhetoric altered the form of [Brontë's] intention."

10. Van Ghent, *English Novel*, pp. 157, 158, 163, developed this same point in discussing the novel's form and function: "Essentially, *Wuthering Heights* exists for the mind as a tension between two kinds of reality: the raw, inhuman reality of anonymous natural energies, and the restrictive reality of civilized habits, manners, and codes." Van Ghent poses a question for the novel—how "to represent dramatically, in terms of human 'character,' its vision of the inhuman"—which I am answering from another perspective, that of the representation of society.

11. Ibid., pp. 163–64.

12. O'Connor, "The Grotesque in Southern Fiction," p. 41.

13. Ibid., pp. 42, 45.

14. Ibid., p. 40.

15. O'Connor, "Everything That Rises Must Converge," p. 408.

16. Ibid., p. 407.

17. O'Connor, *Violent Bear It Away*, chap. 2.

18. O'Connor, "The Grotesque in Southern Fiction," p. 42.

19. Ibid., p. 44.

20. O'Connor, "Revelation," p. 491.

21. O'Connor, "Revelation," p. 500.

22. O'Connor, "Revelation," p. 508.

Chapter 8

1. Faulkner, *Absalom, Absalom!* chap. 1.

2. Vickery, *Novels of William Faulkner*, p. 310.

3. Millgate, *Achievement of William Faulkner*, p. 164, acknowledges this mystery: "Again and again, however, Faulkner stops us short of elucidation . . . by the continual frustration of our desire to complete the pattern of motivation, of cause and effect. . . . it is notable that most of the chapters, including the last, end on such moments of checked resolution."

4. Powers, *Faulkner's Yoknapatawpha Comedy*, p. 106, has made, tangentially, a point similar to mine, "Whether or not [Quentin's] recreation [of Sutpen's story] is truly accurate, or factually verifiable, is beside the point. It is sufficiently true and convincing for Quentin—and that is what matters finally." Powers goes on to argue: "It is, in the full sense of the phrase, Quentin's story, terrifically meaningful for him and for us, since, through Quentin's recreation of Thomas Sutpen's career, we gain Faulkner's most searing penetration into the evil at the heart of the antebellum South's social organization, his most revealing exposure of the rot at the base of the Southern edifice." Indeed this general conclusion about society is one that emerges from the novel—Mr. Coldfield expresses it directly—but I am interested in the way Faulkner preserves a mystery about the role of society, by making it a subject of conjecture and interpretation for each character, not only for Quentin.

5. Brooks, *William Faulkner*, pp. 429–36, has provided a thorough table detailing both facts and events in Sutpen's life and the ultimate authority for those. He also includes a table of important conjectures and who made them about Sutpen.

6. Van Ghent, *English Novel*, p. 164.

7. Brooks, "Thomas Sutpen," p. 296, notes that Thomas Sutpen is, psychologically, a convert. He points out that "the irony of Sutpen's life is

(in part at least) that he was fixated on his image of the plantation which for him was an abstract idea—since he had had scant participation in it as lived experience—and that . . . Sutpen pursued an ideal of gracious ease and leisure, with a breathless ferocity." Brooks makes a corollary point to my thesis that even Sutpen lived out an interpretation or image of society.

8. Brooks, *William Faulkner*, p. 429 n., observes a related point, that when Faulkner was asked whether Sutpen acknowledged Clytemnestra as a daughter, he said, "Well, that would not have mattered because Clytemnestra was a female. The important thing to him was that he should establish a line of dukes, you see."

9. Brooks, "The Narrative Structure of *Absalom, Absalom!*" p. 313, points out that Quentin's and Shreve's attitudes differ strikingly as they attempt to recreate Sutpen's story: "Quentin . . . reacts to the telling of the story with something like fatigue and somber irritation. It is too close to his own life: it is all too painfully real. But Shreve's postponements spring from a diametrically opposite reason. The South is horrifyingly (but delightfully) unreal." Indeed, the parallels between Quentin and Henry are very strong, but Quentin and Shreve are finally *guessing*. My thesis focuses on this fact: the parallels are in part an interpretation whose authority Quentin cannot escape. He must endure the consequences of what he perceives, whether fully accurate or not.

10. Langford, *Faulkner's Revision of "Absalom, Absalom!"* p. 35, notes that this passage is added between manuscript and published book "to emphasize the effect of the story on Quentin." This is one of a number of changes that emphasize Quentin's involvement in the Sutpen story and suggest the imaginative grip of that *interpreted* southern past on Quentin's life.

11. This passage was also added between manuscript and published book, ibid., p. 36.

12. Thomas Mann, "Homage," *The Castle*, by Franz Kafka (New York: Vintage, 1974), p. xvi.

13. Kafka, *Castle*, chap. 2.

14. Mann, "Homage," *The Castle*, p. xiv.

15. Ibid., p. xviii.

16. Goodman, *Structure of Literature*, p. 183.

17. Emrich, *Franz Kafka*, pp. 337–41, has discussed these patterns in Kafka's fiction.

18. Pynchon, *Crying of Lot 49*, chap. 6.

Chapter 9

1. Van Doren, preface, *Dream of the Red Chamber*, p. vii.
2. Ibid., p. vii.
3. Hsueh-chin, *Dream of the Red Chamber*, chap. 4.
4. Eagleton, *Criticism and Ideology*, pp. 110–11.
5. Ibid., p. 161.
6. Ionesco, "Ionesco and the Critics," p. 651.

Bibliography

Allen, Walter. *The English Novel: A Short Critical History*. New York: Dutton Press, 1954.

Alter, Robert. *Fielding and the Nature of the Novel*. Cambridge: Harvard University Press, 1968.

———. "Fielding and the Uses of Style." *Novel: A Forum on Fiction* 1 (Fall 1967): 53–63. Rpt. in *20th Century Interpretations of "Tom Jones."* Edited by Martin Battestin. Englewood Cliffs, New Jersey: Prentice-Hall, 1968.

Anderson, Quentin. "George Eliot in *Middlemarch*." *A Guide to English Literature: From Dickens to Hardy*. Edited by Boris Ford. Harmondsworth: Penguin, 1958.

ApRoberts, Ruth. *The Moral Trollope*. Athens: Ohio University Press, 1971.

Ariès, Philippe. *Centuries of Childhood: A Social History of Family Life*. Translated by Robert Baldick. New York: Alfred A. Knopf, 1962.

Auerbach, Nina. *Communities of Women: An Idea in Fiction*. Cambridge: Harvard University Press, 1978.

Austen, Jane. *The Novels of Jane Austen*. 3rd ed. Volumes 1–5. Edited by R. W. Chapman. London and New York: Oxford University Press, 1932–34.

Bachelard, Gaston. *The Poetics of Space*. Translated by Maria Jolas. New York: The Orion Press, 1964.

Baines, Jocelyn. *Joseph Conrad: A Critical Biography*. New York: McGraw-Hill Book Company, 1959.

Bakhtin, Mikhail. *The Dialogic Imagination*. Translated by Caryl Emerson and Michael Holquist. Edited by Michael Holquist. Austin: University of Texas Press, 1981.

Basch, Françoise. *Relative Creatures: Victorian Women in Society and the Novel*. Translated by Anthony Rudolf. New York: Schocken Books, 1974.

Battestin, Martin. "Fielding's Definition of Wisdom: Some Functions of Ambiguity and Emblem in *Tom Jones*." *English Literary History* 35 (1968): 188–217.

Bedient, Calvin. *Architects of Self: George Eliot, D. H. Lawrence, and E. M. Forster*. Berkeley, Los Angeles, and London: University of California Press, 1972.

Beer, Patricia. *Reader, I Married Him: A Study of the Women Characters of Jane Austen, Charlotte Brontë, Elizabeth Gaskell, and George Eliot*. New York: Macmillan, 1974.

Berger, Morroe. *Real and Imagined Worlds: The Novel and Social Science*. Cambridge: Harvard University Press, 1977.

Berlin, Isaiah. *The Hedgehog and the Fox: An Essay on Tolstoy's View of History*. London: Weidenfield and Nicholson, 1953.

Booth, Bradford. *Anthony Trollope: Aspects of His Life and Art*. Bloomington: Indiana University Press, 1958.

Booth, Wayne. *The Rhetoric of Fiction*. Chicago: University of Chicago Press, 1961.

Brantlinger, Patrick. *The Spirit of Reform: British Literature and Politics*. Cambridge: Harvard University Press, 1977.

Brontë, Charlotte. *Jane Eyre*. Edited by Richard J. Dunn. New York: Norton, 1971.

Brontë, Emily. *Wuthering Heights*. Edited by William M. Sale, Jr. New York: Norton, 1963.

Brooks, Cleanth. "The Narrative Structure of *Absalom, Absalom!*" *William Faulkner: Toward Yoknapatawpha and Beyond*. New Haven and London: Yale University Press, 1978.

———. "Thomas Sutpen: A Representative Southern Planter?" *William Faulkner: Toward Yoknapatawpha and Beyond*. New Haven and London: Yale University Press, 1978.

———. *William Faulkner: The Yoknapatawpha Country*. New Haven: Yale University Press, 1963.

Brown, Douglas. *Thomas Hardy*. London: Longmans, Green, 1954. Reprinted 1961.

Brown, Julia Prewitt. *Jane Austen's Novels: Social Change and Literary Form*. Cambridge: Harvard University Press, 1979.

Butler, Marilyn. *Jane Austen and the War of Ideas*. Oxford: Clarendon Press, 1975.

Cazamian, Louis. *The Social Novel in England, 1830–1850: Dickens, Disraeli, Mrs. Gaskell, Kingsley*. Translated by Martin Fido. London and Boston: Routledge and Kegan Paul, 1973.

Collins, Clifford. "Theme and Conventions in *Wuthering Heights*." *The Critic* 1 (1947): 43–50.

Conrad, Joseph. "Autocracy and War." *Notes on Life and Letters*. Garden City and Toronto: Doubleday, Page and Company, 1921.

———. *Nostromo: A Tale of the Seaboard*. Introduction by Robert Penn Warren. New York: Random House, 1951.

Craig, David. *The Real Foundations: Literature and Social Change*. New York: Oxford University Press, 1974.

Crane, R. S. "The Concept of Plot and the Plot of *Tom Jones*." *Critics and Criticism*. Chicago: University of Chicago Press, 1952.

Daiches, David. *Literature and Society*. London: V. Gollancz, 1938.

Daleski, H. M. *The Forked Flame: A Study of D. H. Lawrence*. London: Faber and Faber. Evanston: Northwestern University Press, 1965.

Davies, H. S. *Trollope*. London: Longmans, Green and Company, 1960.

Demetz, Peter. *Marx, Engels, and the Poets: Origins of Marxist Literary Criticism*. Translated by Jeffrey L. Sammons. Chicago and London: University of Chicago Press, 1967.

Dickens, Charles. *Bleak House*. Edited by George Ford and Sylvère Monod. New York: Norton, 1977.

———. *Our Mutual Friend*. New York: Random House, 1960.

Dreiser, Theodore. *An American Tragedy*. New York: New American Library, 1964.

Duckworth, Alistair. *The Improvement of the Estate: A Study of Jane Austen's Novels*. Baltimore and London: Johns Hopkins University Press, 1971.

Eagleton, Terry. *Criticism and Ideology: A Study in Marxist Literary Theory*. Norfolk: Lowe and Brydone Printers, Ltd., 1975.

———. *Marxism and Literary Criticism*. Berkeley and Los Angeles: University of California Press, 1976.

Edwards, Lee R. "Women, Energy and *Middlemarch*." *Massachusetts Review* 13 (1972): 223–38.

Edwards, P. D. *Anthony Trollope*. New York: Humanities Press, 1969.

Eliot, George. *Adam Bede*. Edited by John Paterson. Boston: Houghton Mifflin, 1968.

———. "Amos Barton." *Scenes of Clerical Life*. Edited by David Lodge. Harmondsworth: Penguin, 1973.

———. *Daniel Deronda*. Edited by Barbara Hardy. Harmondsworth: Penguin, 1967.

———. *The George Eliot Letters*. Edited by Gordon S. Haight. New Haven: Yale University Press, 1954–55.

———. *Middlemarch*. Edited by Gordon S. Haight. Boston: Houghton Mifflin, 1956.

———. "The Natural History of German Life." *Essays of George Eliot*. Edited by Thomas Pinney. London: Routledge and Kegan Paul, 1963.

———. "Three Months in Weimar." *Essays of George Eliot*. Edited by Thomas Pinney. London: Routledge and Kegan Paul, 1963.

Emrich, Wilhelm. *Franz Kafka: A Critical Study of His Writings*. Translated by Sheema Zeben Buehne. New York: Frederick Ungar Publishing Company, 1968.

Faulkner, William. *Absalom, Absalom!* New York: Random House, The Modern Library, 1936.

Fielding, Henry. *Joseph Andrews*. Edited by Martin Battiston. Boston: Houghton Mifflin, 1961.

———. *Tom Jones*. Edited by Sheridan Baker. New York: Norton, 1973.

Fleishman, Avrom. *Conrad's Politics: Community and Anarchy in the Fiction of Joseph Conrad*. Baltimore: Johns Hopkins University Press, 1967.

———. *The English Historical Novel: Walter Scott to Virginia Woolf*. Baltimore and London: Johns Hopkins University Press, 1971.

———. *A Reading of "Mansfield Park": An Essay in Critical Synthesis*. Baltimore and London: Johns Hopkins University Press, 1967.

Forster, E. M. *Aspects of the Novel*. New York: Harcourt, Brace and World, 1927.

———. *Howards End*. New York: Random House, 1921.

Friedman, Alan. *The Turn of the Novel: The Transition to Modern Fiction*. London and New York: Oxford University Press, 1966.

Frye, Northrop. *Anatomy of Criticism: Four Essays*. New York: Atheneum, 1957. Reprinted, 1969.

———. *The Stubborn Structure: Essays on Criticism and Society*. Ithaca: Cornell University Press, 1970.

Garrett, Peter K. *The Victorian Multiplot Novel: Studies in Dialogical Form*. New Haven and London: Yale University Press, 1980.

Gilbert, Sandra, and Susan Gubar. *The Madwoman in the Attic*. New Haven: Yale University Press, 1979.

Goodman, Paul. *The Structure of Literature*. Chicago: University of Chicago Press, 1954.

Graff, Gerald. *Literature Against Itself: Literary Ideas in Modern Society*. Chicago: University of Chicago Press, 1979.

Greene, Donald J. "Jane Austen and the Peerage." *PMLA* 68 (1953): 1017–31.

Gregor, Ian, and Brian Nicholas. *The Moral and the Story*. London: Faber and Faber, 1962.

Grossvogel, David L. *Limits of the Novel: Evolutions of a Form from Chaucer to Robbe-Grillet*. Ithaca: Cornell University Press, 1968.

Guerard, Albert. *Conrad the Novelist*. Cambridge: Harvard University Press, 1958.

Hakutani, Yoshinobu. *Young Dreiser: A Critical Study*. Cranbury, New Jersey: Associated University Presses, 1980.

Harden, Edgar F. "The Discipline and Significance of Form in *Vanity Fair*." *PMLA* 82 (1967): 530–41.

Hardy, Barbara. *The Appropriate Form: An Essay on the Novel*. London: Athlone Press, 1964.

_____. *The Moral Art of Dickens*. New York: Oxford University Press, 1970.

_____. *The Novels of George Eliot: A Study in Form*. New York: Oxford University Press, 1959.

_____. *A Reading of Jane Austen*. New York: New York University Press, 1976.

Hardy, Thomas. *Jude the Obscure*. Edited by Norman Page. New York: Norton, 1978.

_____. *Tess of the D'Urbervilles*. Edited by Scott Elledge. 2d ed. New York: Norton, 1979.

Harvey, W. J. *The Art of George Eliot*. New York: Oxford University Press, 1968.

_____. *Character and the Novel*. Ithaca: Cornell University Press, 1965.

_____. "Criticism of the Novel: Contemporary Reception." *Middlemarch: Critical Approaches to the Novel*. Edited by Barbara Hardy. London: Athlone, 1967.

Hay, Eloise Knapp. *The Political Novels of Joseph Conrad: A Critical Study*. Chicago: University of Chicago Press, 1963.

Holloway, John. "Dickens' Vision of Society." *Listener* (25 February 1965): 287–89.

Hough, Graham. *The Dark Sun: A Study of D. H. Lawrence*. New York: Macmillan, 1957.

House, Humphry. *The Dickens World*. Oxford: Oxford University Press, 1942.

Howe, Irving. Afterword, *An American Tragedy*. New York: New American Library, 1964.

_____. *Thomas Hardy*. New York: Macmillan, 1966.

Hsueh-chin, Tsao. *Dream of the Red Chamber*. Translated by Chi-Chen Wang. New York: Doubleday and Company, 1958.

Ionesco, Eugene. "Ionesco and the Critics: Eugene Ionesco Interviewed by Gabriel Jacobs." *Critical Inquiry* 1 (1975): 641–53.

Iser, Wolfgang. *The Implied Reader: Patterns of Communication in Prose Fiction from Bunyan to Beckett*. Baltimore and London: The Johns Hopkins University Press, 1974.

James, Henry. *The Ambassadors*. Edited by Leon Edel. Boston: Houghton Mifflin, 1960.

_____. *Daisy Miller*. The New York Edition. New York: Augustus M. Kelley, 1971.

_____. Preface, *The Princess Casamassima* in *The Art of the Novel: Critical Prefaces*. Edited by R. P. Blackmur. New York and London: Charles Scribner's Sons, 1934.

Jameson, Fredric. *Marxism and Form: Twentieth-Century Dialectical*

Theories of Literature. Princeton: Princeton University Press, 1971.
————. *The Political Unconscious: Narrative As a Socially Significant Act*. Ithaca: Cornell University Press, 1982.

Kafka, Franz. *The Castle*. New York: Vintage, 1974.

Karl, Frederick. *A Reader's Guide to Joseph Conrad*. New York: Farrar, Straus and Giroux, 1969.

Kendrick, Walter M. *The Novel-Machine: The Theory and Fiction of Anthony Trollope*. Baltimore and London: Johns Hopkins University Press, 1980.

Kermode, Frank. "Novel and Narrative." In *The Theory of the Novel: New Essays*. Edited by John Halperin. New York: Oxford University Press, 1959.

Kettle, Arnold. *An Introduction to the English Novel*. 2 vols. London and New York: Hutchinson's University Library, 1951–53.

Kincaid, J. R. "*Barchester Towers* and the Nature of Conservative Comedy." *English Literary History* 37 (1970): 595–612.
————. *The Novels of Anthony Trollope*. Oxford: Clarendon Press, 1977.

Knoepflmacher, U. C. *Laughter and Despair: Readings in Ten Novels of the Victorian Era*. Berkeley and Los Angeles: University of California Press, 1971.

Langford, Gerald. *Faulkner's Revision of "Absalom, Absalom!": A Collation of the Manuscript and the Published Book*. Austin and London: University of Texas Press, 1971.

Langland, Elizabeth. "A Perspective of One's Own: Thomas Hardy and the Elusive Sue Bridehead." *Studies in the Novel* 12 (1980): 12–28.

Lawrence, D. H. *The Collected Letters of D. H. Lawrence*. Edited by Harry T. Moore. New York: Viking Press, 1962.
————. "Morality and the Novel." *Phoenix: The Posthumous Papers*. Edited by Edward McDonald. New York: Viking Press, 1936.
————. *The Rainbow*. New York: Viking Press, 1970.
————. *Women in Love*. New York: Viking Press, 1969.

Leavis, F. R. *D. H. Lawrence: Novelist*. New York: Simon and Schuster, 1955.
————. *The Great Tradition*. 1948; rpt. New York: New York University Press, 1969.

Levine, George. *The Realistic Imagination*. Chicago: University of Chicago Press, 1981.

Lewes, G. H. "Dickens in Relation to Criticism." *Fortnightly Review* 17 (1872): 143–51. Reprinted in *Charles Dickens*. Edited by Stephen Wall. Harmondsworth: Penguin, 1970.
————. "The Novels of Jane Austen." *Blackwood's Magazine* 86

(1859): 99–113. Reprinted in *Pride and Prejudice*. Edited by Donald Gray. New York: Norton, 1966.

Litz, A. Walton. *Jane Austen: A Study of Her Artistic Development*. New York: Oxford University Press, 1965.

Loofbourow, John. *Thackeray and the Form of Fiction*. Princeton: Princeton University Press, 1964.

Lubbock, Percy. *The Craft of Fiction*. 1921; rpt. New York: Viking Press, 1957.

Lucas, John. *The Literature of Change: Studies in the Nineteenth-Century Provincial Novel*. New York: Barnes and Noble, 1977.

_____. *The Melancholy Man: A Study of Dickens' Novels*. London: Methuen, 1970.

Lukács, Georg. *The Historical Novel*. Translated by Hannah and Stanley Mitchell. London: Merlin Press, 1962.

_____. *Studies in European Realism*. New York: Grosset and Dunlap, 1964.

_____. *Theory of the Novel: A Historico-Philosophical Essay on the Forms of Great Epic Literature*. Translated by Anna Bostock. Cambridge: The MIT Press, 1971.

McMaster, Juliet. *Thackeray: The Major Novels*. Toronto: University of Toronto Press, 1971.

Mann, Thomas. "Homage." *The Castle*, by Franz Kafka. New York: Vintage, 1974.

Marcus, Steven. *Representations: Essays on Literature and Society*. New York: Random House, 1975.

Mathison, John K. "The German Sections of *Vanity Fair*." *Nineteenth-Century Fiction* 18 (1963): 235–46. Reprinted in *The German Sections of "Vanity Fair" and Other Studies*. Edited by Richard L. Hillier. Laramie, Wyoming: University of Wyoming, 1975.

_____. "Nelly Dean and the Power of *Wuthering Heights*." *Nineteenth-Century Fiction* 11 (1956): 106–29.

Matthiessen, F. O. *Theodore Dreiser*. New York: William Sloane, 1951.

Miller, J. Hillis. *Charles Dickens: The World of His Novels*. Cambridge: Harvard University Press, 1958.

_____. *The Form of Victorian Fiction: Thackeray, Dickens, Trollope, George Eliot, Meredith, and Hardy*. Notre Dame: University of Notre Dame Press, 1968.

_____. "Optic and Semiotic in *Middlemarch*." In *The Worlds of Victorian Fiction*. Edited by Jerome Buckley. Cambridge: Harvard University Press, 1975.

Millgate, Michael. *The Achievement of William Faulkner*. New York: Random House, 1966.

Moers, Ellen. *Literary Women*. Garden City, New York: Doubleday, 1976.

——. *The Two Dreisers*. New York: Viking Press, 1969.

Moynahan, Julian. *The Deed of Life: The Novels and Tales of D. H. Lawrence*. Princeton: Princeton University Press, 1963.

Mudrick, Marvin. *Jane Austen: Irony as Defense and Discovery*. Princeton: Princeton University Press, 1952.

——. "The Originality of *The Rainbow*." *Spectrum* 3 (Winter 1959): 3–28. Reprinted in *Twentieth Century Interpretations of "The Rainbow."* Edited by Mark Kinkead-Weekes. Englewood Cliffs, New Jersey: Prentice-Hall, 1971.

O'Connor, Flannery. "Everything That Rises Must Converge." *The Complete Stories of Flannery O'Connor*. New York: Farrar, Straus and Giroux, 1971.

——. "Revelation." *The Complete Stories of Flannery O'Connor*. New York: Farrar, Straus and Giroux, 1971.

——. "Some Aspects of the Grotesque in Southern Fiction." *Mystery and Manners: Occasional Prose*. Edited by Sally and Robert Fitzgerald. New York: Farrar, Straus and Giroux, 1961.

——. *The Violent Bear It Away*. New York: Noonday Press, 1955.

Orr, John. *Tragic Realism and Modern Society: Studies in the Sociology of the Modern Novel*. Pittsburgh: University of Pittsburgh Press, 1977.

Pile, Stephen, reporter. "A Pilgrimage to D. H. Lawrence—Warts and All." *The Sunday Times*, London (20 July 1980): Sec. 1, p. 32.

Polhemus, R. H. *The Changing World of Anthony Trollope*. Berkeley and Los Angeles: University of California Press, 1963.

Powers, Lyall H. *Faulkner's Yoknapatawpha Comedy*. Ann Arbor: The University of Michigan Press, 1980.

Preston, John. *The Created Self: The Reader's Role in Eighteenth-Century Fiction*. New York: Barnes and Noble, 1970.

Price, Martin. "Fielding: The Comedy of Forms." In *To the Palace of Wisdom: Studies in Order and Energy from Dryden to Blake*. New York: Doubleday, 1964. Reprinted in *Henry Fielding*. Edited by Claude Rawson. Harmondsworth: Penguin, 1973.

Pynchon, Thomas. *The Crying of Lot 49*. New York: Bantam, 1967.

Rader, Ralph. "The Comparative Anatomy of Three 'Baggy Monsters': *Bleak House, Vanity Fair, Middlemarch*." English Conference, University of California, Berkeley, Spring, 1975.

——. "The Concept of Genre and Eighteenth-Century Studies." In *New Approaches to Eighteenth-Century Literature*. Edited by Philip Harth. New York: Columbia University Press, 1974.

_____. "Fact, Theory, and Literary Explanation." *Critical Inquiry* 1 (1974): 245–72.

Ray, Gordon N. *Thackeray: The Uses of Adversity 1811–1846*. London: Oxford University Press, 1955.

Sacks, Sheldon. *Fiction and the Shape of Belief*. Berkeley and Los Angeles: University of California Press, 1964.

Sagar, Keith. *The Art of D. H. Lawrence*. Cambridge: Cambridge University Press, 1966.

Said, Edward. *Beginnings: Intention and Method*. New York: Basic Books, Inc., 1975.

_____. *The World, the Text, and the Critic*. Cambridge: Harvard University Press, 1983.

Sammons, Jeffrey. *Literary Sociology and the Practical Criticism: An Inquiry*. Bloomington and London: Indiana University Press, 1977.

Sanders, Scott. *D. H. Lawrence: The World of the Five Major Novels*. New York: Viking Press, 1973.

Schorer, Mark. "Fiction and the 'Matrix of Analogy.' " *Kenyon Review* 11 (1949): 539–60.

_____. "Technique as Discovery." *Hudson Review* 1 (1948): 67–87. Reprinted in *The Theory of the Novel*. Edited by Philip Stevick. New York: The Free Press, 1967.

Sherman, Stuart. "The Barbaric Naturalism of Mr. Dreiser." In *The Stature of Theodore Dreiser: A Critical Survey of the Man and His Work*. Edited by Alfred Kazin and Charles Shapiro. Bloomington, Indiana: Indiana University Press, 1965.

Showalter, Elaine. *A Literature of Their Own*. Princeton: Princeton University Press, 1977.

Shroder, Maurice. "The Novel as a Genre." In *The Theory of the Novel*. Edited by Philip Stevick. New York: The Free Press, 1967.

Spearman, Diana. *The Novel and Society*. New York: Barnes and Noble, 1966.

Squires, Michael. *The Pastoral Novel: Studies in George Eliot, Thomas Hardy, and D. H. Lawrence*. Charlottesville: University Press of Virginia, 1974.

Stevenson, Lionel, ed. *Victorian Fiction: A Guide to Research*. Cambridge: Harvard University Press, 1964.

Stoll, John E. *The Novels of D. H. Lawrence: A Search for Integration*. Columbia: University of Missouri Press, 1971.

Stump, Reva. *Movement and Vision in George Eliot's Novels*. Seattle: University of Washington Press, 1959.

Sussman, Herbert L. *Victorians and the Machine: The Literary Response to Technology*. Cambridge: Harvard University Press, 1968.

Swinden, Patrick. *Unofficial Selves: Character in the Novel from Dickens to the Present Day*. London: Macmillan, 1973.

Taube, Byron. "Contrast as a Principle of Structure in *Vanity Fair*." *Nineteenth-Century Fiction* 18 (1963): 119–35.

Tave, Stuart. *Some Words of Jane Austen*. Chicago: University of Chicago Press, 1973.

Thackeray, W. M. *Vanity Fair*. Edited by Geoffrey and Kathleen Tillotson. Boston: Houghton Mifflin, 1963.

Tillotson, Kathleen. "*Vanity Fair*." In *Novels of the Eighteen-Forties*. London: Oxford University Press, 1954. Reprinted in *Thackeray: A Collection of Critical Essays*. Edited by Alexander Welsh. Englewood Cliffs, New Jersey: Prentice-Hall, 1968.

Tolstoy, Leo. *War and Peace*. Translated by Rosemary Edmonds. Harmondsworth: Penguin, 1957.

Trilling, Lionel. Introduction, *Little Dorrit*, by Charles Dickens. New York and London: Oxford University Press, 1953. Reprinted in *Charles Dickens*. Edited by Stephen Wall. Harmondsworth: Penguin, 1970.

———. *The Liberal Imagination: Essays on Literature and Society*. New York: Viking, 1950.

———. *The Opposing Self: Nine Essays in Criticism*. New York: Viking, 1955.

Trollope, Anthony. *The Warden* and *Barchester Towers*. New York: Random House, 1950.

Van Doren, Mark. Preface, *Dream of the Red Chamber*, by Tsao Hsueh-chin. Translated by Chi-Chen Wang. New York: Doubleday, 1958.

Van Ghent, Dorothy. *The English Novel: Form and Function*. New York: Harper and Row, 1953. Reprinted, 1975.

Vickery, Olga W. *The Novels of William Faulkner: A Critical Interpretation*. rev. ed. Baton Rouge: Louisiana State University Press, 1964.

Warren, Robert Penn. *Homage to Theodore Dreiser*. New York: Random House, 1971.

———. Introduction, *Nostromo*, by Joseph Conrad. New York: Random House, 1951.

Watt, Ian. *The Rise of the Novel: Studies in Defoe, Richardson, and Fielding*. Berkeley and Los Angeles: University of California Press, 1957.

Wharton, Edith. *The Age of Innocence*. New York: Charles Scribner's Sons, 1969.

Williams, Raymond. *The Country and the City*. New York: Oxford University Press, 1973.

———. *Culture and Society, 1780–1950*. New York: Columbia University Press, 1958.

_____. *The English Novel; from Dickens to Lawrence*. New York: Oxford University Press, 1970.

Woolf, Virginia. *The Common Reader*. New York: Harcourt, Brace and World, 1925.

_____. *A Room of One's Own*. New York: Harcourt, Brace and World, 1929.

Zola, Émile. "The Experimental Novel." In *The Experimental Novel and Other Essays*. Translated by Belle M. Sherman. New York: Haskell House, 1964.

_____. *Germinal*. Translated by L. W. Tancock. Harmondsworth: Penguin, 1954.

Index

Characters from novels are indexed under the title of the novel in which they appear.

Absalom, Absalom! (Faulkner), 14, 187, 198, 212; society as source of quest in, 188–90, 194–96, 207–8; presentation of society in, 190, 196; society as characters' interpretations in, 191–94

Ada (Nabokov), 211

Adam Bede (Eliot), 41, 69, 74, 75, 86, 148, 211; compared to *An American Tragedy*, 141–42, 143, 144; compared to *Nostromo* and *Barchester Towers*, 153

Age of Innocence (Wharton), 41

À la recherche du temps perdu (Proust), 202

Alcott, Louisa May. See *Little Women*

Allen, Walter, 224 (n. 14)

Alter, Robert, 231 (nn. 6, 8)

Ambassadors (James), 114, 115, 116

An American Tragedy (Dreiser), 10, 12, 146, 218; society as theme in, 126; compared to *Germinal*, 134–35, 136–37, 139; presentation of society in, 135–37; moral relativity in, 137–38, 142–43; characterization and society in, 139–40, 143–45; moral judgment precluded in, 140–41; compared to *Adam Bede*, 141–42, 143, 144

Anderson, Quentin, 121

ApRoberts, Ruth, 241 (n. 2)

As You Like It (Shakespeare), 94

Auerbach, Nina, 41–42, 230 (n. 18)

Austen, Jane, 9, 12–13, 22, 23, 46, 49, 209; as watershed in formal treatment of society, 25–26; marriage and society in novels of, 27, 103; society as moral yardstick in novels of, 28, 30, 56; presentation of society in novels of, 30, 42–43, 51, 52, 69; social convention and character in novels of, 33, 34–38, 42, 50; narrative commentary in novels of, 38, 39, 44; family as social microcosm in novels of, 39–42. See also *Emma*; *Mansfield Park*; *Persuasion*; *Pride and Prejudice*

Bachelard, Gaston, 227 (n. 39), 230 (n. 13)

Bakhtin, Mikhail, 223 (nn. 1, 2)

Barchester Towers (Trollope), 4, 6, 13; society as formal protagonist in, 148–50; narrative instabilities in, 150–51, 152–55; compared to *Adam Bede*, 153; compared to *Middlemarch*, 154; characterization and society in, 155–60; structure of action in, 160–66; compared to *Pride and Prejudice*, 163; artist's intuition in, 166–67

Battestin, Martin, 232 (n. 12)

Bedient, Calvin, 234–35 (n. 1), 236 (n. 17)

Beliefs in the novel, 8, 224 (n. 13). See also Novel: and value

Berger, Morroe, 22, 226 (n. 31)

Berlin, Isaiah, 3, 10

Bernard, Claude, 127

Bleak House (Dickens), 4, 6, 12, 46, 47, 103, 138, 148, 154, 182, 219; individual freedom from social determinism in, 68, 75–76, 77; presentation of society in, 68–70, 72, 79; characterization and society in, 70–74, 76–77; compared to *Mid-*

dlemarch, 74; compared to *Adam Bede*, 74

Booth, Wayne, 56, 224 (n. 13), 233 (n. 20)

Brontë, Charlotte, 233 (n. 15). See also *Jane Eyre*

Brontë, Emily, 188, 190, 196. See also *Wuthering Heights*

Brooks, Cleanth, 246 (nn. 5, 7), 247 (nn. 8, 9)

Brown, Douglas, 236 (n. 20)

Brown, Julia Prewitt, 228 (n. 1), 230 (n. 15)

Butler, Marilyn, 229 (n. 4)

Castle (Kafka), 14, 187; society as source of quest in, 188–89, 196–97, 201–2, 207–8; presentation of society in, 197–98; society as characters' interpretations in, 198–201; fairy-tale patterns in, 200–201, 203

Cazamian, Louis, 226 (n. 33)

Cervantes, Miguel de. See *Don Quixote*

Character: in the novel, 9; in relationship to presentation of society, 9–10, 149–50. *See also* individual titles

Clarissa (Richardson): society in, 16

Collins, Clifford, 245 (n. 8)

Common Reader (Woolf), 230–31 (n. 19)

Conrad, Joseph, 169; "Autocracy and War," 147, 166. See also *Heart of Darkness*; *Nostromo*

Crane, R. S., 231 (n. 5)

Crying of Lot 49 (Pynchon), 14, 19; society as source of quest in, 188–89, 202–3, 207–8; presentation of society in, 203–4; fairy-tale motif in, 203; society as character's interpretation in, 204–7

Daisy Miller (James), 6, 9, 114

Daleski, H. M., 238 (n. 35)

Daniel Deronda (Eliot), 93–94

Deconstruction, ix, 3–4

Defoe, Daniel, 16, 35. See also *Moll Flanders*; *Robinson Crusoe*; *Roxana*

Dickens, Charles, 19, 33, 48, 66–67, 78–79, 160, 209. See also *Bleak House*; *Great Expectations*; *Hard Times*; *Little Dorrit*; *Our Mutual Friend*

Disraeli, Benjamin, 125

Don Quixote (Cervantes), 214

Dream of the Red Chamber (Hsueh-chin), 211–16

Dreiser, Theodore, 124, 125, 209. See also *An American Tragedy*

Duckworth, Alistair, 229 (n. 2), 231 (n. 19)

Eagleton, Terry, 21, 122, 216–17

Eastern novel: versus Western novel, 211–16. See also *Dream of the Red Chamber*

Egoist (Meredith), 71

Eliot, George, 3, 6, 11, 13, 17, 77, 78, 79, 80, 105, 108, 109, 113, 114, 122–23, 160, 209–10, 217, 233 (n. 15); response to Dickens's characterizations, 67–68, 75; "The Natural History of German Life," 67; "The Sad Fortunes of the Reverend Amos Barton," 84, 92. See also *Adam Bede*; *Daniel Deronda*; *Middlemarch*; *The Mill on the Floss*

Emma (Austen), 27, 29, 30, 31, 35, 38

Faerie Queen (Spenser), 200

Far From the Madding Crowd (Hardy), 95

Faulkner, William, 209, 210, 220; See also *Absalom, Absalom!*

Fielding, Henry, 33, 34, 47, 48, 78–79, 81, 86, 209. See also *Joseph Andrews*; *Tom Jones*

Flaubert, Gustave, 80, 83. See also *Madame Bovary*

Fleishman, Avrom, 228–29 (n. 2), 236 (n. 20), 241 (n. 1)

Ford, Ford Madox. See *The Good*

Soldier
Forster, E. M., 231 (n. 1), 234 (n. 37).
    See also *Howards End*
Friedman, Alan, 7
Frye, Northrop, 224 (n. 14)

Garrett, Peter, 226 (n. 30), 234
    (n. 25), 236 (n. 17), 241–42 (n. 2),
    244–45 (n. 3)
Gaskell, Elizabeth. See *Mary Barton*
Germinal (Zola), 12; society as theme
    in, 126; presentation of society in,
    126–27; characterization and so-
    ciety in, 127–28, 129–31; moral
    relativity in, 128–29, 142; use of
    metaphor in, 131–32; complemen-
    tary narratives in, 132–34; com-
    pared to *An American Tragedy*,
    135, 136–37, 139
Gilbert, Sandra, 229 (n. 2)
Golden Bowl (James), 115–16
Goodman, Paul, 199
Good Soldier (Ford), 9
Graff, Gerald, 224 (n. 15)
Great Expectations (Dickens), 36–37
Gregor, Ian, 242–43 (n. 6)
Grossvogel, David, 224 (n. 13)
Gubar, Susan, 229 (n. 2)

Hakutani, Yoshinobu, 240 (n. 7)
Hard Times (Dickens), 45, 77–78
Hardy, Barbara, 34, 228 (n. 1), 233–
    34 (n. 25)
Hardy, Thomas, 11, 33, 78, 79, 80–
    83, 105, 108, 109, 113, 114, 122–
    23, 209–10; narrator, 66. See also
    Far From the Madding Crowd; *Jude
    the Obscure*; *The Mayor of Caster-
    bridge*; *The Return of the Native*;
    Tess of the D'Urbervilles; *Under the
    Greenwood Tree*; *The Woodlanders*
Harvey, W. J., 17, 115, 224 (n. 15),
    235–36 (n. 14), 239 (n. 42)
Heart of Darkness (Conrad), 202
Historical novel, 23–24
Holloway, John, 233 (n. 25)
Hough, Graham, 107

House, Humphry, 67, 233 (n. 25)
Howards End (Forster), 41
Howe, Irving, 135, 237 (n. 20)
Hsueh-chin, Tsao. See *Dream of the
    Red Chamber*
Humphry Clinker (Smollett): society
    in, 15–16

Ionesco, Eugene, 209, 217–18
Iser, Wolfgang, 231–32 (n. 11), 233
    (n. 18)

Jacobs, Gabriel, 217
James, Henry, 51, 67, 68, 77, 78, 83;
    "The Spoils of Poynton," 6; social
    aesthetic in novels of, 114–17. See
    also *The Ambassadors*; *Daisy Mil-
    ler*; *The Golden Bowl*; *Portrait of a
    Lady*
Jameson, Fredric, 21
Jane Eyre (Brontë), 19–20
Joseph Andrews (Fielding), 45, 49;
    compared to *Wuthering Heights*,
    172–73
Joyce, James, 18–19. See also *A Por-
    trait of the Artist as a Young Man*
Jude the Obscure (Hardy), 69, 75, 77,
    80, 81, 83, 95, 97, 98, 102

Kafka, Franz, 209, 210, 220. See also
    The Castle; *The Trial*
Kendrick, Walter, 244 (n. 11)
Kermode, Frank, 18
Kettle, Arnold, 7, 64, 228 (n. 2), 233
    (n. 17), 237 (n. 20)
Kincaid, J. R., 241 (n. 2)
Kingsley, Charles, 125
Knoepflmacher, U. C., 4, 235 (n. 11),
    242 (n. 5)

Langford, Gerald, 247 (n. 10)
Lawrence, D. H., 11, 79, 80–83, 94,
    103, 122–23, 209–10; "Morality
    and the Novel," 104; "inhuman
    will," 128. See also *The Rainbow*;
    Women in Love
Lazarillo de Tormes, 214

Leavis, F. R., 107
Levine, George, 5, 236 (n. 17)
Lewes, G. H., 34, 68–69
Little Dorrit (Dickens), 68, 70, 76, 79
Little Women (Alcott): compared to *Pride and Prejudice*, 41–42
Lolita (Nabokov), 211
Loofbourow, John, 232 (n. 13)
Lucas, John, 7, 67–68
Lukács, Georg, 118, 123, 224 (n. 14), 239 (n. 46)

McMaster, Juliet, 233 (n. 17)
Madame Bovary (Flaubert), 69, 102–3, 125, 130
Mansfield Park (Austen), 28, 29, 30, 39, 40
Marcus, Steven, 86–87, 88, 226 (n. 31)
Mary Barton (Gaskell), 69, 75
Marxist criticism, 21, 122, 216–20
Mathison, John, 62
Matthiessen, F. O., 240 (nn. 7, 9, 14)
Mayor of Casterbridge (Hardy), 95
Meredith, George. See *The Egoist*
Middlemarch (Eliot), 33, 36–37, 72, 74, 77, 80, 81, 106, 116, 128, 138, 148, 160, 182, 217, 218; presentation of society in, 53, 69, 84–90; narrator in, 66, 90–91, 103; ideal community in, 81–82, 84, 85–87, 93; public opinion and characterization in, 83–84, 87–88, 89, 91–93; compared to *War and Peace*, 117, 119–23; compared to *Nostromo* and *Barchester Towers*, 154
Miller, J. Hillis, 67, 68, 70–71, 85, 225 (n. 16), 234 (n. 31)
Millgate, Michael, 246 (n. 3)
Mill on the Floss (Eliot), 6, 41
Mimesis. *See* Society: and mimesis
Moll Flanders (Defoe), 211; society in, 15
Moore, G. E., 115
Moynaham, Julian, 106
Mudrick, Marvin, 238 (n. 32)

Nabokov, Vladimir. See *Ada*; *Lolita*
Narrators: and relationship to society, 9. *See also* individual titles
Neomarxist criticism, 21. *See also* Marxist criticism
Nicholas, Brian, 242–43 (n. 6)
Nostromo (Conrad), 6, 13, 147, 219; society as formal protagonist in, 148–50; narrative instabilities in, 150–55; compared to *Adam Bede*, 153; compared to *Middlemarch*, 154; characterization and society in, 155–60; structure of action in, 160–66; artist's intuition in, 166–67
Novel: and form, ix–x, 7–8, 9–11; and value, ix–x, 8–9; and structure, 8; as instrument of social criticism, 11; as genre, 15–19

O'Connor, Flannery, 14, 188, 190, 196; society precluded in fiction of, 14, 169–71, 185–86, 196, 197, 209; "Some Aspects of the Gothic in Southern Fiction," 168; "Everything that Rises Must Converge," 181; "The Enduring Chill," 181; "The Lame Shall Enter First," 181; presentation of society in fiction of, 181; conflicting realities in fiction of, 182–85; narrator in fiction of, 183; transcendent consummation in fiction of, 184–85; "Revelation," 184–85. See also *The Violent Bear It Away*
Olivier, Lawrence, 169
Orwell, George, 67
Our Mutual Friend (Dickens), 6, 12, 46, 47, 148; individual freedom from social determinism in, 68, 76; presentation of society in, 68–70; characterization and society in, 73–74, 76–77; compared to *Middlemarch*, 74; compared to *Adam Bede*, 74

Pamela (Richardson): society in, 16

Persuasion (Austen), 27, 28, 29, 30, 31, 34, 35, 38, 40; as distinctive in Austen's canon, 29, 42–43
Polhemus, R. H., 241 (n. 1)
Portrait of a Lady (James), 115
Portrait of the Artist as a Young Man (Joyce), 202
Powers, Lyall, 246 (n. 4)
Preston, John, 232 (n. 11)
Price, Martin, 231 (n. 4)
Pride and Prejudice (Austen), 25–44 passim, 71, 72, 103, 128, 154, 218; compared to *Little Women*, 41–42; compared to *Barchester Towers*, 163
Proust, Marcel, 18–19. See also *À la recherche du temps perdu*
Pynchon, Thomas, 209, 210, 220. See also *The Crying of Lot 49*

Rader, Ralph, 225–26 (n. 30), 243 (n. 7)
Rainbow (Lawrence), 81, 83, 103, 117, 218; presentation of society in, 104–7, 108–9; characterization and society in, 104–5, 106, 107–14, 116; nature and society in, 106–7, 114; narrator in, 108, 112
Ray, Gordon, 232 (n. 13)
Return of the Native (Hardy), 95
Richardson, Samuel. See *Clarissa*; *Pamela*
Robbe-Grillet, Alain, 8
Robinson Crusoe (Defoe): society in, 15
Room of One's Own (Woolf), 19, 20
Roxana (Defoe), 211

Sacks, Sheldon, 53, 231 (n. 9)
Sagar, Keith, 238 (n. 36)
Said, Edward, 223 (n. 3)
Sanders, Scott, 239 (n. 38)
Schorer, Mark, 245 (n. 9)
Science fiction novel, 23–24
Sentimental Journey (Sterne), 16
Shakespeare, William. See *As You Like It*

Sherman, Stuart, 129
Shroder, Maurice, 7
Smollett, Tobias, 16. See also *Humphry Clinker*
Social novel, 125, 126
Social taboos, 210–11
Society: as formal aspect of novel, ix–x, 4, 5, 7, 21–23; and reality, 3, 4, 5, 17–19; and mimesis, 4–5, 6, 12, 21–22, 220–21; defined, 4–7; as background in novel, 8; as function in novel, 8–11; as structural aspect of novel, 9; as medium for individual action in novels, 9, 10, 148, 188; and social status quo, 10; in eighteenth-century novel, 11, 15–17, 18–19; in twentieth-century novel, 17–19, 188; historical versus fictional, 19–21; as theme, 22–23, 126; assumptions about Western society in novels, 210–11; Western versus Eastern in novels, 211–16
Society's formal roles: summarized, 11–14; in George Eliot's *Middlemarch*, 11, 80–94, 117, 122–23, 209–10; in Thomas Hardy's *Tess of the D'Urbervilles*, 11, 80–83, 94–104, 117, 122–23, 209–10; in D. H. Lawrence's *The Rainbow*, 11, 80–83, 103–14, 116, 117, 122–23, 209–10; in Henry Fielding's *Tom Jones*, 12, 46, 48–57, 78–79, 209; in W. M. Thackeray's *Vanity Fair*, 12, 46, 48, 57–66, 78–79, 209; in Charles Dickens's later novels, 12, 46, 48, 66–78, 79, 209; in Jane Austen's novels, 12–13, 25–44, 46, 209; in Émile Zola's *Germinal*, 12, 124–34, 145–46, 209; in Theodore Dreiser's *An American Tragedy*, 12, 124–26, 134–46, 209; in Joseph Conrad's *Nostromo*, 13, 147–67, 209; in Anthony Trollope's *Barchester Towers*, 13, 147–67, 209; in Emily Brontë's *Wuthering Heights*, 13, 168–80, 173, 185–86, 209; in Flannery O'Connor's fiction, 14,

168–71, 180–86, 209; in William Faulkner's *Absalom, Absalom!*, 14, 188—96, 207–8, 210; in Franz Kafka's *The Castle*, 14, 196–202, 207–8, 210; in Thomas Pynchon's *The Crying of Lot 49*, 14, 202–8, 210
Sociological criticism, 21–22
Sociological/naturalistic novel, 12, 64, 82–83, 123, 137, 145, 148; as propaganda, 125–26, 145
Spenser, Edmund. See *The Faerie Queen*
Squires, Michael, 237–38 (n. 22)
Sterne, Laurence. See *A Sentimental Journey*; *Tristram Shandy*
Stevenson, Lionel, 18
Stoll, John, 239 (n. 37)
Structuralism, ix
Sussman, Herbert, 233 (n. 25)
Swinden, Patrick, 17

Tave, Stuart, 230 (n. 12)
Tess of the D'Urbervilles (Hardy), 94, 104, 106, 117, 218; narrator in, 95–96, 98–99, 103; presentation of society in, 96–97; public opinion and characterization in, 96–97, 98–99, 100–101, 102
Thackeray, W. M., 33, 34, 40, 70–79, 81, 160, 209. See also *Vanity Fair*
Tillotson, Geoffrey, 232 (n. 13), 233 (n. 17)
Tillotson, Kathleen, 233 (n. 17)
Tolstoy, Leo, 83. See also *War and Peace*
Tom Jones (Fielding), 9, 46, 103, 128, 219; intrusive narrator in, 46, 49, 50–51, 55–56, 57, 64, 66; presentation of society in, 48–49, 51–52, 53–54, 69; characterization and society in, 50–51, 67, 71, 81, 82, 85; digressions in, 52–53; absence of narrator in digressions of, 53; implied reader in, 56–57
Trial (Kafka), 14
Trilling, Lionel, 7, 68

Tristram Shandy (Sterne): society in, 16
Trollope, Anthony, 169; "An Autobiography," 147. See also *Barchester Towers*

Under the Greenwood Tree (Hardy), 94
Utopian novels, 23

Van Doren, Mark, 211–12
Van Ghent, Dorothy, 65, 167, 177, 191, 230 (n. 13), 233 (n. 17), 236 (n. 19), 242 (n. 6), 245 (nn. 9, 10)
Vanity Fair (Thackeray), 12, 45, 46, 57, 72, 73, 75, 80, 132, 148, 154, 219; presentation of society in, 47, 53, 58–59, 69; intrusive narrator in, 47, 59, 61, 63–66; characterization and society in, 59–61, 67, 71, 81, 82, 85; criticism of Victorian idealism in, 61–63; narrator versus implied author in, 64–66
Vickery, Olga, 190
Violent Bear It Away (O'Connor), 181, 182, 183–84, 220

War and Peace (Tolstoy), 6, 120–23, 127–28, 210–11; presentation of history in, 117–18, characterization and history in, 118–19
Warren, Robert Penn, 240 (n. 7)
Watt, Ian, 214, 226 (n. 32)
Wharton, Edith. See *The Age of Innocence*
Williams, Raymond, 7, 67, 227–28 (n. 41), 234 (n. 25), 237 (nn. 20, 21)
Women in Love (Lawrence), 105, 111, 113; compared to *Wuthering Heights*, 172–73
Woodlanders (Hardy), 95
Woolf, Virginia, 18–19. See also *The Common Reader*; *A Room of One's Own*
Wuthering Heights (Brontë), 9, 182–83, 191, 220; society precluded in, 13–14, 168–71, 173, 185–86, 196,

197, 209; socially normative perspectives in, 171–77; compared to *Joseph Andrews*, 172–73; compared to *Women in Love*, 172; conflicting realities in, 174–77; failures of social communication in, 177–79; transcendent consummation in, 179–80

Zola, Émile, 123, 125, 209; "The Experimental Novel," 124; "A Letter to the Young People of France," 124; novel as science, 127–28, 132. See also *Germinal*